# CONTENTS

# 13 *Program Development: cc, make, lint, cb* *417*

# Preface

This book is about the language C in the UNIX environment. UNIX is an important operating system and has a user interface called a shell, a command interpreter that comes in several varieties and has many of the features of a programming language. The shell is *programmable* and has the usual looping structures, such as while-do statements, for statements and others. It is also equipped with branching statements, such as if then else and case statements. Naturally, C also enjoys all of these structures with a somewhat different syntax.

## UNIX VERSUS OTHER OPERATING SYSTEMS

But why use UNIX as opposed to MS-DOS or other operating systems? The reasons are generic as well as specific to the language C. The generic reason for the choice of UNIX can be summarized briefly by the statement found in the first paragraph, "the shell is programmable." This feature alone makes UNIX an extraordinarily powerful and versatile program development environment.

## LINKAGE BETWEEN UNIX AND C

There is a natural linkage between C and UNIX that is straightforward and easy to implement. It should not be surprising that UNIX and C interface so nicely—they were developed in the same laboratories within a few years of each other. More than 90% of UNIX is written in C, which gives the reader some idea of its power and versatility.

## PURPOSE OF BOOK

The purpose of this book, then, is to assist the reader in learning C coupled with the essentials of UNIX as a program development environment. The essentials of UNIX, in this book, take on three distinct flavors:

1. UNIX utilities that can be executed independently of C programs—basic utilities that copy files, display files, and perform other chores

**2.** Shell programming that improves the productivity of the programmer by storing sequences of UNIX commands, perhaps with looping structures, in a file that can be read and interpreted by the shell

**3.** UNIX system calls and library functions prewritten in C that can be easily accessed from within C programs

## THE APPROACH

Problems thus will be solved in the UNIX environment by writing C programs (possibly with attendant "calls" to UNIX from within the program—this means the technique of using prewritten system calls, which are really just C functions, within a C program); by writing UNIX shell scripts that execute C programs from within; and by using either tool, UNIX or C, separately. But note, the primary emphasis will be on C. No attempt will be made to be encyclopedic in the coverage of UNIX. Only those UNIX features that are the most important will be introduced— the primary emphasis will be on problem solving techniques.

## THE OUTCOMES

When the reader has completed this book, he or she will have developed a clear understanding and comprehension of two powerful computing software tools, the language C and the operating system UNIX, and their connection and relationship. The reader will also be secure with the knowledge that the time spent on this endeavor will be highly profitable. There is good evidence to suggest that C and UNIX will enjoy increasing popularity in the years to come.

## CHAPTER CONTENTS

**Chapter 1** provides an overview of UNIX features, the relationship of C and UNIX, and versions of the UNIX system.

**Chapter 2** discusses the essential utilities of UNIX that are needed to begin programming in C, including an introduction to an editor, the file system, and other elementary topics that are necessary to use UNIX effectively.

**Chapter 3** discusses the editor "vi" in some detail so that the reader can edit C programs or UNIX shell scripts.

**Chapter 4**    covers the Bourne shell for constructing UNIX shell scripts, including methods of execution, environment considerations, signals, pipes, and redirection.

**Chapters 5–9**    are the sections of the book that cover the language C. The essentials of these chapters are independent of UNIX itself and provide a complete discussion of the features of C.

**Chapter 10**    discusses UNIX system calls and library functions and how each can be accessed from within C programs. This chapter also shows the reader how to access UNIX shell scripts from within C programs.

**Chapter 11**    provides further discussion of the UNIX-C interface, including instruction on how to access standard input and open files in a C program, how to provide options, how to process multiple files, how to access system information, and a more detailed analysis of command files. The concept of trapping signals is included here.

**Chapter 12**    gives examples of dynamic memory allocation, file access considerations (including set user-ID), and file locking methods in C programs.

**Chapter 13**    discusses program development tools, including cc, make, lint, and cb.

## *EXERCISES*

Within each chapter there are sets of exercises that the reader is encouraged to complete. Most of these are oriented to solving particular problems, testing an understanding of the concepts, and reinforcing earlier ideas. A sample of these exercises should definitely be assigned and completed.

## *ACKNOWLEDGMENTS*

The author expresses his gratitude and love to his wife, Jean Buddington Martin, for sharing her life. Our children—Christine, Jennifer, Marc, and Clayton—deserve to have their names in at least one book. Dr. Keith Olson also wrote an excellent solutions manual and Holly Harrison painstakingly checked all the programs—and improved many of them.

# CHAPTER 1

# Introduction to UNIX and C

This chapter provides brief glimpses of the essential features of the UNIX operating system, including portability, multiuser operation, background processing, hierarchical file system, command shell, pipes, UNIX utilities, text processing, software development, and electronic mail. An operating system in general is simply that collection of programs that delivers system services to all users, freeing them from the burden and necessity of programming these system applications. The burden of writing an operating system is highly dependent upon the nature of the desired services and considerably more complicated in the case of a multiuser system, where users compete for services of a central processor.

The tools available to user-written C programs are discussed as are the reasons for using the UNIX environment for C programming. Versions of the UNIX operating system are summarized.

## 1.1 MAJOR UNIX FEATURES AND BENEFITS

One of the best features of UNIX is the fact that it is designed to achieve *portability*. As a result, UNIX, or a version of UNIX, is available on a wide variety of machines ranging from microcomputers to supercomputers. Not only does portability decrease the user's learning time when moving from one machine to another, but it also increases options in terms of choices among hardware vendors for a given set of software.

Because UNIX is a portable operating system, many applications that are written in a programming language, such as C, which makes use of the UNIX-C interface, will be portable also. Development time is decreased and software suppliers can offer solutions running on a broad spectrum of systems.

UNIX supports *multiuser operation,* which means that on a given system there can be a number of users sharing processing power and memory. UNIX also supports various security and protection features that permit users to access only the data and programs for which they have permission. This will be explored in Chapter 2.

UNIX supports the concept of multitasking, which allows the user to initiate a task and then proceed to perform other tasks while the original task is being run in the *background.* Long tasks then need not take up computer time and resources to the exclusion of other jobs. This feature can be especially helpful in providing maximum efficiency in the use of the system.

UNIX supports a *hierarchical file system,* which provides the ability to group data and programs in a manner that provides easy management. Users find that data and programs generally can be located with little difficulty. The key is to use appropriate names for files and to organize them in a clear and natural manner. The hierarchical file system will be discussed in Chapter 2. Figure 1.1 shows such a file system.

The user's interaction with UNIX is controlled by the *shell,* which is a powerful command interpreter. The shell is able to interpret over two hundred different commands and has the additional feature of permitting input to and output from those commands to be redirected to places other than the standard default. (Normally, standard input and standard output are both the terminal.) Besides these features, the shell is able to execute any user-defined sequence of commands that has been stored in a file, and has possibly been employed therein with built-in programming language features. Thus, the shell is considered to be a programming language in itself. The main features and attributes of the shell will be studied in Chapter 4 and used in later chapters to provide for enhanced C programming. A single UNIX operating system can actually access several shells: the most common one with System V.3 is the Bourne shell, while Berkeley versions of UNIX often run the C shell.

UNIX supports the concept of a *pipe,* which means that the output from one program can be made the input to another program—with the programs themselves executed sequentially. This mechanism permits the user to sequence elementary programs in such a manner that they can be combined to perform more complex tasks.

There are over two hundred *UNIX utilities* that are the essential tools for accomplishing routine tasks without writing new routines. Only the most often used of these will be explored in Chapter 2. If one wishes to study all of the UNIX commands in depth, there are many excellent books on the subject.

In addition to these stand-alone utilities, UNIX has about 60 system calls (functions that are written in the language C), which are the heart of the UNIX operating system. These system calls provide basic input/output services, access the system clock, determine file permissions, and perform other basic tasks. All of these system calls can be accessed from C programs. Several of the more important system calls will be studied in the latter part of this book to provide the reader with knowledge of how they can be accessed and their essential features. It is important to

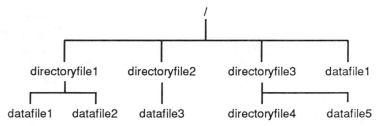

**FIGURE 1.1**    Directory File Structure

understand that the system calls are C functions and can only be accessed (or called) from within C programs. System calls are essentially independent of the UNIX system. The set of system calls available on a UNIX system will appear in Section 2 of the UNIX manual. For example, the system call open() (to open a file) is referred to in the manual as open(2). None of the system calls require special "#include" type code in a C program if they are to be accessed.

Moreover, there are a number of UNIX library functions that are available to the C programmer. These library functions can be thought of as an extension of the basic UNIX system and, in fact, many of the UNIX system calls are the essential building blocks used in the construction of the library functions. The method of accessing UNIX library functions from C programs will be studied, but no attempt will be made to give a complete analysis of these library functions. Just like system calls, library functions can *only* be accessed from within C programs—however, library functions will likely be highly dependent upon the particular UNIX system.

Furthermore, library functions will be available even on non-UNIX systems. The set of library functions available on a UNIX system will appear in Section 3 of the UNIX manual. For example, the library function printf() is referred to in the manual as printf(3S). "S" stands for the standard input and output functions. Many of the library functions require special "#include" type code in a C program if they are to be accessed.

UNIX offers a wide range of *text-processing tools,* including text-editing and text-formatting programs. Because this book deals primarily with C programs, attention is limited to text editing only. One of the more popular editors in use is "vi." A comprehensive introduction to vi is given in Chapter 3.

UNIX includes a number of *software development tools,* which support various phases of the software development process, including editing, debugging, locating potential nonportable code, and helping the programmer track changes in various versions of code. These features are explored in this book, and some of the more important tools include the program maintenance tool "make," the program to locate nonportable code "lint," the C beautifier "cb," and the symbolic debugger "sdb."

*Electronic mail,* a common service of multiuser operating systems, permits users to exchange files, communicate interactively, and exercise various options associated with basic services. UNIX has these general services available with a variety of programs.

UNIX is a relatively mature operating system, even though it continues to go through modifications, with usage dating back to the early 1970s. It is thus relatively bug free and is increasing in popularity and use. The user can be sure that concepts learned here will be beneficial because UNIX is likely to be used increasingly in the future.

The purpose of this book is not to provide an in-depth or complete discussion of UNIX but rather to provide a thorough study of C in the UNIX environment. As such, the reader can expect to see only the most rudimentary features of UNIX explained in the early portion of the text; later, some of the UNIX system calls and UNIX library functions that can be accessed from C programs will be studied.

## 1.2 | *WHY STUDY UNIX AND C TOGETHER?*

UNIX and C were both created at Bell Laboratories and their developments have thus been interwoven. The original UNIX was written in the late 1960s in PDP assembly language. A later version used software written in a language called B, which was developed in 1970. The language B evolved into C, which includes structured programming constructs coupled with the ability to perform both bit- and byte-level manipulation. As such, C is an excellent language for operating system development, and UNIX, in fact, was rewritten in 1973 in the language C. Ninety percent of UNIX is now written in C.

The aim of this book is to provide the UNIX tools necessary to become a productive and efficient C programmer. A C program is modular by nature, with each module consisting of a function performing a simple task. Functions in C perform the same role as those of subroutines, functions, and procedures in languages such as Pascal and FORTRAN.

The tools that can be used in a C program fall into one of three categories:

1. Built-in functions, called *UNIX C functions,* that cannot stand alone, but rather must be part of a C program.

   a. *Type I UNIX C functions.* These are *system calls* and are part of UNIX itself. There are about 60 and they should be standard on every UNIX, or UNIX look-alike, system. They are part of the "kernel" of UNIX, the low-level interface with hardware. System calls are available to C programs automatically and without the necessity to declare them in the C program. One example of a system call is the one to open a file, called open(2).

    b. *Type II UNIX C functions.* These are *library functions,* are add-ons to the operating system, and typically use system calls to perform their tasks. They may not be standard across UNIX systems, but in fact often are. Some but not all of the library functions must be declared in the C program to make them available. One example of a library function is the formatted print function, printf(3S).

2. UNIX commands or sequences of UNIX commands stored in a file called a *shell script* can stand alone in UNIX and can also be called from a C program. In fact, they are called via one of the library functions, the special one that is actually called system.

3. User-written functions

In addition to the powerful hooks from C into UNIX described above, it is quite easy to run a C program from within a sequence of UNIX commands stored in a file. This is often done, for example, to make a C program interactive.

## 1.3 | *VERSIONS OF THE UNIX SYSTEM*

UNIX was once a complete system with source code, but it is sometimes sold as unbundled products and licensed in binary form. UNIX can be thought of as being comprised of the following, which combined would be called the complete system:

1. *run-time system:* the kernel (system calls) and most utilities
2. *software development system:* C compiler, linker and libraries, make, SCCS, yacc, lex, and debuggers (The meanings of these terms are not important at this point.)
3. *text processing system:* nroff, troff, tbl, eqn, and spell
4. *shell functioning as a command interpreter*

There are many versions of UNIX available today and they can be classified according to three major categories: (1) *AT&T versions,* the most common of which is System V Release 2.x running the Bourne shell; (2) *Berkeley versions,* the most recent of which is 4.x running the C shell; (3) *other versions derived from AT&T versions,* including Microport System V/AT, SCO XENIX V.2, IBM XENIX 2.0, and Dynix V 3.0.4.

There is currently no standard, but the differences (exclusive of the shells), from the beginner's standpoint, are usually not great. For example, all of those listed in (3) meet AT&T's published System V Interface Definition (SVID) with only a short list of exceptions. From a practical standpoint, this means that they are compatible with AT&T System V.2 at the system call level, but may not support all the utilities in AT&T System V.2. Thus, most of the utilities mentioned in this book can be considered standard and will run without modification on most systems. However, do be aware that there are major differences in the Bourne shell (developed by AT&T) and the C shell (developed by Berkeley). Each has its advocates. This book covers the rudiments of the Bourne shell, but many systems will use the C shell, and some can use both.

## 1.4 | *CHAPTER SUMMARY*

1. UNIX is a portable operating system, supporting multiuser operation, background processing, and a hierarchical file system.

2. The user interface to UNIX is a shell of which there are several varieties available.

3. Pipes permit the user to combine programs so that the output of one becomes the input to the next.

4. UNIX comes with over two hundred utilities to provide essential routines for the user.

5. UNIX comes with about 60 system calls that are the heart of the operating system and provide essential low-level services.

6. UNIX library functions are available to the C programmer; these provide an extensive set of C routines that is among the building blocks a programmer can use.

7. The development of UNIX and C, in contrast to most operating systems and languages, took place in the same laboratories, within just a few years.

8. C programmers have available built-in functions called UNIX C functions (subdivided into system calls and library functions), user-written functions, and shell scripts.

9. The Bourne shell and the C shell are popular command interpreters that serve as user interfaces to UNIX.

# CHAPTER 2

# The Essentials of UNIX for C Programming

This chapter provides the fundamentals needed to begin using UNIX in an effective manner. The first part of the chapter covers the methods to enter and leave UNIX and how to correct errors when typing in commands at the command line. Only the most rudimentary features of the editor vi will be explored, but enough will be given to write a very simple C program—and then compile and run it. The UNIX hierarchical file system will be discussed along with several of the most commonly used UNIX utilities. The concept of permissions will be introduced and there will be a brief prelude to the world of special characters.

## 2.1 | ENTERING AND LEAVING UNIX

The first order of business is to learn to login and logoff a UNIX-based system. The user needs to be identified as a valid user for the system, in other words, he or she needs at least a user ID and perhaps even a password. The system administrator usually takes care of these details. On this system, the login process is reproduced here. (Be aware that UNIX is sensitive to the distinction between uppercase and lowercase letters.)

```
login: kem
Password: <RETURN>
UNIX System V Release 2.0 3B-2 Version 2
unf4
Copyright © 1984 AT&T Technologies, Inc.
All Rights Reserved
you have mail
news:network
$
```

Some words of explanation:

1. If the system administrator has assigned the user a password, for security the user will not see the password when typing it. If a password has not been assigned, the user should simply press the return key at the password prompt. The next text on the screen might be an optional message of the day (perhaps containing system news written by the system administrator) followed by the "you have mail" message, and the "news: network" message, followed by the default prompt of "$ ".

2. After logging on, the user will typically be running the command interpreter known as the shell, often stored under the name /bin/sh. The shell has many characteristics of a typical programming language, including the ability to interpret shell scripts. One of the most important types of programs that will be run during a session is an editor, permitting the creation of a file that consists of C language statements. The most common editor is called "vi". Also available on some systems is "emacs."

3. The shell runs until it receives an end of input signal, which on most systems can be sent by keeping the control key depressed and then depressing the lowercase d key. This combination of two keystrokes will be denoted ctrl-d in this book.

At this point, typing ctrl-d will end the input to the shell and will log the user off the machine.

## EXERCISES 2.1

1. Log on to a UNIX-based system and try logging off by typing ctrl-d.
2. What is the message of the day on the UNIX system you are using?
3. Look up the UNIX utility called find and attempt to use it to locate the shell—it is typically stored under the name /bin/sh.

## 2.2 | INTERPRETING AND CORRECTING ERRORS IN UNIX

When the prompt "$ " appears the user is at the command line of UNIX and is ready to run a utility or issue a command. A utility is simply a program that enables UNIX to perform some task. For example, a very important utility is pwd, which stands for "print working directory." UNIX will attempt to execute the utility when the name followed by the return key is typed. (This issues a command to the shell.) The set of characters typed before the return key is pressed is called the command line.

There are several kinds of errors that can be made when keying in the command line. They are:

1.  *Errors in the input line that are noticed after the return.* Many times when keying a command on the prompt line an error will be made in the actual command line. If an error is made at this stage and return has already been pressed, the command line typed will be sent for processing and the shell or the invoked utility will issue an appropriate error message. For example,

    **$ pwdd RETURN**

    versus

    **$ pwd RETURN**

    In the first case, the command is misspelled and an error message is received. In the second case, output was displayed (and there is no error message). The output will be explained later. From now on the return will be omitted from the text—but it is always assumed present and follows the command line.

2.  *Errors in the input line noticed before return is pressed.* If the user wishes to backspace and erase the previous character on a command line, the typical way is to type ctrl-h or use the backspace (←) key. This is, however, system dependent and can even vary among installations of the same computer vendor. The system administrator should be consulted if problems are experienced. The ctrl-h can be typed as many times as needed leading the user back, if desired, to the prompt itself. If the user wishes to backspace over the entire command line (and hence erase the entire command line), a faster way than repeat ctrl-h is to type the single character @. Again, this is system and installation dependent.

3.  *Errors in the running or execution of the utility.* Suppose a long-running utility needs to be terminated. In this case, the interrupt execution key labeled del (for delete) should be depressed. UNIX then sends an interrupt signal to the utility and terminates the running of that utility. (This is an example of terminating a process, that is, the running of a program.)

## EXERCISES  2.2

1.  Distinguish between a command line and a utility.
2.  Give three examples of a UNIX utility from the reference manual and state the purpose of each.
3.  How can errors be corrected on the command line before the return key is depressed?

4. Find out which key on your system terminates a process.

5. What is the difference between a process and a program?

6. Go to the UNIX reference manual and find the numeric value associated with the signal to interrupt a process.

## 2.3 | *USING THE EDITOR vi AND RUNNING a First C PROGRAM*

The editor called vi (short for visual and pronounced vee-eye or vigh) is often used to create a file. It is a full-screen editor (in contrast to a line editor), which means that the user can scroll through the document, forward and backward, without the necessity of finding a particular line (or lines) and editing them. This section will simply show how to use vi to create text files—files of data that will typically be C programs—the so-called source code.

The first objective is to create a simple C program called programl.c. This will be accomplished by invoking the editor vi:

```
$ vi programl.c
```

Before the text for programl.c is input, a few instructions are in order. When entering vi, the user is always in command mode (not able to enter text, but only able to issue vi commands). Note that the esc key always returns the user to command mode.

Now, here is how to create that file called programl.c. First, the user needs to enter input mode (only able to enter text, but not able to issue vi commands). To enter input mode, the cursor is positioned at the place in the text where changes are required with an appropriate arrow key (or backspace key if necessary), i (for input mode) is typed, and text may then be entered. Note these five capabilities in vi:

1. The user can move the cursor in command mode by using the return key, the space bar, and the arrow keys. The user can also backspace with ctrl-h.

2. The user can delete a single character by escaping (esc) to command mode, positioning the cursor on the character, and typing x. To delete a word, the user types dw (delete word), and to delete a line, types dd.

3. If the user accidentally makes a deletion, the u command (undo) will restore the text. (This must be done before additional commands are entered.)

4. If the user wishes to insert new text, he or she enters command mode with esc, positions the cursor at the proper place, gives command i (input), enters the new text, and presses esc to return to command mode.

5. The command o opens a blank line below the current cursor position, which is useful for inserting a new line. Similarly, the command o opens a blank line above the current cursor position. Notice that vi is uppercase and lowercase sensitive!

Now, here is the complete set of instructions to enter vi to edit the file programl.c, enter input mode (i), key in the program, return to command mode (the esc key), and save to disk (ZZ from command mode—note UPPERcase).

```
$ vi programl.c
i
main() {
printf("hello there-I have written a program");
}
esc
ZZ
```

If the user tries this and all goes well, he or she should be able to return to command mode with the esc key and save the file to disk by typing ZZ (while in command mode).

The name of the C compiler is cc. To compile the C program programl.c the following will do the job:

```
$ cc programl.c
```

If there were no syntax errors in the program itself, then the executable file a.out is created. (There will only be one such file, so the user must be careful—if two files are compiled only the last one will be saved in a.out.) Execute as follows:

```
$ a.out
```

If there were syntax errors in the program, then the following editing is necessary:

```
$ vi programl.c
```

Use this to correct those errors, then leave the editor, compile, and execute again. A fairly comprehensive coverage of vi will be given in Chapter 3. The purpose here is simply to get started.

1. On many systems, source code in C must be stored under a name that ends with a period followed by a lowercase c (.c). What are the requirements on your system?

2. Introduction to Chapter 3: experiment with vi by learning how to backspace; how to delete a character, a word, or a line; how to undo the previous command; and how to open blank lines for insertion of text.

3. Enter the C program given in the text but modify it to print three lines of output. Now compile the program and run it.

4. Introduction to Chapter 3: read about the C compiler and try to figure out how to save two different executable files—unless special options are given, the previous a.out is overwritten when a new compile occurs.

## 2.4 | *THE UNIX FILE SYSTEM*

A data file is defined as a set of information (data or program) that was created using a text editor or by running a program. For example, the C program that was just constructed using vi is an example of a data file.

A device file is defined as a type of file that is not stored on disk at all but, rather, represents a peripheral device, such as a terminal, disk, tape, or printer.

A directory file (or simply a directory) is a distinctive form of file that maintains a list of all the files assigned to it, including possibly data files, device files, *and* other directory files (called subdirectories).

A file is defined as a data file, device file, or directory file.

In UNIX every actual data file or device file is assigned to (or is the child of) a directory file. In a nutshell, UNIX files use a *hierarchical file system.* The UNIX hierarchical file structure can be visualized in the form of a tree with the directories (except for the top directory called the root and denoted by /) pictured as branches and the data files and device files pictured as leaves attached to the branches. The definition of the UNIX file structure is "recursive," that is, defined in a continued fashion in terms of itself as follows:

1. The top of the UNIX file structure is labeled / and is called the root node.

2. Immediately below the root node, or any other node (called a parent node), are its so-called children nodes (if any), which consist of a finite number of files and/or directory files of which only the directory files may have children nodes.

■ **Example 2.4.1**

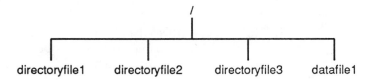

**FIGURE 2.1**    Example 2.4.1

Figure 2.1 is an example of a UNIX file structure that has four directory files (don't forget the root) and one data file, of which only the root (/) has any children (it has four). Note that, if indeed datafile1 is a data file, then it cannot have children. ■

■ **Example 2.4.2**

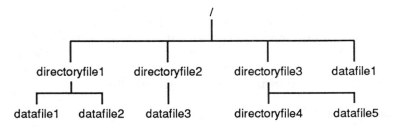

**FIGURE 2.2**    Example 2.4.2

Note that in Figure 2.2 the directories are likely to be /, directoryfile1 through directoryfile4 and the data files are likely to be datafile1 through datafile5. Notice that directoryfile4 is a subdirectory of directoryfile3.

It is the user's responsibility to organize the files in the most efficient and logical manner. Names should be carefully chosen and directories placed logically to insure easy and intuitive access. This point cannot be overemphasized. For example, directoryfile3 might, in practice, hold the contents of Chapter 3, while directoryfile4 might hold the contents of Section 4 of Chapter 3. The best names for them might simply be chapter3 and chapter3.sec4 respectively. ■

Both types of files, whether directories or files, are identified by filenames, which must obey the following rules:

1. They must be 1 to 14 characters in length chosen from A–Z, a–z, 0–9, (_), (.), and (,).
2. The root directory is always named /.
3. Source code in the language C must have a filename that ends with .c.

4. Two invisible files "." and ".." appear in every directory ("." refers to the directory itself and ".." refers to its parent).

5. The UNIX utility to list files in a directory, ls, does not usually display invisible filenames (those that begin with the character ".").

6. The complete pathname of a file is called the file's absolute pathname, while the pathname of a file beginning with the current working directory is called its relative pathname. (Complete pathname means that sequence of filenames, each separated from the next by the symbol /, beginning at the root and following the "tree path" through to the file itself.)

During a UNIX session, the user has what is known as a "working directory" (that he or she also has the ability to change). The working directory can be thought of as the user's association with a particular directory in the UNIX file structure (think of it as the labeled location in the UNIX tree). In general, it is very helpful to choose the working directory carefully, simply because it will afford the opportunity to perform operations with less key strokes by using relative pathnames rather than absolute pathnames. The working directory at the time of login is known as the user's HOME directory.

■ **Example 2.4.3**

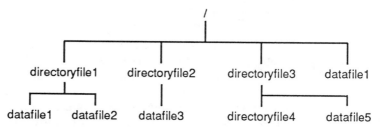

**FIGURE 2.3**    Example 2.4.3

In Figure 2.3 the absolute pathname of datafile3, for example, is /directoryfile2/datafile3. The absolute pathname of datafile1 is /datafile1. If the working directory is directoryfile4 then "." refers to directoryfile4 while ".." refers to directoryfile3. ■

■ **Example 2.4.4**
**(not a complete**
**UNIX file structure)**

The file structure shown in Figure 2.4 indicates a typical (partial) UNIX file structure. For instance, the directory bin under / contains certain UNIX utilities (shown are pwd—print working directory, ls—list, and

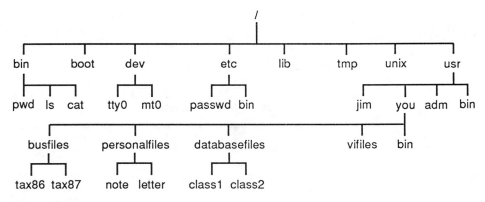

**FIGURE 2.4**    Example 2.4.4

cat—concatenate). Also note that the user-denoted you has files stored under /usr/you. Other users would typically have their files stored under /usr/jim or /usr/fred, and so on. The directory dev under / contains certain device files, in this case tty0 (perhaps a terminal) and mt0 (perhaps a mounted tape). The directory etc under / contains a password file (passwd) and binary files (bin). Administrative utilities for users are housed in /usr/adm and binary files for users are placed in /usr/bin. ∎

## EXERCISES 2.4

1. Discuss the idea of a hierarchical file structure paying particular attention to that of UNIX.

2. Differentiate among data files, directory files, and device files.

3. Where in the file structure is C source code typically stored and under what filenames?

4. Explain the significance of invisible files.

5. Differentiate between relative and absolute filenames.

6. Consider the UNIX file structure (partial) in Figure 2.5.

    a. Give the absolute pathname of every file that is on the same level as busfiles.

    b. Give the relative pathname of vifiles with respect to usr.

    c. Give the relative pathname of tax86 with respect to you.

    d. Give the absolute pathname of the file associated with the file designated ".." in personalfiles.

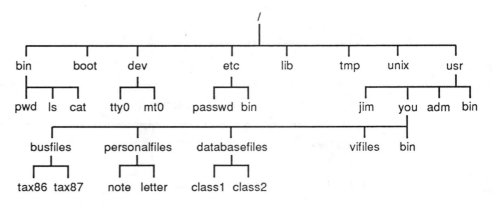

**FIGURE 2.5**    Partial File Structure

## 2.5 | *ESSENTIAL UNIX UTILITIES*

This section will now discuss 12 essential utilities in the UNIX file structure stored under /bin. The general format of each utility will be shown, but generally there will be only a simple, specific example or two. The purpose is not to learn all the options and possible arguments, but rather to get a basic working knowledge of UNIX so that it can be used effectively to do programming in C. If more details are needed, the UNIX manual for a particular system should be consulted.

The format for many of the two hundred or so UNIX utilities is given by the following command line format, which is entered at the prompt ( $ ):

`command [options] [arguments]`

This means that the command is to be applied to the arguments specified (often a file or list of files). The options are used to tailor the output to specific needs and are preceded by a -. (Both options and arguments are optional. They may or may not be selected and are just as implied—optional!) Several options can generally be preceded by a single -.

For Section 2.5, the UNIX file structure in Figure 2.6 will be used to illustrate the concepts. (This will be considered to be the complete file structure.)

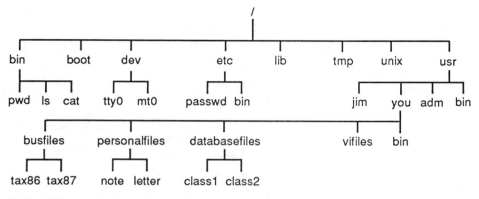

**FIGURE 2.6**    File Structure for Section 2.5

FORMAT: `pwd`

**1.** The pwd (print working directory) UNIX utility allows the user to print the working directory.

```
$ pwd
/usr/you
$
```

No options or arguments can be given to pwd and the absolute pathname of the working directory is the output when the pwd command is issued on the command line.

FORMAT: `ls [options] [file-list]`

**2.** The ls (list) UNIX utility prints the names of the files that are the children of the working directory (including both files and directories) in alphabetical order. The -l (long) option is particularly useful because it generates lots of information, but an example illustrating it will be postponed until the concept of permissions is discussed at the end of this section. The -C option lists the files in the working directory in vertically sorted columns. The optional file-list contains the names of data files, device files, or directories;

relative (to the working directory) or absolute pathnames are acceptable. Suppose the working directory is /usr/you. Here is a representative interchange:

```
$ pwd
/usr/you
$ ls
busfiles
databasefiles
personalfiles
vifiles
$ ls -C
bin            databasefiles     vifiles
busfiles   personalfiles
$ ls -C /etc
   bin              password
$
```

```
mkdir
```

FORMAT: mkdir directory-list

3. The mkdir (make directory) UNIX utility allows the construction of another directory (or even more) in order to provide more detailed organization for files. Suppose the user wants to make the directory shellscripts under /usr/you/vifiles. This can be done by providing the complete pathname as the argument for the command as follows:

*Solution I:*

```
$ mkdir /usr/you/vifiles/shellscripts
$
```

The utility does its work silently and without positive reinforcement.
   The user can provide the relative pathname as the argument if so desired. Hence, if the working directory is /usr/you then the appropriate command line is:

*Solution II:*

```
$ mkdir vifiles/shellscripts
$
```

In either case, the altered file system is as shown in Figure 2.7.

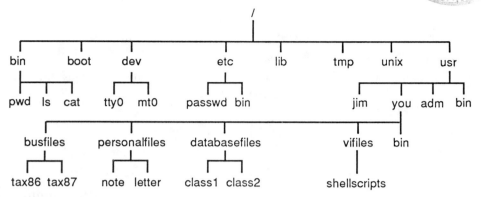

**FIGURE 2.7**    Effect of mkdir

```
cd
```

FORMAT: **cd [directory]**

4. The cd (change directory) UNIX command, which is a built-in command rather than a utility, allows the user to change the working directory. The same comments apply as with the mkdir utility, that is, the user may use complete pathnames or relative pathnames. Remember also that "." refers to the working directory itself and ".." to its parent. It should also be noted that cd with no argument returns the user to the HOME directory.

Suppose the working directory is /usr/you and the user wants to change to /lib.

*Solution I:*

```
$ cd ..
$ cd ..
$ cd lib
$
```

Again the work is done silently. Each command with the optional parent directory (..) takes the user one level higher in the UNIX file system.

*Solution II:*

```
$ cd /lib
$
```

This just uses the absolute pathname to go directly to the desired directory.

*Solution III:*

```
$ cd ../../lib
$
```

Here the user travels up the file system two levels to the root, and then back down to lib.

```
┌─────────┐
│  rmdir  │
└─────────┘
```

**FORMAT:** `rmdir directory-list`

5. The rmdir (remove directory) UNIX utility allows the user to remove a specified directory or a list of directories. Again, the user may use complete pathnames or relative pathnames. However, there are two prohibitions:

   a. You cannot remove the working directory (for safety reasons).

   b. The directory must not have any files in it. Any such files can first be removed with the rm (remove) utility.

Suppose the working directory is /usr/you and the user wants to remove the directory /usr/you/databasefiles. (The user must have removed class1 and class2 first—see remove utility.)

*Solution I:*

```
$ rmdir databasefiles
$
```

*Solution II:*

```
$ rmdir /usr/you/databasefiles
$
```

The UNIX file structure is now as shown in Figure 2.8.

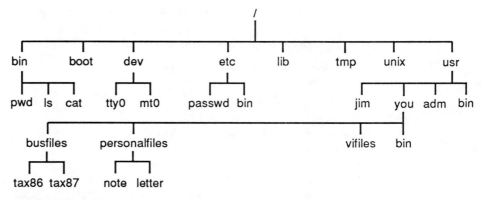

**FIGURE 2.8**   Effect of rmdir

```
rm
```

FORMAT: `rm [options] file-list`

**6.** The rm (remove file) UNIX utility allows the user to remove a specified file or files. Again he or she may use complete pathnames or relative pathnames. The rm command in its most simple form has the list of files to be removed as the arguments.

Suppose the user wants to remove the files class1 and class2 under databasefile and the working directory is /usr/you/databasefiles.

*Solution I:*

```
$ rm class1 class2
$
```

*Solution II:*

```
$ cd /usr/you
$ rm databasefiles/class1 databasefiles/class2
$
```

*Solution III:*

[Here we encounter the famous "wild card" character designated asterisk (∗).] Assume the working directory is now /usr/you:

```
$ rm databasefiles/class∗
$
```

The wild card asterisk will match any character or number of characters including zero characters. It will not, however, match a leading period (.). Thus, solution III also could have been written as:

```
$ rm databasefiles/*
$
```

or

```
$ rm databasefiles/cl*
$
```

or

```
$ rm databasefiles *s*
$
```

The first revised example removes all data files with any name whatsoever. The second removes all files that begin with a cl and may or may not have additional characters in their names. The third removes all files that begin with zero or more characters, followed by the character s, followed by zero or more characters. In any case, the new file structure is as shown in Figure 2.9.

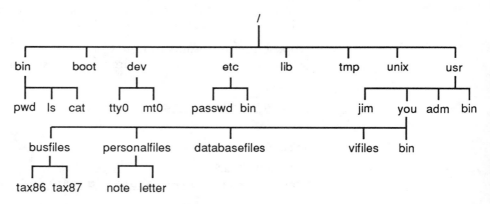

**FIGURE 2.9**   Effect of rmdir

```
                                    ┌─────┐
                                    │ mv  │
                                    └─────┘
```

```
FORMAT: mv existing-file new-file-name
        or
        mv existing-file-list directory
```

**7.** The mv (move file) UNIX utility will allow the user to move (rename) a specified file or files. Again, the user may use complete pathnames or relative pathnames. The mv command in its most simple form has the existing file and the new filename as the arguments. Suppose the user wants to move letter under personalfiles to bigletter under databasefiles and that the working directory is /usr/you.

*Solution:*

```
$ mv personalfiles/letter databasefiles/bigletter
$
```

Note that the user will have only one copy of the file. There will be no file with the name /usr/you/personalfiles/letter. The new file structure is shown in Figure 2.10:

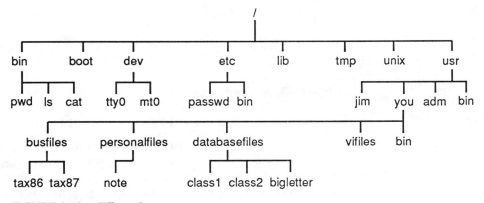

**FIGURE 2.10**    Effect of mv

Now suppose that the user wishes to moves all the databasefiles to the personalfiles directory while having each file (class1, class2, and bigletter) retain its original simple filenames. This is easily accomplished (assume the working directory is /usr/you) by:

```
$ mv databasefiles/class*! 	 personalfiles
$ mv databasefiles/bigletter personalfiles
$
```

The file structure given immediately prior to this changes to that shown in Figure 2.11:

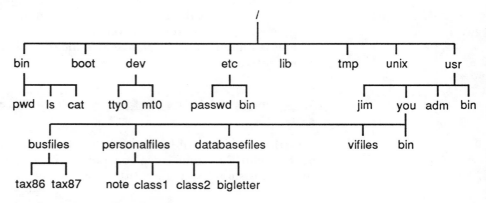

**FIGURE 2.11**    Effect of mv

```
cp
```

FORMAT: **cp source-file      destination-file**
                or
        **cp source-file-list destination-directory**

**8.** The cp (file) UNIX utility will allow the user to make a copy (copy) of a specified file or files. Again, you may use complete pathnames or relative pathnames. The cp command in its most simple form has the existing file and the new filename as the arguments. Suppose the user wants to copy letter under personalfiles to bigletter under databasefiles.

Again assume the working directory is /usr/you:

$ <u>**cp personalfiles/letter databasefiles/bigletter**</u>
$

The user now has two copies of the same file.

Now suppose, on the other hand, that the user's original intention was to copy letter under personalfiles to letter under databasefiles. And again assume the working directory is /usr/you:

$ <u>**cp personalfiles/letter databasefiles**</u>
$

```
 ┌─────────────┐
 │     ln      │
 └─────────────┘
```

FORMAT: `ln existing-file    new-link`
or
`ln existing-file-list directory`

**9.** The ln (link) UNIX utility will allow the user to access a specified file or files. Again, he or she may use complete pathnames or relative pathnames. The ln command in its most simple form has the existing file and the new link as the arguments.

Suppose the following:

**a.** jim gives you permission to write a file to his directory /usr/jim.

**b.** you want jim to have access to your file called /usr/you/personalfiles/letter.

**c.** jim wishes it to be known as /usr/jim/myletter.

The first interaction that follows is performed by "jim" and the second interaction is performed by "you" and the user's working directory is again /usr/you:

```
$ chmod a=+w /usr/jim
$
$ ln personalfiles/letter /usr/jim/myletter
$
```

The chmod utility will be explained more fully later, but for now, it sure makes sense to think that "you" cannot put a file that "you" created, like /usr/you/personalfiles/letter in the directory of jim without his permission. The chmod (change mode) utility is executed by jim, who grants that permission by saying that all (a) have permission to write (w) added (+) into the directory /usr/jim.

Each time the user creates a file, he or she is putting a pointer in a directory. The pointer associates the filename with the address on the disk of the beginning of the actual data in the file. It is quite possible and useful to have several pointers (links to the same file). There are two typical ways that can be useful:

**a.** The user wants to refer to the same file by different names or simply have access to two copies of the same file.

**b.** The owner wants to share a file with another user or group of users.

```
echo
```

FORMAT: `echo message`

   **10.** The echo UNIX utility allows the user to copy the arguments followed by a carriage return to the screen.

Suppose the user wants to echo the message "enter your input now in
standard form" to the screen. Any one of these three commands does
the job:

```
$ echo "enter your input now in standard form"
enter your input now in standard form
$ echo 'enter your input now in standard form'
enter your input now in standard form
$ echo enter your input now in standard form
enter your input now in standard form
$
```

In general, double quotes and single quotes will make a difference if
special characters, like blanks and others, are enclosed. This will be covered later.

```
        lp
     or lpr
     cancel
     lpstat
```

FORMAT: `lp [options] [file-list]`
        `lpr [options] [file-list]`
        `cancel job-id`
        `lpstat [options] [job-id]`

   **11.** The lp and lpr UNIX utilities place one or more files in the line
printer queue, thus permitting several users orderly access to the
printer. Some systems do not support the lp utility. There happens
to also be a pr UNIX utility that paginates a file for printing, including such features as spacing, headers, length, width, and
others. The utility cancel is used to cancel print jobs that have been
submitted, while the lpstat utility is used to check on the status of
print jobs in the print queue. Suppose the user wants to print the
files named memo3 and list4.

```
$ lp memo3 list4
request id is printer_4-385 (2 files)
$
```

If three copies are desired then the number (n) option should be specified:

```
$ lp -n3 memo3 list4
request id is printer_4-386 (2 files)
$
```

Notice that each print job is assigned an identification number. This permits the user to cancel the print job using the cancel utility as follows:

```
$ cancel printer_4-385
$
```

On the other hand, sometimes it is desirable to know which print jobs are still in the print queue waiting to be printed. The lpstat utility permits the user to display the status of jobs that were started with lp or lpr:

```
$ lpstat
printer_4-386 kem 4834  Nov 13 12:40
$
```

Here, job printer_4–386 has in its print queue a job from kem that has process number 4834 and was submitted on Nov. 13 at 12:40.

```
cat
```

FORMAT: cat [options] [file-list]

12. The cat UNIX utility joins files and displays the contents of one or more files on the terminal. Suppose the user wants to display the contents of the files letter1, letter2, and memo3 on the terminal.

```
$ cat letter1 letter2 memo3
  . . .
$
```

## EXERCISES 2.5

1. Use the ls utility with the following options and in each case explain the purpose of the option:
   a. -t option
   b. -l option
   c. -u option
   d. -r option
   e. several options at the same time

2. Make directories called dir1 and dir2 under your user number and within dir1 build files with vi called file1.1 and file1.2 (with any information whatsoever in them); within dir2 make similar files called file2.1 and file2.2.

3. Display the contents of each of the files created in Exercise 2 by using the cat utility.

4. Another way to build files, but without using vi, is to use the cat utility by having it take its standard input from the terminal and redirecting (the > symbol) its standard output to the name of the file specified (newfile in this case), entering the text at the terminal ending with a ctrl-d. The method is:

```
enter text here
end it with ctrl-d
```

Use this technique to build a file without using an editor.

5. Use the cp utility to copy several files from one directory to another where the simple filenames of the new files are (a) the same as the originals and (b) different from the originals.

6. Experiment with the cp utility using the wildcard (*) character to copy several files at once.

7. Experiment with the cd utility. Be sure to use the parent reference (..) in at least one example.

8. What is the purpose of the -r option for the rm utility? What about the -i option? Combine the options in an example and explain the results. Find a directory that has no useful data files or subdirectories and experiment (carefully noting the results) with $ <u>rm *</u>.

9. Rename several of your files.

10. Work with a partner to gain access to each other's files.

11. Discover how making the last characters to be echoed \c affects the placement of the prompt.

12. Send a file to the printer.

13. Send a file to the printer and then cancel the job.

14. Experiment with the lpstat utility.

15. Remove a directory.

16. Explore all the options for the cat utility, particularly -u (unbuffered) with terminal input and -s (silent) for a nonexistent file.

## 2.6 | *PERMISSIONS*

For each directory or file on the UNIX file system, there is an associated set of permissions. These permissions come in three varieties and determine who can do what with the directory or file. They are:

| | | |
|---|---|---|
| read | designated | r with a numeric value of 4 |
| write | designated | w with a numeric value of 2 |
| execute | designated | x with a numeric value of 1 |

> ### read

If you can read a file, it means the file can be cat (see it on the screen) or edited (use vi), but it cannot necessarily have changes made to it. If you can read a directory, it means it is possible to determine which files exist in that directory.

> ### write

When a file has write permission, it is possible to change the contents of the file.

When a directory has write permission, it is possible to change the contents of the directory (i.e., add and remove files in that directory).

> ### execute

When a file has execute permission, it is possible to run the file, usually by typing its name at the prompt or by having the name of the file in a batch file. Of course, the file may or may not do anything useful.

When a directory has execute permission, it is possible to make that directory the working directory and also to search the directory for a file with a known name.

In addition, for each directory or file on the UNIX file system, there are three sets of users associated with it (established by the systems administrator) namely, (1) the owner of the file designated u (user), (2) the group the owner belongs to designated g (group), and (3) all other users designated o (other).

■ **Example 2.6.1**   The ls program (with the -l option) will display the various permissions for a single file or all files in a directory:

```
$ ls -l filename
-rwxr-x--- 1 kem 101 2345 Nov 2 10:00 filename
$
```

■

The output is interpreted as follows:

character 1: can be either d or -; d indicates a directory, - indicates a file

characters 2–4: read, write, and execute permission for owner

characters 5–7: read and execute permission for group

characters 8–10: no permission for other

next field: number of copies (links) to the file (1)

next field: the name of the owner of the file (kem)

next field: the name of the group (system dependent-101)

next field: the size of the file in bytes (2345)

next field: the date and time the file was created or last modified (November 2 at 10 A.M.)

next field: the name of the file (myfile)

The character a (all) can be used to designated u, g, and o. Note also that + is used to add permission, − to remove permission, and = to grant permission to u,g,o, or a and remove permissions from all others.

■ **Example 2.6.2**   Grant read and write permission to all (a) users for file1.

*Solution I:*

```
$ chmod a=rw file1
```

*Solution II:*

```
$ chmod 666 file1
```

Note that read and write are additive in that 4=read and 2=write "add" to 6=(read and write). If the user wanted to set read permission for the user, read and write permission for the group and others, the proper solution would be:

```
$ chmod 644 file1
```

■

■ **Example 2.6.3**   Remove write permission from others for file1.

*Solution:*

```
$ chmod o-w file1
```

■

■ **Example 2.6.4**   Add execute permission for others from file1.

*Solution:*

```
$ chmod o+x file1
```
■

■ **Example 2.6.5**   Remove all permissions for group and others from file1.

*Solution:*

```
$ chmod go= file1
```
■

### EXERCISES  2.6

1. Study the chmod utility in the UNIX manual and become familiar with the octal numbering system for permissions and the symbolic system.
2. Give the octal equivalents that will grant permission for (a) the owner to read and write, (b) the group to write only, and (c) the others to execute only.
3. Research the permission designated "s" that sets the user ID or the group ID.

## 2.7  SPECIAL CHARACTERS

The user should NOT use the following characters on a command line or in a shell script unless their special purposes are known. They will be explained in Chapter 4. These characters are:

   **&**    run a process in the background

   **;**    continue on the same line with another utility

   **|**    pipe symbol—output of first process, input of second process

   **\***    wild card filename generation

   **?**    wild card single character generation

   **'**    to quote a string and not permit shell expansion

   **"**    to quote a string and permit shell expansion

   **`**    to provide in-line execution of a utility

   **[ ]**    to group together

   **( )**    to group together

   **$**    to provide the value of a variable

   **<**    to redirect input to a process

   **>**    to redirect output from a process

If the user does need to keep the shell from interpreting a special character, such as *, then precede it with a backslash. Thus, \* protects * from special interpretation.

■ **Example 2.7.1** The echo utility, when passed the argument asterisk (*), will expand it to be the list of all files in the working directory. Thus, consider Figure 2.12, a partial UNIX file system with working directory /usr/you :

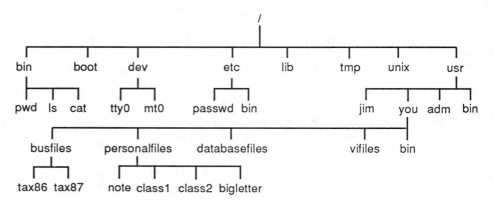

**FIGURE 2.12**  A Typical File System

```
$ echo *
busfiles bin databasefiles personalfiles vifiles
$ echo \*
*
$
```

Thus the character \ does indeed protect the special character *. ■

## EXERCISES 2.7

1. Write a brief description of the usage of each of the special characters of Section 2.7. Illustrate each with an example.
2. An illustration of the use of the wild card character asterisk (*) was given in Exercise 1. Explain the output from the following:

```
$ echo b*
```

## 2.8 | *CHAPTER SUMMARY*

1. The user enters UNIX via an identification number and (perhaps) a password, both assigned by the system administrator. Typically, the shell is then running and provides the user interface to the operating system. The session is terminated by typing ctrl-d or exit.

2. The default prompt is a dollar sign followed by a space ($ ) in System V, and the shell is then ready to execute utilities by keying in the "command line" followed by the RETURN key. The del, discon, break, or rubout keys will, on many systems, interrupt execution of a utility.

3. When the user enters vi, he or she is in command mode and can always return to command mode by depressing the esc key. The command to exit from vi is double Z (ZZ) and the C compiler is usually named double c (cc) with executable code defaulting to the file named a.out.

4. UNIX organizes files in the form of a hierarchy and permits directories, data files, and device files. Relative pathnames can be given instead of absolute pathnames to decrease the amount of key strokes.

5. The pwd (print working directory) UNIX utility returns the name of the working directory to the user.

6. The ls (list) UNIX utility permits the user to print the names of files in the working directory.

7. The mkdir (make directory) UNIX utility permits the user to create a subdirectory of an existing directory.

8. The cd (change directory) shell command permits the user to change the working directory.

9. The rmdir (remove directory) UNIX utility permits the user to remove directories.

10. The rm (remove) UNIX utility permits the user to remove files.

11. The mv (move) UNIX utility permits the user to rename files.

12. The cp (copy) UNIX utility permits the user to make a copy of existing files.

13. The ln (link) UNIX utility permits the user to access specified files.

14. The chmod (change mode) UNIX utility permits the user to modify file access permissions.

15. The echo UNIX utility permits the user to display its arguments on the screen.

16. The lp or lpr (line print) UNIX utility permits the user to print files.

17. The cat (concatenate) UNIX utility permits the user to display contents of files on the screen.

18. The user has the mechanisms available to control read, write, and execute permissions.

19. Three sets of users are associated with each file, namely, the owner, the group to which the owner belongs, and others.

20. Certain special characters need to be used wisely because they have special meanings attached to them; however, these special meanings can generally be protected with the backslash character (\).

CHAPTER **3**

# The vi Editor

## 3.1 INTRODUCTION

The line-oriented editor called ed was the original editor for use in UNIX-oriented systems. Because it was a line editor, and not a full-screen editor, it had disadvantages that hindered extensive editing. In UNIX Version 6, a full-screen editor named ex became available. The editor ex was an extended version of ed.

The ex editor has five different modes of operation. They are (1) vi command mode, (2) vi input mode, (3) vi last line mode, (4) ex command mode, and (5) ex input mode.

The vi modes (modes 1–3) have proved immensely popular and it has now become possible to enter those modes without invoking ex at all. In this text, the emphasis will be on entering vi directly without going through ex, and no attention will be given to ex itself except to say the following:

1. If the user does wish to first enter ex and then select vi (*ex→vi*), the proper commands are ex followed by vi:

   $ <u>ex</u>

      <u>vi</u>

2. If the user enters vi directly from the shell (*shell→vi*), it is still possible then to enter ex by entering the command Q (uppercase, not lowercase):

   <u>Q</u>

There are several ways to begin an editing session for the file named, say, filename. They include the following:

| Goal | Command |
|------|---------|
| Begin editing the first time | `vi filename` |
| Begin editing at line number k (useful for editing a document that has already been written, but needs specific changes) | `vi +k filename` |

| Goal | Command |
|------|---------|
| Begin editing at last line (useful to think of k as being given a large default value) | `vi + filename` |
| Begin editing at the first occurrence of the pattern word | `vi +/word filename` |
| Begin editing after a system crash (the r stands for recover and the author had this experience in the last hour—power failure, not of the author, but of the electric company) | `vi -r filename` |

Note that in the last case the disk may not be totally up to date with the contents of the buffer, hence, some data may have been irretrievably lost when the system crashed.

The four most important rules for entering vi modes will now be given. They should become second nature to the user with just a little practice.

### How to Enter vi Modes

1. When the user begins an editing session, vi is always in command mode:

   **$ `vi myfile`**

   that is to say, the user can now only give a command to the word processor vi, but cannot (yet) enter text into the document that is being edited. Command mode can always be reached (from any point within vi) by pressing the esc key.

2. To enter input mode (and thus be able to enter text into the document), any one of the following commands can be given. The user must be certain to *be in command mode for these instructions to be executed.* After each of these commands has been executed (except r), the user is in vi input mode. The user would then press esc to return to command mode after entering all data.

| Goal | Command |
|------|---------|
| Insert text before cursor | i |
| Insert text before first nonblank character on line | I |
| Append text after cursor | a |
| Append text at end of line | A |
| Open a line below current line | o |
| Open a line above current line | O |
| Replace current character | r |
| Replace characters, beginning with current character (overwrite until esc) or return | R |

3. In addition to vi input and command modes, there is the so-called vi "last line mode." Last line mode is entered by beginning a command with the colon (:). The cursor will then be positioned at the bottom (last line) of the screen ready for the user to key in the command itself. Last line mode commands must be terminated by pressing the return key. This is not necessary in ordinary command mode.

4. Both the change and the replace commands combine command and input modes. This is because both of those commands must also alter the actual text. The change command deletes text and returns the user to input mode. The replace command deletes the characters desired and inserts the desired ones.

From input mode, the erase and line kill keys allow the user to erase text that needs to be corrected. The keystrokes ctrl-W move the cursor to the beginning of the current word being entered:

```
now is the time ctrl-W now is the time
```

However, with ctrl-W, one cannot back up past the beginning of the current line, nor can one back up past the beginning of the text that has been entered since the most recent entry into input mode.

Be especially sure that the beginning letter of the command being entered is either uppercase or lowercase as desired; *vi is case sensitive*.

When the user first begins an editing session on a new file, the contents of the file are actually being manipulated in the working buffer (a portion of internal memory of predetermined size), not on the disk itself. Only at the end of the vi session, or when the working buffer is filled (whichever comes first), does a write to update the disk file take place.

Thus, changes that are made during an editing session *initially* only affect the contents of the working buffer, not the actual file on disk. One needs to be sure that these ideas are well understood. Changes made during the vi editing session that might be unintended, and thus perhaps seem disastrous, are actually only changes in the working buffer. If an editing session is ended without writing the contents of the buffer to disk, the work of that editing session is lost. If it was the user's first session with that file everything is lost, for the file was not actually saved on disk.

An editing session can be ended with the ZZ command, which both saves (dumps) the contents of the working buffer to disk and exits from vi itself:

<u>E s c</u>

<u>ZZ</u>

**$**

ZZ is the usual way to end a session. However, the command (last line mode beginning with a colon)

<u>**:q!**</u>

simply instructs vi to quit and not save the contents of the working buffer to disk. In that event, the disk copy will not be updated and, if no intermediate saves were made, may be identical to the copy retrieved when the editing session for that file began.

If the user enters vi at the prompt, does not specify the filename, enters input mode (i), enters text, and then eventually escapes to command mode to issue the save and exit sequence ZZ, then the message "No current filename" will be displayed as shown here:

| i |
|---|
| enter text |
| Esc |
| ZZ |

**No current filename.**

Similarly, if the user attempts the save and exit command ZZ and does not have write permission to that file, then the message "Permission denied" will be delivered as follows:

$ vi filename

| i |
|---|
| enter text |
| Esc |
| ZZ |

Permission denied.

Hence, the user is prohibited from writing to a file if its name is not specified or if write permission has not been granted. The former problem can be remedied by issuing the last line mode write command :w filename:

## EXERCISES  3.1

1. How would the user begin editing the file containing the login identifications of all the users at the point of the first occurrence of his or her own login identification? Note: a typical user probably does not have write permission to this file. Check with the system administrator if the name of the file containing the login identifications is not known.

2. Build a file called myfile that has the following text:

```
The line-oriented called ed was the original editor
for use in UNIX-oriented systems. Because it was a line
editor, and not a full-screen editor, it had
obvious disadvantages that hindered extensive
editing. Anyone who has worked with a line editor
can appreciate those difficulties. In UNIX
6, a full-screen editor named ex became available.
editor ex was an axtended bunion of ed.
```

Experiment with the various methods of entering vi input mode to correct the text.

   a. Position the cursor in the proper place and use i to insert the word "editor" before "called" in line 1.

   b. Position the cursor in the proper place and use I to insert the word "The" at the beginning of the last line.

   c. Position the cursor in the proper place and use a to append the word "old" between "The" and "editor" on the last line.

   d. Position the cursor at the end of the third last line and use A to put in the word "Version."

   e. Position the cursor somewhere on the first line and use o to open an additional line below it. Leave that new line blank.

   f. Position the cursor somewhere on the first line and then use O to open an additional line above it. Leave that new line blank.

g. Position the cursor at the appropriate character on the last line and use r to correct the spelling of "axtended."

h. Position the cursor at the appropriate character on the last line and use R to correct the spelling of "*bun*ion" to become "*ver*sion."

3. Try the write command in last line mode.

4. Experiment with the change and the replace commands in vi.

## 3.2 | *THE DISPLAY*

The last line displayed on the screen is the status line, which, as in many word processing packages, is used to display information about the current status of the file being edited. This includes error messages that may be generated by an improper use of an edit command, information about blocks of text that have been added or deleted, and other details. In addition, last line mode commands, those that begin with a colon (:), are also displayed on this line.

The text editor vi adheres to the philosophy that the screen display will be refreshed infrequently, and consequently the contents of the screen *may* or *may not* be the same as the corresponding contents of the working buffer. Thus, a block of text may have been successfully deleted from the working buffer, but still appear on the screen. The advantage of this approach is that the user does not have to endure long pauses that would be necessary if the screen were always faithfully being updated. This economy can be particularly important when telecommunications is taking place—access time is expensive.

The down side is that the screen may or may not be congruent with the corresponding contents of the buffer. For example, if a line has been successfully marked for deletion, the editor may simply display the at symbol (@) on the left of that line, but *keep the line on the screen*. The @ symbol itself is not written to the working buffer or to the disk. The user, fortunately, always can exercise the option of refreshing the screen at any instant; simply esc to command mode, and issue either ctrl-R or ctrl-L depending on the terminal type:

<u>Esc</u>
<u>ctrl-R or ctrl-L</u>

Another useful screen display is the tilde ($\sim$) symbol. The tilde symbol is displayed prior to each line on the screen that is beyond the current end of the disk file. So when the user initially calls the vi editor in order to eventually create a file, every line except for the first one will display a tilde (because the file can be thought of as having zero lines since nothing has been saved yet).

## EXERCISES  3.2

1. Experiment with the ctrl-R and ctrl-L keystrokes on your terminal to determine which one refreshes the screen you are using.

2. List the advantages and disadvantages of having the display screen in vi refreshed infrequently.

## 3.3 | COMMAND MODE

From command mode, the user can display on the screen any portion of the working buffer and also can move the cursor to any character on the screen. Thus, the entire working buffer is available for full-screen editing. Hence, the user must be able to (1) scroll the display through the buffer, (2) locate the proper portion to be edited, and (3) move the cursor through the visible text.

### Moving through Text

Scrolling The Display

| Goal | Method |
| --- | --- |
| Move the screen down a half screen of new text. | **ctrl-D** (for down) |
| Move the screen up a half screen of new text. | **ctrl-U** (for up) |
| Move the screen down a full screen of new text. | **ctrl-F** (forward through the text) |
| Move the screen up a full screen of new text. | **ctrl-B** (backward through the text) |
| Move the cursor to the last line of the buffer. | G (for goto) |
| Move the cursor to the kth line of the buffer. | k  G |

The cursor can be moved quickly through various units of text. These units are defined as character, word, line, sentence, paragraph, and screen. The screen unit has already been discussed. Each of the units can be preceded by a so-called *repeat factor,* which specifies how many units the cursor should be moved.

| Goal | Method |
|---|---|
| To move the cursor forward by the smallest unit, the character, repeated k times. | **k l** (k is the number of characters, l is the letter "ell"—the space bar or the right arrow can be used instead of l.) |
| To move the cursor backward by the smallest unit, the character, repeated k times. | **k h** (k is the number of characters, h is the letter "h"—the left arrow can be used instead of h.) |
| To move the cursor forward to the first character of the next word(s). | **k w** (k is the number of words, w stands for word—a group of punctuation marks counts as a single word.) |
| To move the cursor backward to the first character of the preceding word(s). | **kW** (k is the number of words.) |
| To move the cursor down by lines. | **RETURN** takes cursor to beginning of next line— the j key or the down arrow moves the cursor to the character directly below the cursor. Note that the cursor will not move beyond the last line of text. |
| To move the cursor up by lines. | The *k* or the up arrow should be used. |
| To move the cursor forward (backward) to the beginning of the next (current) sentence. | Use the command **)** . |
| To move the cursor forward (backward) to the beginning of the next (current) paragraph. | Use the command **(** . |
| To move the cursor to the top (left), middle, or last line of the screen. | **H, M, or L**—these respectively stand for home, middle, and lower. |

Command mode also provides the user with the mechanisms to delete and change text, typical word processing features. This ability to modify text can be extremely valuable during program modification sessions. The user thus needs to be proficient using these features.

As we have indicated, the vi commands work on chunks of text called units of text. It is necessary to understand the precise and technical definition of these units.

### Units of Text

A *white space* character is defined as either the space character, or the tab character, or any nonprinting character.

A *character* is defined as any single character, either a printable character or a white space character.

A *word* is defined as either (a) one or more characters that is (are) *immediately preceded* by a punctuation mark, space, tab, digit, or newline *and immediately followed* by one character from the same group; (b) a group consisting of only one or more punctuation marks.

■ **Examples 3.3.1**

| Text | Count | Words | | | |
|------|-------|-------|---|---|---|
| dog | 1 | dog | | | |
| 3dog night | 2 | 3dog night | | | |
| !.dog nite | 3 | !. | dog | nite | |
| !dog! nite | 4 | ! | dog | ! | nite ■ |

A *blank delimited word* is defined as a word including any adjacent punctuation. Blank delimited words are separated by space, tab, or newline; that is, they are *delimited* by *blanks*.

■ **Examples 3.3.2**

| Text | Count | Blank Delimited Words | | | |
|------|-------|-----------------------|---|---|---|
| dog | 1 | dog | | | |
| dog!. | 1 | dog!. | | | |
| !dog nite | 2 | !dog | nite | | |
| !dog ! nite | 3 | !dog | ! | nite | |
| dog, ! ! ! | 4 | dog, | ! | ! | ! ■ |

A *line* is defined as a string of characters bounded on each side by the newline character. Note that a line may not appear to be as such on the screen—it may in fact occupy several "screen lines" because of wrap.

A *sentence* is defined as just what it normally is in English; that is, a sentence is textual matter that always ends with a period, exclamation point, or question mark, followed by at least two spaces or a newline. Note that the two spaces and newline are not part of the sentence, but its ending punctuation is. This can be confusing unless one remembers that sentences need hard separation (newline) or long separation (two spaces).

A *paragraph* is defined as text that is preceded and followed by at least two newlines (super separation). Be careful that indentation is not confused with newlines.

A *screen* is what is seen on the display terminal.

FORMAT: Summary

| Unit | Delimiters |
|------|------------|
| word | punctuation, white space, or digit |
| blank delimited word | white space |
| line | newline |
| sentence | newline or two spaces |
| paragraph | two newlines |
| screen | portions of the buffer |

## Repeat Factor and Delete

In addition to the units of measure, commands may include a repeat factor option. Thus, for example, while w represents the unit word, 5w represents five words. The repeat factor defaults to one.

The basic *delete commands* are denoted by the single characters d and x. Remember that d and x are commands, and the user must be in command mode to execute them. To enter command mode from input mode, press esc.

Now, the basic philosophy is to enter the command, followed by the repeat factor (defaults to one), followed by the unit of measure.

| Goal | Method |
|------|--------|
| To delete k characters, beginning with the current character. | **k x** For example, to delete five characters beginning with the cursor character, use 5x. |
| To delete k units from the buffer. | **d k u** For example, to delete five words from the buffer, use d5w. Other units available include right parenthesis,), for sentences and left brace,{, for paragraphs. |
| To delete k lines. | **k dd** Note that k defaults to one and that 2dd can alternatively be given as simply d. Deletion always begins with the current line. |

■ **Example 3.3.3**    The d command can be used in a very powerful way by changing either the repeat factor, the unit of measure, or both. For example, to delete from the current line through the end of the buffer use dG (G for global). Similarly, to delete from the current line back through the beginning of the buffer, use d1G. Likewise, dH (H for high) will delete from the top line on the screen through the current line, while dL (L for last or low) will delete from the current line through the last line of the screen. ■

■ **Example 3.3.4**    The command d{ will delete from the current character back through the beginning of the paragraph, while d} will delete from the current character forward through the end of the paragraph. The repetition factor can be used: thus d5{ deletes from the current character back through the beginning of the fifth preceding paragraph. Similar patterns hold for the sentence unit designated by ), going forward, and (, going backward. ■

■ **Example 3.3.5**    The command dW will delete to the end of a blank delimited word, while dB will delete back to the beginning of a blank delimited word (W can be thought of as designating a kind of super word, and capital B takes the user back to the beginning of a super word). Using the repeat factor, d5W will delete through the fifth blank delimited word. Lowercase w and lowercase b are used for "standard" words. ■

### Changing and Replacing

Besides deleting text, the user will often want to change or replace text. One phrase can replace another, several lines can replace a single line, a character can replace a paragraph—the possibilities are endless. The change command is the single character c. The idea is: enter command mode, press c (change) followed by the repeat factor (defaults to one), followed by the unit of text. After this, vi automatically reverts to input mode. While in input mode, enter the new text and press esc—presto, the old text (the repeat factor applied to the unit is replaced by the interactively entered text)! Note that the text is not deleted from the screen immediately; instead, a $ sign appears at the end of the text that will be changed, and the user remains in input mode. Text that appears to be overwritten will be restored upon pressing esc (except for that actually deleted by c).

| Goal | Method |
|------|--------|
| To change k words, beginning with the current word. | **c k w** For example, to change to end of fifth word beginning with the cursor, use c5w. |
| To change to end of kth sentence. | **c k )** For example, to change to end of fifth sentence (from cursor), use c5). Similarly, to change to beginning of fifth preceding sentence, use c5(. |
| To change k lines. | **k c c** For example, to change five lines starting with the current line, use 5cc. Note that k defaults to one and that deletion always begins with the current line. |

The c command can be used in a very powerful way by changing either the repeat factor, the unit of text, or both. For example, to change from the current line through the end of the buffer use cG (G for global). Similarly, to change from the current line back through the beginning of the buffer use c1G. Likewise, cH (H for high) will change from the top line on the screen through the current line, while cL (L for last or low) will change from the current line through the last line of the screen.

■ **Example 3.3.6** The command c{ will change from the current character back through the beginning of the paragraph, while c} will change from the current character forward through the end of the paragraph. The repetition factor can be used; thus, c5{ changes from the current character back through the beginning of the fifth preceding paragraph. Similar patterns hold for the sentence unit designated by ), going forward, and (, going backward. ■

■ **Example 3.3.7** The command cW will change to the end of a blank delimited word, while cB will change back to the beginning of a blank delimited word (W is thought of again as designating a super word, and capital B takes the user back to the beginning of a super word). Using the repeat factor, c5W will change through the fifth blank delimited word. Lowercase w and lowercase b are used for "standard" words. ■

## EXERCISES 3.3

1. Edit a file and practice at least six different ways to scroll the display.

2. Practice moving the cursor forward and backward by single characters and by words.

3. Count the number of words and blank delimited words in the following paragraph:
The command cW will change to the end of a blank delimited word, while cB will change back to the beginning of a blank delimited word (W is thought of again as designating a super word, and capital B takes the user back to the beginning of a super word). Using the repeat factor, c5W will change through the 5th blank delimited word. Lowercase w and lowercase b are used for "standard" words.

4. Practice with the repeat factor applied to the d command on the paragraph given in Exercise 3.

5. Practice with the repeat factor applied to the c command on the paragraph given in Exercise 3.

## 3.4 | INPUT MODE

There are four basic commands that allow the user to enter input mode: insert, append (two versions), open (two versions), change, and replace (two versions). Each has its own particular use.

The *insert command,* i, permits the user to insert text, which has the effect of pushing forward the text beginning at the cursor character. It literally allows insertion between chunks of text. The cursor is designated in the following examples by an underscore character.

■ **Example 3.4.1**

| Text | Command |
|---|---|
| now is the time all good men | Esc  i |
| now is the time for_all good men | ■ |

■ **Example 3.4.2**

| Text | Command |
|---|---|
| now is the time for all good men to me to | Esc  i |
| now is the time for all good men to come to | ■ |

The *append command,* a, permits the user to enter text that also pushes text forward. However, insertion begins at the character following the cursor. The A command is similar except that insertion begins after the last character on the current line.

■ **Example 3.4.3**

| Text | Command |
|---|---|
| now is the time for all good men to com to the | Esc  a |
| now is the time for all good men to come to the | ■ |

The *open command,* o, permits the user to open a blank line below the cursor and places the cursor at the beginning of that line. Similarly, O opens a blank line above the cursor and places the cursor at the beginning of that line.

■ **Example 3.4.4**    *Text:*

```
now is the time for all good men to come to the
aid of their party. Now is the time for all good
men to come to the aid of their party.
```

*Command: Esc O*

```
now is the time for all good men to come to the

aid of their party. Now is the time for all good
men to come to the aid of their party.
```

*Command: Esc o*

```
now is the time for all good time to come to the

aid of their party. Now is the time for all good

men to come to the aid of their party.
```

Thus, to insert a new line between old lines 1 and 2 use O, but to insert a new line between old lines 2 and 3 use o. ■

The *replace command,* r, followed by a single character, causes the character at the cursor to be overwritten with that character (user is returned to command mode). However, R, followed by any string of characters, causes the character at the cursor and subsequent characters to be overwritten with that string (user must then press esc to return to command mode). Be especially careful with TABs—a TAB is a single character.

■ **Example 3.4.5**    *Text:*

```
now is the time for all goody men to go to the
aid of their party.
```

*Command: R and decentEsc*

```
now is the time for all good and decent to the
aid of their party.
```
■

## EXERCISES 3.4

1. Experiment with the commands i, a, and A.
2. Experiment with the commands o and O.
3. Experiment with the commands r and R.

## 3.5 | *SEARCHING AND SUBSTITUTING*

The vi editor permits forward or backward searches through the buffer for a particular string or for a string with certain characteristics. The forward slash, /, initiates forward searches, while the question mark, ?, initiates backward searches. After the / or the ?, the user immediately follows with the string sought (all of which will appear on the status line).

To find the next occurrence of the string "now is the time," press esc (to return to command mode if necessary), press /, and type the phrase "now is the time" followed by a return:

**Esc/now is the timeRETURN**

Successful searches will position the cursor on the first character of the desired string. If the string is not found by the time the search has reached the end of the buffer (/) or the beginning (?), the search will wrap and continue at the beginning of the buffer (/) or the end (?).

The n and N keys permit the user to repeat the previous search either in the same direction (n) or the opposite (N).

### Special Characters

Some characters, when included in the search string, have a special meaning that permits greater power in searches. These characters include:

caret: ^

dollar sign: $

period: .

end of word indicator, which is the backward slash followed by the greater than symbol: \>

beginning of the word indicator, which is the backward slash followed by the less than symbol: \<

character class definition, which uses square brackets: [ ]

There is no way to turn off the special meaning of the caret and the dollar sign, however, the others can have their special meanings disabled. The method to disable the special meanings will be discussed later.

■ **Example 3.5.1**  The caret placed at the beginning of the search string forces the search string to appear at the beginning of a line for a successful search to take place. Thus,

> `/^now`

will only find the next occurrence of now if it appears at the beginning of a line while

> `/now`

will find the next occurrence of now regardless of its position on the line. ■

■ **Example 3.5.2**  The dollar sign placed at the end of the search string forces the search string to appear at the end of a line for a successful search to take place. Thus,

> `/party.$`

will only find "party." if it appears at the end of a line (forward match). ■

■ **Example 3.5.3**  The period will match any character and must be repeated for multiple matches. Thus,

> `/l..er`

will find words like lover, liver, loner, and laker (forward match). ■

■ **Example 3.5.4**  The pair of characters \> will match the end of a word. Thus,

> `/es>\`

will find words like cheeses, fries, and tingles (forward match). ■

■ **Example 3.5.5**  The pair of characters \< will match the beginning of a word. Thus,

> `/\<house`

will find the next word that begins with house, such as houseboat, houses, or houseflies. ■

■ **Example 3.5.6**  Square brackets enclosing two or more characters match any individual character found between the brackets. Thus,

> `/l[aeiou]er`

will find the next occurrence of laer, leer, lier, loer, and luer. ■

■ **Example 3.5.7**  A caret (^) and a dash (–) inside square brackets have special meaning. If the caret is the first character inside, then the match occurs for any character *except* those listed. The dash, on the other hand, indicates a range of characters to match. Thus,

`/[^aeiou]xy`

will find the next string that begins with a single nonvowel followed by the string xy. Contrast that with

`/^aeiouxy`

which will find the next line that begins with "aeiouxy". ■

■ **Example 3.5.8**  Because the dash inside square brackets indicates a range, the command

`/[^1-47-9]a.e`

will find the next string that begins with the digit 0,5,or 6 followed by the character a, then any character, then the character e; for example 5abe is matched. ■

■ **Example 3.5.9**  The command

`/^.[14]$`

will match any line that begins with any character (.), followed by a single character (because of the [14], which must end the line because of the dollar sign). Thus, the only string it will find is a line with exactly two characters, the last of which is a one or a four. ■

The purpose of the search commands given above is to find strings that can then be removed, replaced, or otherwise edited. Many times in programming it is desirable to substitute one string with another. This combines the search and change commands. The substitute command begins with a colon ":" (last line command) and has the following general format:

`:[address]s/search-string/replace-string/[/g]`

where address indicates the portion of the buffer to be searched, s is the substitute command itself, search-string is the string sought, replace-string is the substituted string, g is the global flag.

The editor uses the *address* to search only those lines specified by that address. The lines represent lines of the buffer. If the address is not specified, it defaults to the *current* line. The current line is indicated by its number or the character ".". The last line in the buffer is indicated by its number or the character "$". Relative (to the current line) increments can be obtained by using plus or minus signs. The line numbers given are separated by a comma.

■ **Example 3.5.10**

| Command | Result |
|---|---|
| `:5,5s/x1/y1` | On line five only, substitute x1 with y1, but only for the first occurrence of x1 (g flag omitted). Note that 5s/x1/y1 will do the same. |
| `:10,23s/six/6/g` | On lines 10 through 23, substitute six with 6 for all occurrences (the g option). |
| `:1,.s/\<house\>/ home/g` | On lines one through current line (.), substitute the word house with the word home for all occurrences (note that houseboat will not become homeboat because of the \>. Also, boathouse will not become boathome because of the \<. |
| `:1,$s/city/town` | On lines one through end ($) of buffer, substitute the word city with the word town, first occurrence only on each line. |
| `:.,.+20s/city/ town/g` | On the current line (.) and through the next 20 lines, substitute each and every occurrence (g) of city with town. |

■

## EXERCISES 3.5

1. Which character is used to initiate searches backward through the buffer?

2. Explain the meaning of the dollar sign and the caret (^) when used in searches.

3. How would you search for all lines that end with the word party?

4. How would you find all lines that begin with the word now and also end with the word party?

5. How would you find which of the next 20 lines contains the three-letter word that begins with the character b, ends with the character t, and has a vowel in between?

6. How would you find which of the previous 20 lines contains the four-letter word that begins with an even digit, followed by the three-letter word specified in Exercise 5?

7. How would you substitute the word program with the word procedure on lines 40 through 80 (all occurrences)?

8. Do Exercise 7 for the previous 40 lines.

## 3.6 | *READING AND WRITING FILES*

Disk files are brought into the work buffer by calling vi from the shell. When the ZZ command is given, the vi editing session is terminated and the contents of the work buffer are written back to the disk file. Thus,

    **vi**          work buffer ←———— disk file

invoked at the prompt $, and

    **ZZ**          disk file ←———— work buffer

invoked from within vi provide the basic I/O.

There are, however, many variations in this theme.

Sometimes in the course of writing a program the author wishes to import a disk file into the file currently being edited. This imported file might be a common set of declarations used in several programs, or perhaps a function that does a sort or has some other useful output. In order to import the disk file, the user positions the cursor at the appropriate place in the edited file (the imported file will be inserted following the current line) and gives the last line command

    `:r [filename]`

where r means read, and filename is the pathname of the file that the user wants to import. Filename defaults to the file that is currently being edited (which generally is not what is intended to be imported). Remember, because this is a last line command, the entire command beginning with the colon appears on the status line.

Similarly, the author might wish to export or write a portion (or all) of the work buffer to a disk file. The portion wanted is specified by an address, which defaults to the entire work buffer; the name of the disk file to receive the portion of the work buffer defaults to the file being edited, thus updating the edited file on the disk. The appropriate command is the write command with the format

    `:w [address][!] [filename]`

Remember that the address is optional and defaults to the entire work buffer. But, for example, to write lines 10 through 100 of the work buffer to the existing disk file /usr/you/saveit, simply issue the command:

    `:w 10,100 ! /usr/you/saveit`

The exclamation point is necessary when the user is writing a portion of the file being edited to itself (which can be very dangerous) or when overwriting another existing file, such as /usr/you/oldfile as in:

    `:w 10,100 ! /usr/you/oldfile`

The point is (no pun intended) that the exclamation point is a safety feature to prevent possible overwriting catastrophes. If, on the other hand, the user simply wishes to write the entire work buffer to the file being edited, the appropriate command is:

:w

which is a good idea during a long editing session. The exclamation point also is not needed when a portion or all of the work buffer is being written to a new file called /usr/you newfile, such as in:

:w 10,100 /usr/you/newfile

## EXERCISES 3.6

1. What is the purpose of the exclamation point when used in the write (w) command of vi?
2. What is the format of the read command?
3. Explain why an error message might be received when a read or write is attempted even though the file in question exists.

## 3.7 PARAMETERS

It is very common for a particular user to have a unique set of criteria that he or she wishes vi to meet. This can include such features as always numbering lines during editing sessions, providing automatic and consistent indentation for C programs, providing the display of invisible characters, and other tasks. The best way to provide these services is to set various parameters in a file called .profile (Bourne shell), so that they are automatically initialized upon logon. A more cumbersome way to set parameters is from within vi by entering last line mode with the colon (:) in order to issue the set command

:set parm1 parm2 parm3...

where parm1, parm2, and so on are replaced with specific parameters.

Again, the best way is to put the commands in the .profile file in the user's home directory. This works with the aid of a variable called EXINIT, which is always read by vi upon invocation. The vi editor receives the values set by EXINIT by having them exported with the export verb. The general format by this method is:

EXINIT='set parm1 parm2 parm3...'
export EXINIT

where parm1, parm2, and so on are replaced with specific parameters.

The user can determine the current list of parameters and their values by giving the last line command named set (from vi):

`:set all`

This can be used if the terminal is behaving strangely and corrective action is needed.

Another useful approach is to display the line number associated with each line of text. This can help immensely in the editing process when addresses are required. To display line numbers, replace any parm with the word "number"; to return to no line numbers, replace any parm with the word "nonumber." In any case, the line numbers are simply for display purposes and are not stored on the disk file.

The editor vi will automatically break text at a specified number of characters *from the right margin* by inserting a newline at the boundary of the last available blank delimited word. The user then does not need to insert newlines after each line of input. This parameter is called *wrapmargin* and is set by replacing any parm by:

`wrapmargin=mm`

where mm is the minimum number of characters from the right side of the screen. Thus, setting

`wrapmargin=05`

insures that words that would normally extend closer than five characters from the right side must be displayed entirely on that line or they will be put entirely on the next line. Right justification is not performed. If the user, on the other hand, writes

`wrapmargin=00`

then this feature is disabled.

One of the most useful features (particularly for beginners) is the *showmode* parameter, which displays the phrase "input mode" when the user is in input mode. This can be extremely valuable because often a command will be attempted when the user is still in input mode. The message "input mode" is displayed when any parm is replaced by

`showmode`

and not displayed when any parm is replaced by

`noshowmode`

Along the same lines, common errors are to press esc even though the user is already in command mode (no harm done), or to give an invalid command while in command mode. In each instance the user will normally hear a short beep (the default). This sound can be changed to a flash by substituting any parm with

**flash**

and can be changed back to the default (beep) by replacing any parm with

**noflash**

As mentioned in the section on searches, vi *does* distinguish between uppercase and lowercase letters. To eliminate this distinction, replace any parm with

**ignorecase**

and to change back to the default (case sensitive), replace any parm with

**noignorecase**

UNIX provides that the following characters (or character pairs) normally have special meanings when used in searches:

.      \<      \>      [ ]

These can be disabled as special characters during searches by replacing any parm with

**nomagic**

and can be changed back to the default with

**magic**

Be aware that the ^ and $ characters always have special meanings in searches—they cannot be overridden.

Invisible characters can be a headache if they are inadvertently put in text. TABs, for example, and newlines are generally not visible. This can be overridden by replacing any parm with

**list**

which will cause a TAB to be displayed as ^1 and a newline to be displayed as $. The default method of display can be invoked by simply replacing any parm with

**nolist**

In the course of editing a file, the user may want to search for a string that occurs anywhere in the document. The default procedure is that in forward searches the search will begin at the current position, go forward, and wrap (continuing the search) to the beginning of the work buffer. In backward searches, the default begins at the current position, goes backward, and wraps (continuing the search) to the end of the work buffer. These can be overridden so that searches stop at the end of the work buffer by replacing any parm with

`nowrapscan`

and can be returned to default by replacing any parm with

`wrapscan`

Automatic indentation can be achieved by replacing two parms with

`shiftwidth=mm autoindent`

and using ctrl-T in input mode to move to the next indentation position, or ctrl-D to move back to the previous indentation.

The mm is replaced by the spacing of the indentation positions. For example, shiftwidth=05 will set the tabs every five spaces. The feature returns to default by replacing any parm with

`noautoindent`

## EXERCISES 3.7

1. Explain the purpose of the set command and find all the options for its parameters in the vi manual.
2. What is the main advantage of using the set command in the profile file?
3. Explain the purpose of the EXINIT variable.
4. Explain the purpose of the nomagic parm.
5. Set automatic indentation in your profile to satisfy your needs in writing C programs.

## 3.8 MISCELLANEOUS

The status of the current file being edited can be displayed by the command *ctrl-G*. The information displayed includes the name of the file, the current line number, the number of lines in the buffer, and the percentage of the buffer preceding the current line.

Another useful command is the plain, old *period* (.). The period command repeats the most recent command that made a change in the buffer. For example, suppose the user has most recently given the command d) to delete to the end of the sentence. After moving the cursor to the appropriate place, the same command can be repeated with the single keystroke period (.). This command can also be effectively used to perform selective substitutions throughout the text.

In addition to the working buffer, vi has 26 additional buffers, called *alphabetic buffers,* named a through z, and a *general purpose buffer* for a total of 27. The alphabetic buffers permit the user to have extensive file and block manipulation capabilities during an editing session. The additional buffers must be explicitly requested in order for them to be used. One can imagine the fruitful benefits of being able to temporarily store text in alternative buffers during an editing session for a C program that needs debugging, and then being able to move that text back into the C program at another desired location. This ability on more recent vintage word processors is known as "block copy and move" capability, and the particular buffer in most instances is simply hidden from the user (because only one is often available).

The text most recently changed or deleted from the working buffer is automatically stored in the general purpose buffer. This buffer permits the user to restore text into the working buffer via the undo command.

If the user thinks back to the discussion of delete commands given earlier, the text was actually deleted from the working buffer; however, the text was also temporarily saved (until the next change) in the general purpose buffer. The *yank* commands are similar to the delete commands except that the text is not deleted from the working buffer—it is simply copied to the general purpose buffer from which the user may put (or Put) a copy of it back to any desired place in the work buffer.

### The General Purpose Buffer

Text that is deleted, changed, or yanked is put into the general purpose buffer. The next such action of any of these types destroys the previous contents of the general purpose buffer. Thus, for example, the undo command actually moves text from the general purpose buffer back into the work buffer. In summary (with the effect upon the work buffer shown):

| | |
|---|---|
| **Delete** | general purpose buffer ← work buffer (altered) |
| **Change** | general purpose buffer ← work buffer (altered) |
| **Yank** | general purpose buffer ← work buffer (no change) |
| **Undo** | work buffer ← general purpose buffer (no change) |

### The Put Commands

The Put and put commands both move certain contents of the general purpose buffer back into the work buffer. In summary, with the effect upon the general purpose buffer shown:

**Put**    work buffer ← general purpose buffer (no change)
(Words and characters are placed in the work buffer
before the current character; lines, sentences, and
paragraphs are placed in the work buffer before the
line the cursor is on.)

**put**    work buffer ← general purpose buffer (no change)
(Words and characters are placed in the work buffer
after the current character; lines, sentences, and
paragraphs are placed in the work buffer after the line
the cursor is on.)

The idea is to combine the delete, change, and yank commands with
the Put and put commands to move text from one place in the work buffer
to another. Because the Put and put commands do not change the contents of the general purpose buffer, the same text may be put back into
the work buffer at several locations. The user must be aware that each
delete, change, and yank command will refresh the general purpose
buffer entirely; thus, the user must be very careful not to change the
general purpose buffer between modifications (like delete, change, and
yank) and puts (put and Put).

## The Delete Commands

The delete commands (described in Section 3.3) place the deleted text
in the general purpose buffer, from which it can be placed back in the
work buffer with a put or Put command at any designated place by proper
movement of the cursor. The yank commands behave exactly as the delete
commands except that only a copy of the yanked text is placed in the
general purpose buffer—the contents of the work buffer are unchanged.
Remember the distinction between d RETURN and dd. The same applies to y RETURN and yy; the former yanks two lines, the latter yanks
only the current line.

## The Alphabetic Buffers

The movement of text back and forth between the work buffer and the
general purpose buffer (with a delete, change, yank or put) can be overridden so that movement occurs between the work buffer and any of the
alphabetic buffers. Considerable flexibility is achieved, including the
opportunity to overwrite an alphabetic buffer or simply to append to it.
The general idea is to precede the usual command with a double quote
and the name of the alphabetic buffer, lowercase or uppercase. But note,

lowercase letters signal vi to overwrite the alphabetic buffer when it deletes text from the alphabetic buffer or yanks text into the alphabetic buffer; uppercase letters, on the other hand, signal vi to append to the alphabetic buffer the newly deleted or yanked text.

■ **Example 3.8.1**    `"bDelete`    b buffer ← work buffer (altered) (delete from the work buffer and place in the b buffer, overwriting) ■

■ **Example 3.8.2**    `"BDelete`    b buffer ← work buffer (altered) (delete from the work buffer and place in the b buffer, appending) ■

■ **Example 3.8.3**    `"bYank`    b buffer ← work buffer (no change) (yank from the work buffer and place in the b buffer, overwriting) ■

■ **Example 3.8.4**    `"BYank`    b buffer ← work buffer (no change) (yank from the work buffer and place in the b buffer, appending) ■

Note that text can be collected from many places in the work buffer and placed together in a single alphabetic buffer or buffers by using uppercase letters.

The user has several additional features available in vi, including the ability to "mark" up to 26 different places in the text for easy reference. The markers are labeled a–z and can be used to mark various lines. For example, to mark line 34 with the marker b, position the cursor on line 34, esc to command mode, and enter the command

<u>mb</u>

where m stands for mark, and b is the marker itself. To move to the line marked by b from anywhere in the work buffer, give the command

<u>'b</u>

The user also has the ability to delete text from the current line to the line marked by b by giving the command

<u>d 'r</u>

The user can also do substitutions with reference to markers. For example, to delete all text from the current line to the line with marker b, issue the command

<u>: d 'b</u>

The real power of the marker idea comes in substitutions. Suppose the user has begun an editing session and immediately marked the line with marker b. Then imagine that the user has typed one hundred additional lines and notes that throughout the new text a word, say, category, has been misspelled as catagory. No problem! Simply issue the following command, applied from the line marked with b to the current line (.), to substitute catagory with category for every occurrence:

`:'b,.s/catagory/category/g`

Note that when the work buffer is written to disk and the editing session has ended, the markers are not retained in the file.

A great deal of power is available with the last line e command (e for edit). The user has the ability to issue a last line e command to edit any file. For example, to edit the previously saved file called oldfile, during the editing of newfile, the user should save the work buffer to newfile and issue the edit command as follows:

`:w newfile`

`:e oldfile`

On the other hand, if the work buffer does not need to be written to disk, then the proper command is

`:e! oldfile`

Furthermore, oldfile defaults to the file currently being edited. So if the user wants to begin a new editing session, without writing the work buffer to disk, then the proper command is

`:e!`

Now, however, comes the interesting part. The :e command does *not* destroy the contents of the alphabetic buffers; it does, however, destroy the contents of the general purpose buffer. So suppose that the user has four blocks of text in oldfile that will be needed in other files, file1 through file4. The user can store single blocks in buffers a through d while editing oldfile. Then issue the command

`:e file1`

and subsequently move the text from buffer a (for example) to file1. Repeat the same procedure with the other files.

Finally, the power to execute shell commands is available to the user in vi. While in vi, issue the last line command

`:sh`

which creates a new shell. Now, issue whatever shell command is needed (for example ls or cat), and then when it is time to exit the new shell, press ctrl-d, as usual (end of input to that shell). Remember, however, that even though the user has produced a new shell, vi is still, for all intents and purposes, editing the old file. This is because vi was only temporarily suspended. In particular, vi still is working with the old work buffer. It is usually a bad mistake (there are of course no good mistakes) to begin editing the same old file again because vi will associate a brand new work buffer with that file, and the contents of the old work buffer will be destroyed. This is because each invocation of vi creates a new work buffer. It is also possible to issue a shell command that will return the user at the completion of the utility to vi. For example, to execute the ls utility and return to vi upon completion, enter the last line command

> `:!ls`

But there's more! The user can even send the output of a shell command into the text that is being edited—note that the current line of the text is actually replaced, so it is best to put the cursor on a blank line before doing this. To put the output from the previous ls in the text, position the cursor where the output should be sent, and issue the command

> `!!ls`

In the last case, the cursor moves to the status line after the second ex-clamation point.

What!! There's even more! How about making the input to a shell command as part or all of the file being edited and, at the same time, making the output from the command replace the input. Suppose that the input should be that portion of the file between the cursor and the marker b. First, mark the appropriate place with the command

> `mb`

Now, move the cursor to the beginning of the block of text that will be the input. Then, for example, sort that portion of the text in reverse order by giving the command

> `!'bsort -r`

which means to mark the text from the cursor to the b marker and make that text the input to the sort utility, sorted in reverse order (-r).

Similarly to sort the *entire* text, move the cursor to the beginning of the text, and give the command

> `!Gsort`

which means to sort globally (the entire text).

Remember, the undo command can retrieve the original results, if necessary.

## *EXERCISES* 3.8

1. Specify all the buffers available in a vi session and their possible uses.
2. Distinguish among the delete, change, and yank commands.
3. Distinguish between the put and Put commands.
4. Distinguish between using uppercase versus lowercase letters in reference to alphabetic buffers.
5. Write four chunks of text in a single file, save each chunk in different alphabetic buffers, and then store them in reverse order in a new file.
6. Explain how the input to a shell command can be given in a file and then also have the output from the command replace the input.

## 3.9 | *CHAPTER SUMMARY*

1. The user typically enters the editor vi by typing vi filename, where filename is the name of the file to be edited; the user is initially placed in command mode, and can enter it at any time by pressing esc.
2. The typical ways to enter input mode are via the i or a commands.
3. ZZ is the typical way to save to disk from a vi editing session.
4. The display can be scrolled with ctrl followed by D, U, F, or B.
5. Cursor movement can be controlled by units of measure (text) and repeat factors.
6. The editor vi permits forward and backward searching and substitution.
7. Addresses within files can be specified for writing selected portions of files to other files.
8. Parameters for vi can be set from last line mode, from the shell itself, or most conveniently within the .profile file.
9. The editor vi has 28 different buffers that the user can use.
10. The delete, change, and yank commands move text from the work buffer to the general purpose buffer; the put and Put commands move text in the other direction.
11. The shell can be accessed from vi, including using edited text as input to a command, and output from the command as a replacement for that text.

### A Summary of Some Important Facts

| | |
|---|---|
| Begin editing the first time | `vi filename` |
| Begin editing at line number k | `vi +k filename` |
| Begin editing at last line | `vi + filename` |
| Begin editing at the first occurrence of the pattern "word" | `vi +/word filename` |
| Begin editing after a system crash | `vi -r filename` |
| Insert text before cursor | `i` |
| Insert text before first nonblank character on line | `I` |
| Append text after cursor | `a` |
| Append text at end of line | `A` |
| Open a line below current line | `o` |
| Open a line above current line | `O` |
| Replace current character | `r` |
| Replace characters, beginning with current character (overwrite until esc) or return | `R` |
| Move the screen down a half screen of new text. | `ctrl-D` (for down) |
| Move the screen up a half screen of new text. | `ctrl-U` (for up) |
| Move the screen down a full screen of new text. | `ctrl-F` (forward through the text) |
| Move the screen up a full screen of new text. | `ctrl-B` (backward through the text) |
| Move the cursor to the last line of the buffer. | `G` (for goto) |
| Move the cursor to the kth line of the buffer. | `k G` |
| To move the cursor forward by the smallest unit, the character, repeated k times. | `k l` (k is the number of characters, 1 is the letter "ell"—the space bar or the right arrow can be used instead of 1) |

| | |
|---|---|
| To move the cursor backward by the smallest unit, the character, repeated k times. | **k h** (k is the number of characters, h is the letter "h"—the left arrow can be used instead of h) |
| To move the cursor forward to the first character of the next word(s). | **k w** (k is the number of words, w stands for word—a group of punctuation marks counts as a single word) |
| To move the cursor backward to the first character of the preceding word(s). | **k W** (k is the number of words) |
| To move the cursor down by lines. | **RETURN** takes cursor to beginning of next line— the "J" key or the down arrow moves the cursor to the character directly below the cursor. Note that the cursor will not move beyond the last line of text. |
| To move the cursor up by lines. | The **k** or the up arrow should be used. |
| To move the cursor forward (backward) to the beginning of the next (current) sentence. | Use the command **)** |
| To move the cursor forward (backward) to the beginning of the next (current) paragraph. | Use the command **(** |
| To move the cursor to the top (left), middle, or last line of the screen. | **H, M, or L**—these respectively stand for home, middle, and lower |
| To delete k characters, beginning with the current character. | **k x** For example, to delete five characters beginning with the cursor character, use 5x |
| To delete k units from the buffer. | **d k u** For example, to delete five words from the buffer, use d5w. Other units available include right parenthesis,), for sentences and left brace,{, for paragraphs |

| | |
|---|---|
| To delete k lines. | **k dd** Note that k defaults to one and that 2dd can alternatively be given as simply d. Deletion always begins with the current line |
| To change k words, beginning with the current word. | **c k w** For example, to change to end of fifth word beginning with the cursor, use c5w |
| To change to end of kth sentence. | **c k )** For example, to change to end of fifth sentence (from cursor), use c5). Similarly, to change to beginning of fifth preceding sentence, use c5( |
| To change k lines. | **k cc** For example, to change five lines starting with the current line, use 5cc. Note that k defaults to one and that deletion always begins with the current line |
| **:5,5s/x1/y1** | On line five only, substitute x1 with y1, but only for the first occurrence of x1 (g flag omitted). Note that 5s/x1/y1 will do the same |
| **:10,23s/six/6/g** | On lines 10 through 23, substitute six with 6 for all occurrences (the g option) |
| **:1,.s/\<house\>/home/g** | On lines one through current line (.), substitute the word house with the word home for all occurrences (note that houseboat will not become homeboat because of the \>. Also, boathouse will not become boathome because of the \< |

| | |
|---|---|
| `:1,$s/city/town` | On lines one through end ($) of buffer, substitute the word city with the word town, first occurrence only on each line |
| `:.,.+20s/city/town/g` | On the current line (.) and through the next 20 lines, substitute each and every occurrence (g) of city with town |
| `vi` | work buffer ◄——— disk file |
| | invoked at the prompt $, and |
| `ZZ` | disk file ◄——— work buffer |
| | invoked from within vi provide the basic I/O |
| `Delete` | general purpose buffer ← work buffer (altered) |
| `Change` | general purpose buffer ← work buffer (altered) |
| `Yank` | general purpose buffer ← work buffer (no change) |
| `Undo` | work buffer ← general purpose buffer (no change) |
| `Put` | work buffer ← general purpose buffer (no change) (Words and characters are placed in the work buffer before the current character; lines, sentences, and paragraphs are placed in the work buffer before the line the cursor is on.) |

| | |
|---|---|
| `put` | work buffer ← general purpose buffer (no change)<br><br>(Words and characters are placed in the work buffer after the current character; lines, sentences, and paragraphs are placed in the work buffer after the line the cursor is on.) |
| `"bDelete` | b buffer ← work buffer (altered)<br><br>(delete from the work buffer and place in the b buffer, overwriting) |
| `"BDelete` | b buffer ← work buffer (altered)<br><br>(delete from the work buffer and place in the b buffer, appending) |
| `"bYank` | b buffer ← work buffer (no change)<br><br>(yank from the work buffer and place in the b buffer, overwriting) |
| `"BYank` | b buffer ← work buffer (no change)<br><br>(yank from the work buffer and place in the b buffer, appending) |

CHAPTER  **4**

# The Bourne Shell for C Programming

This chapter sets forth fundamental techniques needed to do shell programming. The command line and its arguments will be discussed. Standard input and output will be considered along with the concept of redirection. Techniques to generate filenames will be given that provide for efficiency and selection. The concept of executable files will be examined along with types of variables and their domains. The creation and control of processes will be shown. The control structures available in the shell will be explained, as will the concepts of signals and trapping. Finally, standard error will be surveyed.

The C shell has most of the features of the Bourne shell and, indeed, has some features that are not available in the Bourne shell. Both the Bourne shell and the C shell provide interfaces between the user and UNIX and, in many instances, give the user a choice of which interface to use. (Even with UNIX System V the C shell may be an alternative available to the user.)

## 4.1  THE COMMAND LINE

When the user has received the prompt (dollar sign plus blank: $ ) the shell is available to execute any program. A command is given next via the command line, that set of characters entered after the prompt and terminated with a return. Pressing the return key initiates an attempt to execute the command. The correct format for a command line is

```
command_name [arg_1] [arg_2]... [last_arg] RETURN
```

Arguments are filenames, strings of text, or other entities that modify the output of the command, or that the command acts upon.

It is the user's responsibility to select the proper command_name to perform the needed task and also to specify the arguments, which may or may not be optional depending upon the command. It is not necessary to specify arguments for certain commands. Thus, for example, entering the date command

$ <u>date</u>

has as its output the time and date and is complete by itself—no arguments whatsoever need be given. Many commands, however, permit arguments, called options, that alter the effect of the command and by convention follow immediately after the command. The options are typically preceded by a hyphen (-) and the specific rules for their placement are determined by the command. For example, ls -rC is the usual way to give the ls command and the r and C options; however, ls -r -C is valid, as is ls -C -r. Repeat: the rules for options *are determined by the command itself.*

When a command line is passed to the system by terminating it with a return, the operating system passes the command line to the shell. The shell is a command interpreter, and must locate the appropriate command specified on the command line and attempt to process it. The shell ignores leading white space (those spaces immediately following the prompt) and processes the contiguous nonwhite space following it as the name of the program that is to be executed. That is, it must find a program with that name, which must be executable. Then and only then does the shell make the options and arguments available to that program.

If the shell cannot find a program with the specified name, say, for example, pwdd was mistakenly entered, an error message is returned. In the case of pwdd the following dialogue would take place:

```
$ pwdd
pwdd: not found
$
```

or in the case of the C shell (% is the default prompt)

```
% pwdd
pwdd: Command not found.
%
```

In some cases the program will be located by the shell, but the user does not have permission to execute it. Suppose the command is "bigdeal," but execute permission has not been given. A message will be returned:

```
$ bigdeal
bigdeal: execute permission denied
$
```

or in the case of the C shell

```
% bigdeal
bigdeal: permission denied.
%
```

But if the shell successfully locates the program and it is executable, the shell will pass the options and arguments to the command, which is then faced with dealing with those options and arguments. Thus, it is the program itself that has the responsibility of processing options and arguments, ignoring them if they are incorrect, or issuing appropriate error messages. Error messages resulting from options and arguments are by-products of the command being executed, not the shell.

Assume then that the program is being executed with the options and arguments fed to it by the shell. During this *process,* which in UNIX is defined as an execution of a program, the shell waits in an inactive state called *sleep* for the process (executing) to be completed. When it is completed, the shell awakens, or returns to an active state, and issues a prompt—yes indeed—it is ready to process another command!

The scenario above is usually expressed by saying that the shell being executed, labeled a *parent process,* has spawned a new process (called a *child process*) and is waiting for its completion. The new process is the child of the parent and can be visualized in much the same way as one visualizes a data file or subdirectory as being a child of another directory. Upon completion of the child process, the child itself dies and its existence is over. More information about processes is given in a later section of this chapter.

## EXERCISES  4.1

1. Give the correct syntax for a command line and indicate the purpose of each of the entities.
2. What role does the hyphen (-) play in the command line syntax?
3. Give two reasons why the shell might not pass the options and arguments specified on the command line to the command itself.
4. Define the concepts of a process and sleep.
5. Experiment with command lines, illustrating examples for Exercise 3.
6. Define what it means to spawn a process and draw a simple diagram illustrating the life span of a spawned process.

The terminal (as well as printers and disk drives) is an example of a device file that usually is a child of the /dev directory in UNIX, say, perhaps, /dev/tty03. The user can locate the name of the device file associated with his or her terminal by issuing the who command as follows:

```
$ who
     kem     tty2     June 28     13:19
$
```

The output is the user's login name (kem), the filename associated with the terminal (tty2), and the current date and time. So, if the user moves to another terminal, the output of who will only be constant for the login name.

Many programs require input and/or produce output during their execution. For example, the cat utility in its simplest form has a source file as its input (the file to be displayed). In this case, the output is automatically directed by the shell to the terminal. Input and output for programs typically default to the terminal, which is called both the *standard input* and the *standard output*.

■ **Example 4.2.1**
```
$ cat file1
... contents of file1 displayed here
. . .
. . .
$
```

The input to cat in this case is file1 and the output defaults to the terminal. This example assumes that file1 exists. ■

■ **Example 4.2.2**
```
$ cat
The crazy dog jumps over the brown fence
ctrl-d
The crazy dog jumps over the brown fence
$
```

The input to cat defaults, in this case, to the standard input (the terminal) because no file is specified. The output also defaults to the standard output (the terminal). The user in this case typed in an input file consisting of the single line "The crazy dog jumps over the brown fence" followed by ctrl-d. The keystrokes ctrl-d terminate the input to the standard input (the terminal). The output of cat defaults to the standard output (the terminal), hence, the contents of the standard input appear on the terminal again. ■

## *EXERCISES* 4.2

1. Define the concepts of standard input and standard output.
2. Find the filename associated with a terminal you have used.
3. Experiment with various options available to the cat utility. In particular, use the -u (unbuffered output) option and the -s (silent) option.
4. What is the standard input to the pg utility?
5. Generally, if no filenames are specified for a command, the standard input is processed. This can be particularly valuable for checking to see how commands work. Experiment interactively with the sort utility with no filenames specified. Also try sort with the -r (reverse) option and the -o filename (output filename) option.

## 4.3 *REDIRECTION*

Although input and output for programs typically default to the terminal, input and/or output can be altered (or redirected) to any file. Redirection of input is accomplished by using the less than symbol ($<$) and redirection of output is done with the greater than symbol ($>$). The general format of a command line with redirected input and/or output is thus

```
program [arguments] <file1 >file2
```

where program is defined as any executable program (application program or UNIX utility), arguments are optional arguments, file1 is the new input file, and file2 is the new output file.

The <file1 and >file2 may appear anywhere on the command line after the program itself, but it is customary to follow the program with arguments (if any), and then the redirected input, and finally the redirected output.

Notice that there is a subtle difference between

```
$ cat file1
```

and

```
$ cat <file1
```

In the former, file1 is an argument to cat that displays its contents. In the latter, the string <file1 causes the shell to redirect the standard input for cat to now come from file1.

The technique of redirecting input and output can be a very powerful tool but must be used with some caution. For example, redirection of output to files will cause the contents of any previously existing files with the same name to be destroyed. Thus,

```
$ cat <file1 >file2
```

causes the shell to redirect input for cat to come from file1, and then the shell redirects the output (the contents of file1) to go to file2. Thus, file1 and file2 will now be identical to file1, regardless of any previously existing file2. However, please note that the utility cat worked with its standard input (which had been redirected by the shell). As indicated above, cat itself does *not,* in this case, work with file1 as an argument, rather the shell performs the redirection of standard input to cat.

Contrast the above with

```
$ cat file1 >file2
```

In this case, file1 is an argument to the utility cat. The net effect is the same as above, except that the shell in this case does not do redirection. Cat does deal with file1 as an argument.

Several utilities in UNIX take their input from any file specified on the command line. If such a file is lacking on the command line, the utility conveniently takes its input from the standard input (terminal). This same principle can apply to output. This provides a convenient mechanism for testing utilities—simply omit the input file, have it default to the terminal, enter the data interactively, and examine the results. The next example may not, however, work on some systems.

■ **Example 4.3.1**

```
$ sort
```

Any command named sort can't be too mysterious. The reader is invited to enter a set of data lines terminated with a ctrl-d and view the output. (Remember that the input is defaulting to standard input—the terminal—and also remember that files end with a ctrl-d.) And, quite well and good, the output is also redirected to the terminal. ■

The user has additional options for capturing output. Imagine an instance in which C object code saved under a.out has been previously run and the output captured in a file called results. Now the user wishes to run the program again with a new set of input data, called, say, newdata, but also wishes to append the new output to the end of the old output. The symbol to do this is >>. The entire command to accomplish this is

```
$ a.out <newdata >>results
```

But, once again, there is even greater versatility available. UNIX gives the user the concept of a *pipe,* symbolized by |, which allows the standard output of one program to become the standard input to another. The format of a command line using a pipe is the same as that of two ordinary command lines joined with the symbol |:

```
program1 [arguments] | program2 [arguments]
```

The output of program1 is redirected to be the input of program2. The pipe symbol can be used with those UNIX utilities or ordinary executable programs that accept input from a file specified on the command line or from the standard input.

■ **Example 4.3.2**    Suppose the user has two different programs of C object code, one that does sorting, called sorter, of lines from any input file, and another called counter that counts the number of lines of a sorted input file that begin with each letter of the alphabet. Note that the counter program only works with sorted files. It can be made to work with any file, say one called oldfile, and deposit the final results in a file called finalresults by using the combination of sorter and counter connected via the pipe:

```
$ sorter <oldfile | counter >finalresults
```
■

■ **Example 4.3.3**    The same results can be accomplished, albeit in a less elegant and efficient manner, by using an intermediate file, called, say, temp, to capture the output of sorter and then serve as the input to counter. Naturally, one would ordinarily destroy temp after its function has been served:

```
$ sorter   <oldfile >temp
$ counter <temp      >finalresults
$ rm temp
```
■

In addition to using redirection and pipes, programs and UNIX utilities can run in the *background,* permitting the user to perform other tasks during particularly long runs. For example, to run the C object code a.out in the background, follow it with an ampersand (&) as follows:

```
$ a.out &
$
```

The problem is that if the output of a out is to be sent to the standard output, then the output will appear at the terminal when the job is completed, no matter what job is currently running. To avoid this, redirect the output to another file, say, results, as follows:

```
$ a.out >results &
$
```

It is also worth mentioning that if a background task needs input from the standard input, the null string ("") is supplied by default. Thus, if a.out needs standard input, capture it in a file called myinput and continue to capture the output in results:

```
$ a.out <myinput >results &
$
```

## EXERCISES 4.3

1. Define the purpose of < and > when used on a command line. When they are used, does the command or the shell itself interpret them?
2. What is the purpose of >> when used on a command line?
3. What is the purpose of the pipe (|) symbol?
4. Experiment with the cat and sort utilities connected with a pipe.
5. What is the difference between terminating a command line with the return key versus the ampersand (&)?
6. Run the echo command as follows:

```
$ echo 'now is the time
>
```

What is the difference between the greater than symbol shown here and that of redirection?

## 4.4 FILENAME GENERATION

UNIX provides the option of capturing many files with a wild card option. This option is based on the special characters, question mark (?), asterisk (*), and brackets ([ and ]). They can be used with both application programs and UNIX utilities.

The ? metacharacter generates filenames by matching any single character in the name of an existing file.

■ **Example 4.4.1** Suppose the user has C object code called a.out, which takes its input from any file (or set of files) that begins with the name file8 and has exactly six characters with the last one an even digit, and sends its output to the file called results. The worst way to run a.out against all such files is:

```
$ a.out file80 > results
$ a.out file82 >>results
$ a.out file84 >>results
```

```
$ a.out file86 >>results
$ a.out file88 >>results
```

Not *quite* as bad:

```
$ a.out file80 file82 file84 file86 file 88 >
results
```

The best way to generate all such filenames with the metacharacter ? is:

```
$ a.out file8? >results
```                                                                ∎

The ? metacharacter can also be used with UNIX utilities as in the following, which joins file80 and are to each other resulting in the file called newfile, and finally pipes the large newfile to the printer:

```
$ cat file8? >newfile ! lp
```

The * metacharacter generates filenames by matching any number of characters, including zero characters, in the name of an existing file.

∎ **Example 4.4.2**   Suppose the user has C object code called a.out, which takes its input from any file or set of files that have the name file in it somewhere (beginning, middle, or end). Suppose these files are afile, bfile, abfile, thefile, files, filed, and thefilers. Suppose, further, that the output is to be deposited in the file called results. The worst way to run a.out against all such files is:

```
$ a.out afile        > results
$ a.out bfile        >>results
$ a.out abfile       >>results
$ a.out thefile      >>results
$ a.out files        >>results
$ a.out filed        >>results
$ a.out thefilers >>results
```

Not *quite* as bad:

```
$ a.out afile bfile abfile thefile files filed
thefilers > results
```

The best way, however, is to generate all such filenames with the metacharacter *

```
$ a.out *file* >results
```                                                                ∎

The user does need to realize that * does not match a file that begins with a period (.). Thus *file does not match .file.

The * can also be used with UNIX utilities as in the following, which joins all files whose names include file8 to each other resulting in the file called newfile:

```
$ cat *file8* >newfile
```

The pair of square brackets defines a character class that will match any single character given within the brackets or any range of characters separated by a hyphen (-). Note that only a single character can be replaced within a character class.

■ **Example 4.4.3**   Suppose the user has C object code called a.out, which takes its input from any file or set of files that begin with the name file and has exactly five characters with the last one an even digit. Suppose, further, that the output is to be deposited in results. A good way to do this is:

```
$ a.out file[02468] >results
```

If it is desired to use only file1, file2, file3, file6, file7, file8, and file9, then use:

```
$ a.out file[1236-9] >results
```

or

```
$ a.out file[1-36-9] >results
```

■

All three generation methods can be combined for more complex combinations. Illustrations follow.

■ **Example 4.4.4**
```
$ a.out *file?[a-d] > results
```

In this case, matching is successful with any file that begins with zero or more occurrences of any character or characters, followed by file, followed by any single character, followed by any single character a, b, c, or d. Thus, the name of the matched files will have six or more characters. ■

## *EXERCISES* 4.4

1. Distinguish between the special characters, ?, *, and [ combined with ].
2. Find an easy way to use special characters to locate files whose names have exactly three characters beginning with the letter f and ending with an odd digit.
3. Find an easy way to use special characters to locate files whose names have three or more characters beginning with the letter f and whose third character is an odd digit.

**4.** Find an easy way to use special characters to locate files whose names have exactly four even digits (and perhaps other characters) with the added condition that the first digit is not zero.

**5.** Find an easy way to use special characters to locate files whose names have three vowels, followed by an odd digit, followed by any character.

## 4.5 | *EXECUTABLE FILES*

A shell script enables the user to sequence commands stored in a file, possibly with control structures, such as if then, if then else, if then elif, for in, for, while, until, break, continue, and the case statement. These control structures will be defined and discussed later. Because shell scripts can also have arguments (just like other commands on the command line) and have their own variables (called shell variables), it is correct, in a fundamental sense, to use the phrase "shell programming." Metacharacters and redirection are also available within the shell script. The user can customize a particular environment by combining various commands with or without control structures in a single shell script, and then can execute them in the desired fashion by making the file itself executable. Thus, the name of the executable file (containing the shell script) together with any options and arguments entered at the command line (terminated with a return, as usual) begins execution of the shell script.

Executable files are those files which someone or some group of users has permission to execute. Such files typically fall into one of three classes: (1) *compiled application programs,* such as those defaulting to a.out; (2) *compiled UNIX utilities,* such as cat, pwd, or even the editor vi; and (3) *shell scripts.*

If the user simply builds a file with a set of command lines in it, then tries to execute that file, the system will respond with a message indicating that the file is not executable.

■ **Example 4.5.1** Suppose the user has built the file called myfile and tries to execute it as follows:

```
$ cat mybackup
cp *.c /usr/kem/mycfiles
$ mybackup
mybackup: execute permission denied
$
```

In this case, apparently the user attempted to execute the shell script called mybackup whose purpose was to take every source file of C program code (namely, those files ending in .c) and copy each of them to the same name in the directory /usr/kem/mycfiles but was denied permission to do so. If successful, each .c file in the working directory would have been copied to a file with the same relative name. For example, program1.c would be backed up to /kem/mycfiles/program1.c, silly.c would be backed up to /kem/mycfiles/silly.c, and so on.

The problem is simply that the user does not have execute permission with respect to the shell script mybackup. The user can have execute permission as the owner, as a member of a group, or as a member of the general public (other). The user can check on status by using the ls utility with the l (long) option on mybackup:

```
$ ls -l mybackup
-rw-r--r-- 1 kem class 10 Jan 4 11:22 mybackup
```

Characters 4, 7, and 10 in the output line from the ls command provide the user with a status with respect to the file called mybackup. In this case, the owner of the file (which may or may not be the user running the ls command) does not have execute (x) permission (because character 4 is a -), nor does the group to which the owner belongs (because character 7 is a -), nor does a member of the general public (because character 10 is a -). The user can quickly remedy the situation (assuming he or she is the owner of mybackup) by adding (+) execute (x) permission to the user (u):

```
$ chmod u+x mybackup
```

and can check the results by running the ls command again:

```
$ ls -l mybackup
-rwxr--r-- 1 kem class 10 Jan 4 11:23 mybackup
```

Now mybackup will silently do its work:

```
$ mybackup
$
```

## EXERCISES 4.5

1. Discuss the meaning of the term "executable" with respect to classes of users.
2. Define three classes of files for which the term "executable" can be useful.

**3.** Experiment with changing the permissions on a file like mybackup; change them for the owner, the group, and then the others. Also change them for all. In each case, use symbolic notation.

**4.** Repeat Exercise 3 using absolute (octal) notation.

## 4.6 | *VARIABLES*

The Bourne shell has variables available to it just as many programming languages do. These are *always* string variables only, that is, they can only have the value of a string of characters. The types of variables available to the shell fall into three classes, shown in Figure 4.1, with the types of actions that can be taken on each class of variable specified according to whether the user or the shell itself can perform those actions.

|  | Can Declare | Can Initialize | Can Read | Can Change |
|---|---|---|---|---|
| User Vars. | user | user | user | user |
| Shell Vars. | shell | shell | user | user |
| Read-only Shell Vars. | shell | shell | user |  |

**FIGURE 4.1**   Actions on Variables

Thus, for example, user variables can be declared, initialized, read, or changed by the user on the command line or within a shell script. The naming convention of such variables is liberal: any sequence of nonblank characters will do. Declarations, initializations, and changes are accomplished in the following way:

```
var_name=value
```

where no spaces are permitted around the equal sign (=).

■ **Example 4.6.1**

```
$ category=apples
$ echo $category
apples
$
```

In this case, the user variable called category has been declared and initialized with the value apples; then the value of category is echoed back to the terminal. Note that the declaration and initialization can also appear in a shell script. The variable category can be taken out of commission by using the unset command (after which its implied value is the null string):

```
$ unset category
$ echo $category
$
```
∎

Reading is accomplished by the following format:

```
read var_name1 var_name2 var_name3 ...
```

When the read statement is encountered, one line is read from standard input and assigned to one or more variables. The values assigned to the variables begin with the first nonwhite space entered, except that the last variable will be assigned any remaining string (including white space between strings).

The echo utility will help check results here because it copies its arguments to standard output; the format is

```
$ echo arg1 arg2 ....
```

However, when $var_name is an argument to echo, as in Example 4.6.1, the echo utility simply substitutes the present value of var_name and displays that value.

∎ **Example 4.6.2**     Suppose the user wishes to assign the variable myfile the value program1.c. This is accomplished with a single statement and the value of myfile is echoed to the screen by using the echo utility with the value of myfile ($):

```
$ myfile=program1.c
$ echo $myfile
program1.c
$
```
∎

It can be a very effective systems programming tool to assign filenames to be the value of user variables. The assignment and initialization could also have been made within a shell script.

∎ **Example 4.6.3**     Suppose the user wishes to assign the variable myfile the value program1.c program2.c. Blanks between strings can be accommodated as follows:

```
$ myfile='program1.c program2.c'
$ echo $myfile
program1.c program2.c
$
```
∎

■ **Example 4.6.4**   The user can suppress the meaning of the metacharacter dollar sign ($) by preceding it with a backslash (\):

```
$ myfile=program1.c
$ echo \$myfile
$myfile
$ echo $myfile
program1.c
$
```
■

■ **Example 4.6.5**   Double quotations and single quotations behave differently when it comes to substitution—double quotations will not prevent the substitution, while singles will.

```
$ myfile=program1.c
$ echo '$myfile'
$myfile
$ echo "$myfile"
program1.c
$
```
■

A user variable can be assigned a value and *then* be declared read-only. This has the effect of fixing its present value and prohibiting the user from changing it. This can be particularly valuable if hidden in a shell script that a novice user cannot see or modify.

■ **Example 4.6.6**
```
$ myfile=program1.c
$ echo $myfile
program1.c
$ readonly myfile
$ myfile=program2.c
myfile: is read only
$ readonly
readonly myfile
$
```

Note that it was impossible to change the value of myfile to program2.c after it was made readonly. Also, as the third last line indicates, a readonly command without arguments displays a list of all readonly variables. Thus, readonly with arguments is completely different from readonly without arguments. ■

■ **Example 4.6.7**   Suppose the writer of a shell script wishes to prompt the user to enter a name at a certain point, and then display the entered name, last name first, then first name, then middle initial. The technique is to build the following statements within the script, called prompter:

```
$ cat prompter
echo 'enter first name, middle, then last name:'
read first mid last
echo 'your name on our list is:' $last ',' $first $mid
$
```

Before prompter will execute, it must be made executable. A sample run is:

```
$ prompter
enter first name, middle, then last name:
John P. Jones
your name on our list is: Jones, John P.
$
```

■ **Example 4.6.8**   It is also possible to read the name of a command into a variable, then execute that command by preceding its name with the dollar sign ($), thus yielding its value. Consider lister, which, with redirected output, will put the names of the working directory files in a file called myfiles:

```
$ cat lister
echo 'enter the command ls:'
read command
$ command
$
```

A sample run of lister with redirected output is (don't forget to make lister executable):

```
$ lister >myfiles
enter the command ls:
ls
$
```

Myfiles now contains the names of the files in the working directory. This can be checked as follows:

```
$ cat myfiles
```

The concept of a *read-only shell variable* permits the user to capture the name of the command and the arguments on the command line as the values of variables. These variables are labeled:

$0   name of the command

$1   name of the first argument following the command

$2   name of the second argument following the command

...

$9   name of the ninth argument following the command

Only nine arguments are accessible at any given time, however, there is an easy way to force the tenth argument to be assigned to $9 and, at the same time, make the original first argument inaccessible—simply use the shift command with no arguments:

```
shift
```

The shift command also accepts numeric arguments to enable the user to move the argument "down" by an integral value. Thus,

```
shift 3
```

will make

...

Argument 12————————→$9

Argument 11————————→$8

Argument 10————————→$7

...

Argument  4————————→$1

Argument  3, argument 2, and argument 1 are lost.

The user cannot assign values to any of these read-only shell variables by writing, for example, $1=newvalue. However, the set command accepts arguments that become the values of $1 up to $9. Set without arguments simply displays the names of the shell variables (to be covered next) and the others that have been set with the set command.

In addition, it is possible to keep track of the number of arguments on the command line with the variable $# and to represent all the command line arguments with the variable $*:

```
$# number of command line arguments
$* all command line arguments
```

■ **Example 4.6.9**   Consider prompter again from Example 4.9.7 with the additional line

```
echo this command was $0
```

Here is the complete revised version:

```
$ cat prompter
echo 'enter first name, middle, then last name:'
read first mid last
echo 'your name on our list is:' $last ',' $first $mid
echo 'this command was' $0
$
```

A sample run is:

```
$ prompter
enter first name, middle, then last name:
John P. Jones
your name on our list is: Jones, John P.
this command was prompter
$
```
■

■ **Example 4.6.10**   Suppose a shell script called copy exists with the following first few lines:

```
echo 'the programs to be copied are' $1 $2 $3 $4 'and'$5
echo 'there are' $# 'programs to be copied'
echo 'the programs to be copied are' $*
echo 'the value of' $5 'is:'
```

Now, a typical session using copy might be (be sure to change the access mode first by "chmod 755 copy"):

```
$ copy program1 program2 program4 program3
the programs to be copied are program1 program2
program4 program3 and
there are 4 programs to be copied
the programs to be copied are program1 program2
program4 program3
the value of is:
```

Note that $5 has been assigned the null string because there was no fifth argument on the command line. ■

■ **Example 4.6.11**    Suppose the shell script called copy is modified as follows:

```
$ cat copy
echo 'the programs to be copied are' $1 $2 $3 $4 'and' $5
shift 2
echo 'there are' $# 'programs to be copied'
echo 'the programs to be copied are' $*
echo 'the value of' $5 'is:'
$
```

Now a typical session using copy might be:

```
$ copy program1 program2 program4 program3
the programs to be copied are program1 program2
program4 program3 and
there are 2 programs to be copied
the programs to be copied are program4 program3
the value of is:
$                                                    ■
```

Now for a couple of examples using *set*. Remember that set without arguments displays a list of all variables that are set while set with argument sets the arguments to the variables $1, $2, and so on.

■ **Example 4.6.12**    Suppose there is a file called combinefiles as follows (be sure to change access mode by "chmod 755 combinefiles"):

```
$ cat combinefiles
set file1.c file2.c file3.c
cat $1 $2 $3 >bigfile.c
$ combinefiles
```

The output of combinefiles will be file1.c, file2.c, and file3.c appended in that order and becoming the latest version of bigfile.c (redirected output from cat). ■

When the user logs on to the system, the typical situation is that the system administrator has allowed him or her to execute /bin/sh. The Bourne shell, that is /bin/sh, then reads the files /etc/profile and .profile (in that sequence) and executes the commands therein in the same environment as the shell itself. The usual situation is that the shell variables are assigned values at that time, although it is also possible to assign these variables values from the command line or even from within other shell scripts. The most important of these shell variables are HOME, PATH, PS1, PS2, and IFS. Each will be illustrated.

The shell variable HOME has as its value a particular (user chosen) directory in the UNIX file system. There are two distinct uses: (1) The user's initial working directory at log on is the value of the HOME variable. (2) The user can change to the directory given by $HOME by issuing the change directory (cd) command without arguments.

■ **Example 4.6.13**  Suppose HOME has been assigned the value /usr/you either in /etc/passwd or in profile. Now presume that the user wants to make /usr/you/mycfiles the working directory:

```
$ cd
$ echo $HOME
/usr/you
$ HOME=/usr/you/mycfiles
$ pwd
/usr/you
$ cd $HOME
$ pwd
/usr/you/mycfiles
$ HOME=/usr/you
$ pwd
/usr/you/mycfiles
$
```

■

The next shell variable, PATH, allows the user to define the paths in the file structure that should be searched, as well as the order in which these paths should be searched to attempt to execute a command. Thus, the user might have several files of executable C code in the UNIX file structure, with the same relative file name, say prog1:

```
/usr/you/mycfiles/prog1
/usr/you/oldcfiles/prog1
/usr/you/prog1
```

Assuming that prog1 (each of them) is executable, the particular one executed by

```
$ prog1
```

depends on the value of the PATH variable. PATH should be assigned the directories, separated by a colon (:), in the order in which they should be searched. Beginning the assignment with a colon (:) means that the working directory should be searched first. Any search stops when the file is found.

■ **Example 4.6.14**   Suppose the user wishes to search the file system in the same order as listed above to execute programs. Consider:

```
$ PATH=/usr/you/mycfiles:/usr/you/oldcfiles:/usr/
you:/bin:/usr/bin
$ prog1
```

In this case, the shell will look for prog1 (or any other file if it is specified on the command line) first in /usr/you/mycfiles, and *if it does not find it there,* search in /usr/you/oldcfiles, and *if it does not find it there,* search in /usr/you, and *if it does not find it there,* search in /bin, and *if it does not find it there,* finally search in /usr/bin.   ■

If, on the other hand, the user wishes the search to begin in the working directory, then a colon (:) is inserted immediately after the equal sign in the assignment to PATH. In any case, the PATH variable should be set carefully because it will be used to search for whatever file is specified on the command line, including UNIX utilities.

Thus, the standard places to find files such as /bin and /usr/bin among others, must be specified somewhere, or the shell will report that it cannot find the file. But if the user wants to customize the shell so that user-defined programs are given the same names (but in different directories) as standard UNIX utilities, then in order to give these user-defined programs precedence over their UNIX counterparts, it will be necessary to specify /bin and /usr/bin last on the path search list. Obviously, an inappropriate sequence of paths assigned to PATH will result in inordinately long searches and adversely affect performance.

The Bourne shell default prompt is a dollar sign followed by a space ($). The shell variable called PS1 holds this value and it can be modified by the user. Similarly, PS2 holds the secondary prompt (defaults to the greater than symbol >) that the shell uses when a command carries over to the next line.

■ **Example 4.6.15**
```
$ PS1='ready '
ready echo 'the prompt has just been changed'
the prompt has just been changed
ready PS2='more '
ready echo 'the secondary prompt has just been
more changed to more'
the secondary prompt has just been changed to more
ready
```

In this example, it is seen that the new primary prompt has been set to "ready " and that the new secondary prompt has been changed to "more ". These changes will only be effective for the life of the session. ∎

The usual way to separate arguments on the command line is with a SPACE or TAB. The shell internal-field separator variable, called IFS, can be used to change this character to something more convenient.

**∎ Example 4.6.16**  Suppose a comma (,) is desired to separate the internal fields on the command line. The following will then copy prog1.c, prog2.c, and prog3.c into the directory named /usr/mycdirectory.

```
$ IFS=','
$ cp prog1.c,prog2.c,prog3.c /usr/mycdirectory
$
```
∎

## EXERCISES 4.6

1. Distinguish among user variables, shell variables, and read-only shell variables.
2. Experiment with the read statement from the command line and check your results with the echo command.
3. What is the essential difference between using single and double quotation marks in the echo command?
4. How can the metacharacter dollar sign ($) be disabled?
5. What would be the purpose in making a variable read-only?
6. Specify the technique to execute a command from within a shell script.
7. How many arguments can be accessible at a given time from a shell script?
8. What is the purpose of the shift command?
9. Write a shell script using the set command.
10. What two files are read by the shell at log on? Why are there two such files; what are their purposes? Print the contents of these files and study them.
11. Change your HOME directory at the command line; now edit a certain file so that it will be changed the next time you log on to the system.
12. Experiment with the PATH variable by putting three files with the same relative name in three separate directories. Record the results of running your program each time PATH is changed.
13. Edit your  profile to change your primary and secondary prompts.

## 4.7 | *PROCESSES*

A process is defined as a command or program in the state of being executed. Users can initiate processes, as can the operating system. When a command is entered on the command line, UNIX begins a process, the execution of that command.

Just as there is a UNIX file system described as a tree, there is also a process structure that can be visualized as a tree. When UNIX is first booted, a root process (visualized in the same way as the root of the file system) is initiated, and it is assigned a process identification number called its PID. This first process has a PID of 1. When a particular user logs on, that user is usually running the shell, which is also assigned a PID. The PIDs assigned to the shells of users have a common ancestor in the process structure—the process with PID 1. The PID number assigned to the running of the shell will not change during a user session.

The purpose here is to understand how processes are created and identified, as well as how to control their environment. The user has the ability, for example, to declare, initialize, read, and change variables within a given process or to export variables to processes.

When the user enters a command on the command line, the parent process forks (or spawns) another process, causing the parent process to be inactive (or go to sleep). When the child process completes its execution, the parent process reactivates and the shell prompts for another command.

■ **Example 4.7.1**

```
$ cp program1.c newname.c
$
```

While the user is entering the command line above (prior to pressing return), the process executing /bin/sh is running. When return is pressed, the process executing cp runs and is a child of its parent process (executing /bin/sh), which is deactivated. When the next prompt appears, the child process is completed and the process running /bin/sh, its parent, reawakens. ■

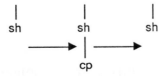

The user also has the option to execute a long-running command in the background by ending the command with an ampersand (&). In that case, the shell forks a child process, but does not go to sleep, and thus does not wait for the child process to be completed. The process ID of the child is shown on the screen.

■ **Example 4.7.2**

```
$ lp *.* &
28435
$
```

The above is, of course, very dangerous, but efficient. The lp command is applied to every file (*.*) in the working directory (dangerous), but it is run in the background (&). The process ID associated with lp is 28435 and the prompt is returned immediately enabling the user to begin another process. ■

As indicated above, each process is associated with a PID that is assigned at the beginning of the process. Thus, even though different processes may be run after the login shell is initially activated, when the user returns to the shell it has the same PID number as it had initially.

The user does have the ability to keep track of processes and their hierarchy. One method is to invoke the ps (process status) utility. Using the long (-l) option with it is especially useful. The ps delivers the name of all processes that are running, their PIDs, the PIDs of each process' parent (PPID), and other useful information.

In addition to the ps utility, the shell variable $$ stores the PID number of the process that is executing. The shell variable $!, on the other hand, stores the PID number of the last process that was executed in the background. It is important to remember that output from background processes that is directed to the screen will appear there and might just interfere with the expected screen display.

■ **Example 4.7.3**

Suppose the user has a long-running print job that is to be run in the background.

```
$ lp bigjob &
24445
$ echo $!
24445
$ echo $$
24000
$
```

In this case, 24445 is the PID of the line printing of bigjob that is being run in the background. This is confirmed as the last process run in the background by the command echo $!; 24000 is the PID of the process that is executing the shell. ■

When a process ends, it returns a condition code (sometimes called a return code or exit status) to its parent process. This condition code is stored in the shell variable $? and, by convention, is zero meaning true (the command terminated successfully) or nonzero meaning false (the command failed). It turns out that in C, just the opposite holds: zero means false and nonzero means true. Be aware!

The possibilities for the condition code returned may also be captured in the code itself with the exit command followed by an integral value. For example, exit 5 will force an exit from the shell script and return a condition code of five. If no exit statements are embedded in the code, then the condition code returned is the condition code returned by the last command executed.

■ **Example 4.7.4**

```
$ cat backup
cp *.c /usr/you/yourcfiles
$ backup
$ echo $?
0
$
```

Assuming that the directory /usr/you/yourcfiles exists, backup simply stores an additional copy of all C programs of the working directory in the directory /usr/you/yourcfiles. The variable $? has been assigned the value zero indicating that backup ran successfully. On the other hand, if /usr/you/yourcfiles did not exist making the cp utility unable to perform its function (and hence backup itself fails), then the value stored in $? will be one as shown below:

```
$ cat backup
cp *.c /usr/you/yourcfiles
$ backup
$ echo $?
1
$
```

■

■ **Example 4.7.5**   In the case specified here, the condition code returned is 2, no matter whether cp is successful or not, because exit 2 is written into the code. This would *not* be a typical use of the exit command; more often, it would be used with different arguments attached to various possibilities for failure (perhaps an *if then else* statement).

```
$ cat backup
cp *.c /usr/you/yourcfiles
exit 2
$ backup
$ echo $?
2
$
```
■

There are five techniques to execute a program using the UNIX operating system.

1. *Write a shell script and make it executable using the chmod utility.* **When this script is invoked, the shell does spawn a new process (child).**

2. *Use `command`.* This instructs the shell to replace the command with the output of the command.

3. *Use . command.* This enables the shell to execute the command as part of the current process and then return to the original script. Compiled programs cannot be handled by this method and the user is not required to have execute permission for the shell script.

4. *Use exec command.* This enables the shell to execute the command as part of the current process and then overlays the original script (unconditional goto). Compiled programs can be executed and the user is required to have execute permission for compiled programs and shell scripts.

5. *Use sh command.* This spawns a new process (the one executing a new shell sh), which in turn spawns another new process executing the command itself. The user is not required to have execute permission to run the command.

■ **Example 4.7.6**   This example combines methods 1 and 2. Note that the date utility displays the time and date:

```
$ date
Fri May 29 09:11:34 EST 1987
$
```

This can be improved (with a better format) to include the working directory.

```
$ cat dir_and_time
dir=`pwd`
echo 'the working directory is ' $dir
set `date`
```

```
echo 'it is ' $2 $3, $6
$ chmod +x dir_and_time
$ dir_and_time
the working directory is /usr/you
it is May 29, 1987
$
```

Notice that the user defined variable dir captures the output of the pwd utility (method 2) and then the echo utility outputs a string followed by the value of dir. The output from the date utility becomes the arguments to set: thus, the command line arguments ($1 through $6 in this case) are assigned values by set. The chmod utility illustrates how to make a shell script executable (method 1). Finally, dir_and_time is executed. ■

■ **Example 4.7.7**    The method using . command permits the user to execute a new shell script while staying in the current process. Thus, the invoked shell script has access to the same variables with inherited values. Remember that variables are local to processes, but there is only one process in this case.

```
$ cat dir_and_time
dir=`pwd`
echo 'the working directory is ' $dir
set `date`
echo 'it is ' $2 $3, $6
$ pwd
/usr/you
$ cat sample.command
dir='this assignment will be changed in dir_and_time'
dire='this assignment is inherited by dir_and_time'
. dir_and_time
echo 'this line is reached'
echo $dire
$ chmod +x sample.command
$ sample.command
the working directory is /usr/you
it is May 29, 1987
this line is reached
this assignment is inherited by dir_and_time
$                                                          ■
```

■ **Example 4.7.8**    The method using exec command permits the user to execute a new shell script while staying in the current process. Thus, the invoked shell script has access to the same variables with inherited values. All of this is the same as with . command. However, here no return is made to the original script.

```
$ cat dir_and_time
dir='`pwd`'
echo 'the working directory is ' $dir
set `date`
echo 'it is ' $2 $3, $6
```

```
$ cat exec_command
dir='this assignment will be changed by dir_and_time'
dire='this assignment is inherited by dir_and_time'
exec dir_and_time
echo 'this line is not reached'
echo $dire
$ chmod +x exec_command
$ exec_command
the working directory is /usr/you
it is May 29, 1987
$
```
■

The final way to execute a program is actually to spawn a new shell (by using sh) and command it to execute a shell script.

■ **Example 4.7.9**
```
$ cat dir_and_time
dir='`pwd`'
echo 'the working directory is ' $dir
set `date`
echo 'it is ' $2 $3, $6
$ sh dir_and_time
the working directory is /usr/you
it is May 29, 1987
$
```

There is an essential concept that needs to be grasped here: the original shell spawns a new shell (via sh). The original shell is now inactive. The new shell spawns a process that runs dir_and_time and the new shell also becomes inactive. When dir_and_time finishes execution, the new shell awakens. Then the new shell dies, and wakes the original shell, which issues a prompt. ■

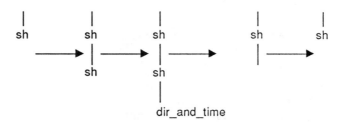

Turning to a new subject, a brief introduction follows on the idea of *environment* and *exporting variables*. Several examples will illustrate various key points. These are:

1. A child process does not automatically receive the value of a variable declared and initialized in its parent.
2. The value of a variable that has not been declared is the null string.
3. A variable declared in a child process has no effect on the value of a variable with the same name in a parent process, that is, variables are local to processes.
4. The export command can be used to pass the value of a variable to a child process. This is pass by value, and, hence, any changes made by the child do not affect the parent's copy.
5. The . command technique can be used to force scripts to share variables because a new process is not generated.

These points cannot be overemphasized. Examples will now be given to illustrate them.

■ **Example 4.7.10**

```
$ chmod +x child grandchild
$ cat child
childvar=bobby
echo $0 $$ $childvar
grandchild
echo $0 $$ $childvar
$ cat grandchild
echo $0 $$ $childvar
$ child
child 54321 bobby
grandchild 54322
child 54321 bobby
$
```

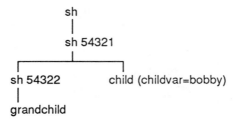

This illustrates points 1 and 2. Grandchild is called from within child and *does not* receive the value of childvar, which was declared in child; hence, childvar has the value of a null string in grandchild. Note, also, that the PIDs are displayed by $$, which gives the PID of the shell process that is executing it. Grandchild *is* executed by a new shell. There would not have been a new shell (and process) if grandchild had been replaced by either ". grandchild" or "exec grandchild" as modified below. ■

■ **Example 4.7.11**

```
$ chmod 755 notchild
$ cat child
childvar=bobby
echo $0 $$ $childvar
.notchild
echo $0 $$ $childvar
$ cat notchild
echo $0 $$ $childvar
$ child
child 54321 bobby
notchild 54321 bobby
child 54321 bobby
$
```

sh
|
sh 54321
|_____
          |
    child (childvar=bobby)

```
$ cat child
childvar=bobby
echo $0 $$ $childvar
exec notchild
echo $0 $$ $childvar
$ cat notchild
$ child
child 54321 bobby
notchild 54321
$
```

```
sh
|
sh 54321
└────────┐
         child (childvar=bobby)
```

■ **Example 4.7.12**    This example illustrates point 3. Notice that grandchild is run by a new process and hence it does not inherit the value of childvar declared in child. Grandchild does declare and initialize a variable called childvar, but it is entirely local to grandchild and has no effect on the childvar local to child.

```
$ cat child
childvar=bobby
echo $0 $$ $childvar
grandchild
echo $0 $$ $childvar
$ cat grandchild
echo $0 $$ $childvar
childvar=sue
echo $0 $$ $childvar
$ child
child 54321 bobby
grandchild 54322
grandchild 54222 sue
child 54321 bobby
$
```

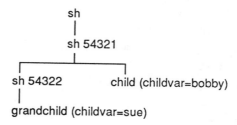

■ **Example 4.7.13**   This example illustrates point 4. Grandchild is run by a new process and it does have its own childvar; it does inherit via the export command the value of childvar from child, but it can change its own childvar, which has no effect on the childvar of child.

```
$ cat child
export childvar
childvar=bobby
echo $0 $$ $childvar
grandchild
echo $0 $$ $childvar
$ cat grandchild
echo $0 $$ $childvar
childvar=sue
echo $0 $$ $childvar
$ child
child 54321 bobby
grandchild 54322 bobby
grandchild 54322 sue
child 54321 bobby
$
```

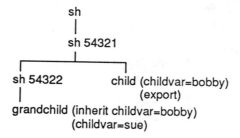

■ **Example 4.7.14**    To reinforce point 5, child will now be modified to call .notchild and then exec notchild (export is not needed—no new process is run by using . notchild or exec notchild). These are like subroutines, with and without a return to the main program, respectively.

```
$ cat child
childvar=bobby
echo $0 $$ $childvar
.notchild
echo $0 $$ $childvar
$ cat notchild
echo $0 $$ $childvar
childvar=sue
echo $0 $$ $childvar
$ child
child 54321 bobby
child 54321 bobby
child 54321 sue
child 54321 sue
$


sh
|
sh 54321
  └──────┐
           child (childvar=bobby)
           (pass control to notchild)

$ cat child
childvar=bobby
echo $0 $$ $childvar
exec notchild
echo $0 $$ $childvar
$ cat notchild
echo $0 $$ $childvar
childvar=sue
echo $0 $$ $childvar
$ child
child 54321 bobby
notchild 54321
notchild 54321 sue
$
```

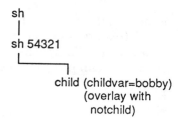

```
sh
|
sh 54321
└───────┐
        child (childvar=bobby)
              (overlay with
                 notchild)
```

■

## EXERCISES 4.7

1. Define the concept of a process.
2. How is a process run in the background?
3. Define the purpose of the shell variables $$, $!, and $?.
4. What is the purpose of a condition code—and what are the conventional values used in its regard?
5. Give five techniques that can be used to execute a program using the UNIX operating system.
6. Illustrate each of the techniques given in Exercise 5. Pay special attention to $$, $!, and $?.
7. What is meant by the phrase "spawning a new process"? Give an example.
8. What is meant by the statement "variables are local to processes"?
9. Discuss the purpose of the export command.
10. Is an error message printed when the value of a nondeclared variable is asked to be printed?
11. Distinguish between . command and exec command techniques.
12. Suppose that process is an executable process. Explain why the following logs the user off the machine: $ <u>exec process</u>.

## 4.8 COMMAND SEPARATION

Interactive shell commands and shell scripts follow certain rules in terms of separation and grouping of commands. These are:

1. Pressing the return key, either on a command line or within a shell script, separates the previous command from the next command to be entered.
2. Entering the pipe symbol ( | ) separates commands and makes the output from the previous command the input to the next command.

**3.** Entering the background task symbol (&) separates commands and forces the shell to execute the task in the background.

**4.** Entering the semicolon (;) separates commands entered on the same command line—execution still depends upon pressing the return key.

**5.** Enclosing commands within parentheses enables the shell to treat the group of commands so enclosed as a single job while still spawning processes to execute the individual tasks.

■ **Example 4.8.1** The following sends the output of cat (which is normally sent to the terminal) to be the input to program2, which in turn sends its output to become the input to program3.

```
$ cat file1 | program2 | program3
```

Contrast the above with:

```
$ cat file1 | program 2 | program3 &
```

The same principle applies with the additional proviso that program3 is run in the background. ■

■ **Example 4.8.2** The following runs both program1 and program2 in the background, but program3 in the foreground:

```
$ program1 & program2 & program3
```
■

■ **Example 4.8.3** The following runs program1, followed by program2, followed by program3 (execution does not begin until the return key is pressed):

```
$ program1 ; program2 ; program3
```

On the other hand, the following runs program1 and program2 as a single job in the background (program1 followed by program2) and then runs program3 in the foreground:

```
$ (program1 ; program2 ) & program3
```
■

It should be noted that when the shell simultaneously executes several tasks in the background, the exact order of the output will vary from run to run because of the scheduling that UNIX must do.

## *EXERCISES* **4.8**

**1.** Give four methods to separate commands.

**2.** Illustrate each of the methods given in Exercise 1.

## 4.9 | CONTROL STRUCTURES

There are assorted control structures available to modify the flow of control within a shell script. Seven of these follow. The seasoned programmer will recognize them as the classical tools available in many programming languages (the portions in **bold** are user supplied). Note that test **command** employs the **test** utility to yield an exit status. It is also possible to simply use **command** in certain instances to inform the shell of the success (zero) or failure (nonzero) of a command.

| Statement | Comment |
|---|---|
| **1.** if test **command**<br>    then **commands**<br>  fi | If test **command** returns a true, then execute **commands**—otherwise, transfer control to the next statement following "fi". |
| **2.** if test **command**<br>    then **commands**<br>    else **commands**<br>  fi | If test **command** returns a true, then execute **commands** after then; otherwise, execute **commands** after else—and then, in either case, transfer control to the next statement following "fi". |
| **3.** if test **command**<br>    then **commands**<br>    elif test **command**<br>        then **commands**<br>        else **command**<br>  fi | If test **command** returns a true, then execute **commands** following initial then and transfer control to the next statement following fi—otherwise, test the next **command** and execute **commands** following then (if true is returned) and **command** following else (if false is returned)—then, in either case, transfer control beyond fi. |
| **4.** for **loop-index** in **argument_list**<br>  do<br>    **commands**<br>  done | For each and every value of the **argument_list**, assign it to **loop-index** and execute **commands**. The word "in" and the **argument_list** can be omitted, in which case **argument_list** defaults to the command line parameters ($1, $2, etc.). If the **argument_list** is specified as *, then the **argument_list** becomes the files in the working directory. |
| **5.** while test **command**<br>  do<br>    **commands**<br>  done | **a.** Examine the exit status returned by test **command.**<br>**b.** If false, transfer control to the next statement following done. Otherwise, execute **commands** between do and done and then repeat step a. |

| Statement | Comment |
|---|---|
| **6.** until test **command**<br>    do<br>        **commands**<br>    done | **a.** Examine the exit status returned by test **command.**<br>**b.** If true, transfer control to the next statement following done. Otherwise, execute **commands** between do and done and then repeat step a. |
| **7.** case **string** in<br>    **pattern1) commands1;;**<br>    **pattern2) commands2;;**<br>    **...**<br>    **patternk) commandsk;;**<br>  esac | Examine the **string,** find the first **pattern** it matches, and execute those **commands** associated with that pattern. Then transfer control to the first statement following esac; if there is no match, transfer control to the first statement following esac. |

Before examples of each of the control structures are provided, the reader should note that a break statement consists of the single phrase "break" and can be inserted as a command within a for, while, or until loop. If a break is executed, control is transferred to the statement following done. Similarly, a continue statement consists of the single phrase "continue" and can be inserted as a command within a for, while, or until loop. If continue is executed, control is transferred to the done statement, which provides for continued execution of the loop.

■ **Example 4.9.1**    This first illustration will be of the *if then statement.* Suppose the user has object code for a C program in the file program1, and that program1 reads an existing file, and its output is the number of characters in that file. The following shell script called readable will check that the file exists and that the user has read permission; then, if affirmative, it will prompt for whether the program should be run; if yes, it will display the output on the terminal. Note that the output of program1 is captured in the variable named ans.

```
$ cat readable
echo 'which file does program1 read from ? : \c'
read readfile
if (test -r "$readfile")
        then echo 'the user has read permission for '
            echo $readfile
            echo 'is the user ready to run program1'
            echo 'y or n ?:'
            echo '\c'
```

```
                    read prompt
                    if (test "$prompt" = "y")
                        then ans='program1'
                        echo 'the no. of chars in' $readfile 'is' $ans
                        fi

        fi
```

$ <u>chmod 755 readable</u>

In this case, the user is testing whether he or she has read permission and whether the filename stored in readfile exists (-r tests both). The test utility evaluates an expression and returns a condition code demonstrating whether the expression is true (zero) or false (nonzero). ∎

Other useful possibilities that can be tested include:

| | |
|---|---|
| -w **filename** | **filename** exists and user has write permission. |
| -x **filename** | **filename** exists and user has exec permission. |
| -f **filename** | **filename** exists and is a data file |
| -d **filename** | **filename** exists and is a directory |
| -s **filename** | **filename** exists and size in bytes $> 0$ |
| -n **string** | **string** has length $> 0$ |
| **string** | **string** is not null string |
| -z **string** | **string** has length zero |
| **string1** = **string2** | same strings |
| **string1** !=**string2** | different strings |
| **integer1** op **integer2** | integer1 compared to integer2 with op replaced by -gt (greater than), -ge (greater than or equal to), -eq (equal to), -ne (not equal to), -le (less than or equal to), or -1t (less than) |

Criteria can be combined with the AND operator (-a), the OR operator (-o), or negated with the exclamation point (!). Special characters should be quoted so that the shell does not interpret them.

■ **Example 4.9.2**    The *if then else statement* will now be illustrated with an example whose purpose is to make a backup (with suffix "bak") of the second argument on the command line and, in the case when the first argument calls for a display (-d), display the file to be backed up on the screen. Note that a nonzero exit status of one is selected to be returned if the number of arguments is incorrect. This value is stored in the variable denoted by $?.

```
$ cat backup
if (test $# != 1 -a $# != 2)
        then echo 'the user must supply one or two args '
                exit 1
fi
if (test $1 != "-d" )
        then cp $1 $1.bak
        else shift 1
                cat $1
                cp $1 $1.bak
fi
$ chmod +x backup
```
■

■ **Example 4.9.3**   The following shell script expands upon Example 4.9.2 by permitting the option to be a usual display (-d) of the file as before, or a display using the page option (-p), or no display whatsoever (but backed up in any case):

```
$ cat backup
if (test $# != 1 -a $# != 2)
        then echo 'the user must supply one or two args '
                exit 1
fi
if (test $1 != "-d" -a $1 != "-p")
        then cp $1 $1.bak
                exit
        elif ( test $1 = "-d")
                then shift 1
                        cat $1
                        cp $1 $1.bak
                else shift 2
                        pg $1
                        cp $1 $1.bak
fi
$
```
■

■ **Example 4.9.4**   The following example will recompile each C program of source code (assumed to have a suffix of .c) in the working directory and store the compiled version in a file with the same name as the source code, but with the suffix .c replaced by .out!

```
$ chmod +x compile
$ cat compile
for file in *.c
      do
              cc -o $file.out $file
      done
$
```
■

On the other hand, if the user only wants to compile those C programs given on the command line as arguments to compile2, then compile2 would be written as follows:

```
$ cat compile2
for file in $*
      do
              cc -o $file.out $file
      done
$
```

The compile program can be made even less powerful by coding in the shell script the names of the files to be compiled:

```
$ cat compile3
for file in program1.c program2.c program3.c
      do
              cc -o $file.out $file
      done
$
```

The *while do command* provides a powerful mechanism to loop through a list. Remember that control is transferred to the statement after the done when the exit status of test **command** is false (nonzero). It is possible that the **commands** never get executed because the initial exit status is false.

■ **Example 4.9.5**    The following shell script counts the number of files in the working directory:

```
$ cat count
number=0
while (test $1 )
     do
            number=`expr $number + 1`
            shift 1
     done
echo 'the number of files in' `pwd` 'is' $number
$ chmod +x count
```

This script will be called with the command line as shown:

```
$ count *
```

The * expands to the names of all filenames in the working directory. Then the first argument is tested to see if it is not null (if it is not then zero is returned and the statements between do and done are executed). Note that the expr utility is used to do the arithmetic; this is because all shell variables have string values, and, hence, must be converted to a number. The output of expr is captured and assigned to the variable number. Then each argument on the command line is shifted one to the left, and finally in the echo statement the output of pwd is also captured to be displayed. ■

The *until do statement* continues to loop until the test **command** returns a true or nonerror condition. The following shell script should be run with one argument, namely the user ID of the person checked on. The script will notify the author when that person has logged on to the system. The output of who is piped to the grep utility, which finds the lines in the output of who that have the value of $1 in them. The lines that match are then redirected to /dev/null, the null file, so as not to clutter the screen.

The sleep utility causes the current process (shell script) to stop executing for the time specified (60 seconds in this case). Note that grep returns an exit status of zero only if it finds a match. Thus, the looping will continue until the match is found, that is, until the user sought has logged on. This nicely illustrates the idea that each utility returns an exit status—the trick is to use it appropriately. (Both the grep and sleep utilities are explained in the UNIX manual.)

■ **Example 4.9.6**

```
$ cat is_he_on
until who | grep $1 >/dev/null
        do
                sleep 60
        done
echo $1 'logged on in the last minute'
$ chmod +x is_he_on
```

Now, to find out when "jones" logs on, have the following job running:

```
$ is_he_on jones
```
■

The next example will use the *case statement* to generate a menu-driven shell script to provide three options for compiling a C program. Other options are available and will be discussed in a later chapter. The script does the following: (1) prompts for source code, (2) tests for existence of file containing source code and generates exit status of 2 if it does not exist, (3) displays menu, (4) prompts for choice, and (5) generates particular compile based on user's choice.

■ **Example 4.9.7**

```
$ newcc
echo 'enter the name of the program to be compiled'
read programname
if ( test ! -f $programname)
    then echo $programname 'does not exist'
        exit 2
fi
echo 'enter the number of the desired option'
echo ' 1   simple compile with executable'
echo '       code in a.out'
echo ' 2   simple compile with executable'
echo '       code in mycfile'
echo ' 3   simple compile with object file'
echo '       only (.o) created'
read choice
```

```
case $choice in
    1) cc $programname;;
    2) cc -o mycfile $programname ;;
    3) cc -c $programname;;
    *) echo 'wrong choice given--try newcc again ' ;;
esac
$
```

There are several points worth emphasizing with regard to the case statement:

**1.** An asterisk (*) is typically used for the default case because it matches any string.

**2.** A question mark (?) matches any single character.

**3.** Square brackets ([]) define a character class and an attempt is made to match any single character within them—a range of characters to be matched can be specified with a hyphen (-).

**4.** The pipe symbol ( | ) is used to separate alternate choices.

## EXERCISES  4.9

**1.** Write a shell script named inform to report the number of users logged in. Try to improve it to also report the number of all active processes in the system.

**2.** Write a shell script that reports the number of arguments passed to the script, the arguments themselves, and the process ID of the script.

**3.** Write a shell script that accepts as arguments the user's first and last names, and then prints them in reverse order, separated by a comma.

**4.** Write a shell script that prompts the user for month (mm), day (dd), and year (yy) on separate lines, and then prints out the date (as mm/dd/yy) on one line.

**5.** Write a shell script that copies two files passed as arguments to the old filenames with .copy appended. Print an error message and terminate the shell script if it did not receive at least two arguments.

**6.** Write a shell script that consists of three command lines that will print the number of currently logged-in users, your entry from the file /etc/passwd, and your current working directory.

7. Write a shell script that prints the sum of the numbers from 1 to 10 (on one line), prints the quotient and remainder of this sum when divided by 3, and prints the number of characters in the name of the directory (use expr).

8. Write a shell script that prompts for a word per line until the word is FINISHED. For each line the script should determine if the first character is uppercase or lowercase, and if the line has exactly eight characters. Print the totals for each of the three categories.

9. Write a shell script that, for every file in the login directory ending in a digit, copies the file to a new file whose name is the old filename with .dig appended.

10. Write a shell script that reports whether the sum of the integers from one to any positive number (to be read) is odd or even.

11. Write a shell script that prompts the user for name, age, and salary, and then invokes another script without passing arguments. Be sure that it is impossible for the second script to modify salary, and have it print the name, age, and salary.

## 4.10 │ *SIGNALS AND STANDARD ERROR*

When a UNIX process is executing, it is able to receive certain signals. The normal effect of many signals is to stop the process that received it, but the user can alter the effect of a signal by using the *trap command* within a shell script. A very common signal results from pressing the ctrl-C key or the DEL key while a process is running. This typically will interrupt the process and the assigned numeric value of this signal is 2. Other useful signals and their assigned values are the *kill signal* (assigned 9—which, incidentally, cannot be trapped) and the *software termination signal* (assigned 15).

The trap command has the following format:

<u>trap ['commands'] signal_numbers</u>

The commands part is optional and specifies explicitly what actions are to be taken if one of the signal_numbers is received. Thus, if the shell script is being executed, the line containing the trap command has been read, and then one of the signal_numbers is received, the commands (if any) will be executed and the process will then resume after the point in the script that was being executed when the signal arrived. A signal, say 2, can thus be ignored entirely by using no commands:

<u>trap ' ' 2</u>

■ **Example 4.10.1**    Suppose the user wants to set a trap to prohibit exit from a potentially long-running shell script by merely pressing the DEL key (normally DEL *will* stop the process). This could be done by putting the following at the beginning of that script to insure that it is read immediately:

```
trap 'echo PLEASE DO NOT PRESS THE DEL KEY--DISABLED' 2
```

On the other hand, this process could still be sent signal 9 (although not able to be trapped), thus ending the process by determining its PID with the ps utility (say it is 46377) and then using:

```
$ kill -9 46377
```

The user might also decide to keep the normal effects of the DEL key (by using the exit command), but also provide a nice (harsh) error message and exit status (say 2) by using:

```
trap ' echo the user pressed the DEL key ; exit 2' 2
```

In addition to the standard input and standard output associated with a shell script, there is also a *standard error,* which can be used to capture error messages. It is the programmer's responsibility to redirect the standard error (or the standard output) if it seems desirable to separate the two. Standard input has a file descriptor of zero, standard output of one, and standard error of two. Typically, all of these default to the terminal. Using this file descriptor of two plus redirection, the user can keep the standard error from appearing on the terminal. ■

■ **Example 4.10.2**    Suppose the user has two files called file1 and file2, but there is no file3. Their contents are as follows:

```
$ cat file1
file1 is a short file
$ cat file2
file2 is a short file
$ cat file3
cat: cannot open file3
$ cat file1 file2 file3 1>joined 2>errors
$ cat joined
this is file1
this is file2
$ cat errors
cat: cannot open file3
$
```

The notation 2>&1 will cause the standard error to be directed to the standard output (which in turn may also be redirected):

```
$ cat file1 file2 file3 1>silly 2>&1
$ cat silly
cat: cannot open file3
file1 is a short file
file2 is a short file
$                                                    ∎
```

1. Read about the kill utility in the manual and then experiment with it.
2. What is the purpose of the optional commands in the trap command?
3. What three files are typically open during a process and what are their respective file descriptors?

## 4.11 | CHAPTER SUMMARY

1. The syntax of the command line calls for a command name, followed by options and arguments and terminated by a return.
2. The processing of the command line results in the spawning of a child process.
3. Standard input and standard output for programs typically default to the terminal.
4. Redirection is a technique to alter standard input (<) or standard output (>).
5. The pipe symbol (|) redirects the standard output of one program to be the standard input to the next.
6. Filenames can be generated with the special characters, ?, *, and [ ].
7. Executable files can be run as commands from the command line. The chmod utility can be used to change the permission status of files.
8. The shell employs user variables, shell variables, and read-only shell variables.
9. The readonly command fixes the present value of a variable.

10. Read-only shell variables include the command and the arguments on the command line ($0 through $9). The shift command moves the arguments forward by a desired integral amount.

11. The shell variables HOME, PATH, PS1, PS2, and IFS are typically set by the user in the file .profile.

12. The ps utility permits the user to keep track of processes and their hierarchy.

13. When a process ends, it returns an exit status of zero (for successful) or nonzero (for failed).

14. The five techniques to execute a program using UNIX are: shell scripts, `command`, . command, exec command, and sh command.

15. The environment of a process can be controlled by the method of invocation and by exporting variables.

16. Commands can be terminated with a return key, pipe symbol, background task symbol, or semicolon.

17. The control structures available in the shell are the if then statement, the if then else statement, the if then elif statement, the for do statement, the while do statement, the until do statement, and the case statement. Break and continue statements can be used to alter the flow of control.

18. The test utility can be used to yield an exit status for conditions applied to control structures.

19. Signals can be received by processing and the trap command can be used to change the default actions associated with signals.

# CHAPTER 5

## Types, Operators, and Expressions in C

### 5.1 | IDENTIFIERS AND VARIABLES

An identifier is defined to be a sequence of any finite length (but greater than or equal to one), consisting of letters, digits, and the underscore (_) character *and* beginning with a letter or an underscore. (The length is limited to 14 in System V.) Identifiers generally are used in C programs for the following purposes:

1. as keywords (discussed in the next section)

2. as names of functions from a standard library, such as the input and output functions scanf and printf, respectively. The function name main, it should be noted, is always used to designate that function executed first in a C program

3. as names of functions that are user defined and are the building blocks for C programs

4. as names of constants, typically consisting of all uppercase letters

5. as names of variables

Examples of each of these uses follow.

■ **Example 5.1**
1. The keyword *while* is always used to begin a particular looping structure and cannot be used for any other purpose.

2. The function *printf* is used to format output from C programs.

3. A user might write a C program with each of certain functions performing specific tasks; for example, get_input might be used to obtain the test scores for a class of students; average_scores might be used to average those scores; perhaps sort_scores sorts the scores in descending order; and print_results displays the sorted scores along with the average.

4. The programmer might use constant definitions in a C program to identify quantities that do not change throughout the program; for

example, the tax rate may be fixed at 28% and the number of work-days at three hundred:

```
#  define  TAX_RATE    .28
#  define  NUMBER      300
```

This technique of defining constants is helpful in that such constants are easily recognizable throughout the entire program, and unexpected changes in their values over time necessitate only single changes in the program code (rather than scattered throughout the program). Furthermore, lengthy values for constants need not be laboriously reproduced throughout the program.

5. A programmer might wish to use variables, such as wages and hours_worked, to designate entities whose values change over time (pardon the pun) or from employee to employee. ■

Variables are used in programs to hold data; their values can be changed, used in calculations without any effect on the value of the data itself, and assigned to other variables.

Variables are declared in C programs. The effect is to associate a memory location with the name of the declared variable, and then permit the user to assign values to that variable. For example, the declaration

```
int  x;
```

declares x to be of data type integer and sets aside (typically) four bytes for that integer. Then the statement

```
x=4;
```

assigns x the integer value 4.

The names that can be chosen for variables in C programs are generally subject to the following guidelines:

1. Use only letters (uppercase or lowercase), digits, and "_". The underscore symbol is considered to be a letter in the context of variable names—3-x is invalid since the hyphen cannot be used.

2. Start its name only with a letter —3x is invalid.

3. Do not use keywords reserved for special meaning. These cannot be redefined. (For example, *auto* is not a valid variable name.)

4. Do not use standard library function names, such as *scanf* and *printf,* for ordinary variables.

5. Uppercase and lowercase characters are distinguishable in most implementations of C. Note that xy3 is different from Xy3.

6. The length of (internal) variables is not limited but only the first eight characters are significant so, a123456789 and a1234567 are the same.

7. The length of external variables, such as function names, and external variables is dependent upon system loaders and assemblers, but should be unique within the first seven characters to be safe.

8. Symbolic constants are typically given identifying names consisting of all uppercase letters. This is only a tradition, but it is thus not a good idea to use variable names consisting only of uppercase letters.

### EXERCISES 5.1

1. Comment on the valid lengths of variables (internal) and contrast these restrictions with the restrictions for external variables.

2. What is the traditional use of a name in a C program composed only of uppercase letters?

3. Give examples of potential sources of problems for each of the eight general guidelines for naming variables.

## 5.2 | KEYWORDS

Reserved words, those that can be used only in a predefined context, are called *keywords*. C has a relatively small number of such words compared to other languages. The reserved words are:

| | | | | | |
|---|---|---|---|---|---|
| *auto* | *default* | *extern* | *int* | *sizeof* | *union* |
| *break* | *do* | *float* | *long* | *static* | *unsigned* |
| *case* | *double* | *for* | *register* | *struct* | *void* |
| *char* | *else* | *goto* | *return* | *switch* | *while* |
| *continue* | *enum* | *if* | *short* | *typedef* | |

Note that these are lowercase and that they cannot be used as the names of variables. Each of these will be explained later in the text. The programmer should also note that some implementations of C also set aside additional keywords such as *asm, ada, pascal,* and *fortran.* It is better to err on the side of caution and not choose names of other languages as variable names.

### EXERCISES 5.2

1. Check your implementation of C and determine exactly which keywords are reserved.

2. Choose five keywords from the list and conjecture what their meanings might be; verify or negate your conjecture by looking up their actual meanings.

3. Compare the number of keywords in C with other languages, including at least one of Cobol, Pascal, and Ada.

## 5.3 | OPERATORS AND SEPARATORS

Operators are used in combination with one or more identifiers to provide "pointing to" members, grouping of quantities, and subscripting in arrays. Several other uses include (1) to negate, increment, decrement, and calculate memory size of stored quantities; (2) to return addresses and perform indirection; (3) to perform arithmetic operations; (4) to do bit shifting in memory; (5) to do comparisons of expressions; (6) to do logical comparisons; (7) to make assignments; and (8) to sequentially evaluate expressions. *Don't worry if a lot of this doesn't make sense now—it will as you go through the book.*

The following is a complete list of operators and associativity for the language C. The precedence level goes from top to bottom. Again, each of these will be explained later in the text, but the user should have, even at this point, some idea of which operators are permitted in C so that they are not unintentionally used.

|  | Operators | | | Associativity |
|---|---|---|---|---|
| 1. | ( ) | [ ] | -> | left to right |
| 2. | ! | ++ | -- | right to left |
|  | sizeof | - | * |  |
|  | & | ~ |  |  |
| 3. | * | / | % | left to right |
| 4. | + | - (binary) | | left to right |
| 5. | << | >> | | left to right |
| 6. | < | <= | > | left to right |
|  | >= | | | |
| 7. | == | != | | left to right |
| 8. | & | | | left to right |
| 9. | ^ | | | left to right |
| 10. | ! | | | left to right |
| 11. | && | | | left to right |
| 12. | !! | | | left to right |
| 13. | ?: | | | right to left |
| 14. | = | += | -= | right to left |
|  | *= | /= | | |
| 15. | , | | | left to right |

There are a couple of subtle points worth mentioning. First, the order of evaluation for operations that are theoretically associative and commutative is machine dependent. Thus a+b could be different from b+a (noncommutative). Also, when a particular operation inadvertently produces overflow or underflow, the results are unpredictable. Notice, also, that the longest operator is two characters in length and that most associate left to right. For example, a+b+c associates left to right, which means that it is equal to (a+b)+c. Here are some examples.

■ **Example 5.3.1**

| Expression | | Equivalent Expression | Rules |
|---|---|---|---|
| d / b % a | is | (d / b) % a | level 3 |

In this example, only the division and modulus operators are used (level 3) and the associativity goes from left to right. Modulus is the remainder after the division takes place; for example 7 % 4 is 3. ■

■ **Example 5.3.2**

| Expression | | Equivalent Expression | Rules |
|---|---|---|---|
| a=b=c=0 | is | a= ( b=(c=0) ) | level 14 |

Again, the only operator present is the level 14 assignment (=) operator with associativity, however, going from right to left. If the associativity had been from left to right, then the equivalent expression would have been:

(((a=b)=c)=0)    ■

■ **Example 5.3.3**

| Expression | | Equivalent Expression | Rules |
|---|---|---|---|
| 9/c + − 20 / d | is | (9 / c) +((−20) / d) | levels 2,3, and 4 |

Here the expression involves operators at different precedence levels: level 2 (unary minus (−)), level 3 (division), and level 4 (addition). Thus, the equivalent expression is generated in the following sequence:

(−20)              level 2
(9/c)              level 3 left to right
((−20)/d)          level 3
(9/c)+((−20)/d)    level 4    ■

■ **Example 5.3.4**

| Expression | | Equivalent Expression | Rules |
|---|---|---|---|
| x > y * z | is | x > (y * z) | levels 2 and 6 |

The sequence of evaluations to generate the equivalent expression is:

(y * z)            level 2
x > (y * z)        level 6    ■

It is not necessary to separate operands and operators by white space. This is different from the situation in UNIX in which white space is not permitted around certain operators. It is also important to realize that the context in which an operator appears can determine its usage. For example, the dash or minus ($-$) character can be used in several differing contexts:

| | |
|---|---|
| x $-$ y | Here minus serves as the subtraction symbol. |
| $--$x | Here the adjacent minus signs serve as a single "decrement" operator (meaning to decrease x by 1). |
| x $-=$y | Here the adjacent minus and equals signs serve as a single special assignment operator, which is shorthand for x = x $-$y. |
| p $->$ x | Here the adjacent minus sign and greater than sign serve as a single "pointer operator." |

## EXERCISES 5.3

1. Find the fully parenthesized equivalents for the following expressions using the precedence chart and the associativity rules:
   a. 1 $*$ 2 $+$ 3 $-$ 20 / 5
   b. x % y ? z : k $+$ 4
   c. j $<<$ 2 $<<$ 1
   d. $*$k = ($*$z) $*$ ($*$k)
   e. x $>$ y $<<$ z $*$ a && q $==$ b
2. Give examples of the level 6 operators.
3. Look up the difference between the $==$ and $=$ operators.

## 5.4 CHARACTERS AND STRINGS

Each character is stored in a single byte, which usually consists of eight bits. Thus, it is possible to store 256 (two to the eighth) different bit combinations in a byte. Many of these possibilities correspond to printed characters, some correspond to nonprinting characters, while others are not presently assigned to anything. In ASCII, a popular code for storing characters, the following holds:

1. 0000 0000 through 0001 1111 (0 through 31) are nonprinting characters.
2. 0010 0000 (32) is a space.
3. 0011 0000 through 0011 1001 (48 through 57) represent 0 through 9.

**4.** 0100 0001 through 0101 1010 (65 through 90) represent A through Z.

**5.** 1100 0001 through 1111 0010 (97 through 122) represent a through z.

**6.** 1000 0000 through 1111 1111 (128 through 255) are unused.

Some nonprinting and hard-to-print characters must be escaped (literally to escape the usual meaning of a character), by using a \ followed by a single character, when used in a C program. Examples of these are null, backspace, tab, newline, formfeed, carriage return, double quote, single quote, and backslash. For example, the tab character has ASCII value 0000 1001 (9) and would be written \t or \9, while the formfeed character has ASCII value 0000 1100 (12) and would be written \f or \12.

When a value of a variable that has been assigned a character is printed from a C program with the function printf, the output will depend upon the format, which will be %c (as a character) or %d (as a decimal).

**■ Example 5.4.1**    Here is an example of a complete C program with two variable declarations; bigone is declared to be an ordinary integer, and littleone is declared to be a character. Various printing is performed.

```
/************************/
/*  CHAPTER 5  5.4.1.C  */
/************************/

main()
{
   int bigone;
   char littleone;
   littleone = 'A';
   bigone = 256;
   printf("\nThe value of littleone is %c\n",littleone);
   printf("The value of bigone is %d\n",bigone);
   printf("The integer value of littleone is %d\n",littleone);
   printf("The next value of littleone is %c\n",littleone+1);
}



/**********/
/* OUTPUT */
/**********/
The value of littleone is A
The value of bigone is 256
The integer value of littleone is 65
The next value of littleone is B
```

Notice that A + 1 printed as a character (using %C) is B while A + 1 printed as a decimal (using %d) is 65. ■

A string in C is a sequence of characters surrounded by double quotation marks. If it is necessary to include a double quotation mark within the string, represent that character as the backslash followed by a double quotation mark (\"). Note carefully that it is the convention in C that each string has an implicit extra character written \0 (end of string character with ASCII value 0—called the null character). A string is simply an array of characters.

Examples follow:

■ **Example 5.4.2**  "good "  The characters are g followed by o followed by o followed by d followed by blank followed by hidden character \0. Thus, there are six, not five, characters in this string. The character \0 is understood to be a single character whose ASCII value is zero. ■

■ **Example 5.4.3**  'g'  This is not a string because the letter g is not enclosed in double quotation marks. It is, instead, simply a character. ■

■ **Example 5.4.4**  "a+b"  This is a string of four characters (a, +, b, and the null character). No arithmetic can be performed because the double quotation marks make it a string—a single entity.

"a\""  This is a string with three characters: a, ", and \0. ■

## EXERCISES 5.4

1. If a character were stored in two bytes, how many bit combinations would be possible to store different characters?
2. What is the absolute difference between the ASCII value of an uppercase letter and a lowercase letter?
3. The bit patterns representing ASCII values 128 through 255 have one bit whose value is constant. Which bit is it and what is its value?
4. Run a program similar to the one in this section experimenting with the character (%c) format to attempt printing some hard-to-print or nonprinting characters.

## 5.5 COMMENTS AND CONSTANTS

Comments consist of any set of characters placed between /* and */. They can be placed anywhere a blank or a newline can appear. A comment cannot be nested within another comment such as:

    /* ... ... /* .....*/........*/

Comments are ignored by the compiler and are used to document a program. Comments should help explain the code to both the author of the program and to readers (such as faculty) of the program, but most important of all, comments provide an important mechanism to assist in the maintenance of programs.

Examples of C code followed by a comment are given next.

■ **Example 5.5.1**

```
takehome = salary * .93;
```
/* deduct for social security*/

```
income = salary + tips;
```
/*add salary and tips—this is not a useful comment because it is basically a restatement of the C code*/

```
x=x+y*2;
```
/*comments should be written at the time the original code is written, not as an afterthought to satisfy faculty members*/ ■

A common error is to forget the closing */, in which case a very large chunk of supposed C code might be considered as simply one large comment. An example of this follows.

■ **Example 5.5.2**

```
a = b+ c;
```
/*compute earnings

```
x = y+ z;
```
/*compute deductions—the end of the first comment is at the next slash*/

/*note that x =y+z never gets executed*/                                  ■

Comments are typically used "in line," or immediately prior to a chunk of code (which in C might typically be a function or a loop). An example of the latter would be as follows.

■ **Example 5.5.3**

```
/*the following code will compute the final take-
home pay for a person with any number of
deductions and any salary up to $50,000. It is
assumed that credit union and other miscellaneous
deductions will be computed here*/
```

The function itself would follow this code. Note that the comment runs across the line as opposed to "in line" comments, which typically appear on the right side of C code. ■

*Constants* have a particular value. They would include such quantities as 29 (an integer), 29.4 (a floating point number), and "good23" (a string of seven characters including the null character), and 'g' (a single character). There are various other forms in which numbers can occur (scientific notation, hexadecimal, etc.) and these will be discussed fully in later sections of this chapter.

## EXERCISES 5.5

1. The following code is an example of a C program with no comments and horrible indentation.

```
main() { int a,b,
c; printf("enter three integers--no decimal
points--on the same line")
;
          scanf
( "%d %d %d", &c,&b
,&a); printf("computed average is %d",
(c +
b+a)/3;}
```

   a. Compile and execute the program.

   b. Rewrite the program with comments, indentation, and appropriate use of white space to make it readable.

   c. Compile and execute the program again.

2. Write a short essay giving a clear distinction between characters and strings.

## 5.6 DECLARATIONS

In general, variables must be declared before they can be used in a C program. They may also be initialized (subject to some restrictions given later) at the time of declaration as with the variable called tips below.

**■ Example 5.6.1**

```
main()
{
int salary, wages;      /*salary and wages are declared to be of
                          type integer*/

float deductions;       /*deductions is declared to be a real
                          number with "single precision"*/

int i,j,k;

int x,y,z;              /*these really need comments—variable
                          names are rather cryptic*/
```

```
int tips = 0;          /*tips is declared and initialized to 0 */
                       /*executable code goes here */

}
```

Declarations serve two purposes:

**1.** The compiler sets aside an appropriate amount of space in main memory to hold any particular values that may be assigned to these variables. Thus, when the declaration

```
int salary;
```

is made the compiler associates a memory location with the identifier called salary and then expects that only integer values will ever be stored in that location.

**2.** The compiler can perform operations correctly with any operator that uses these variable names. Thus

```
i = j +k
```

instructs the compiler to take the integer values stored in j and k, add them as integers, and store the integer result in the variable k. This kind of arithmetic is implemented quite differently from a statement of the form

```
x = y + z
```

where all variables in sight are of type float. One needs to be especially careful to instruct the compiler properly in the declarations and to see that in the "executable" code, assignments and arithmetic operations are as desired. In other words, mixing data types is generally not a good idea unless the user fully understands how the code will be translated into machine instructions. ∎

## EXERCISES 5.6

**1.** The following program should be compiled and run on your machine to test for integer arithmetic (note that 1 is always true and hence the user may wish to change the condition):

```
main()
{
      int a,b;  /*the operands in the arithmetic*/
while(1) {
      printf("\n\n\n  enter two integers: ");
      scanf("%d %d", &a,&b);
      printf("\n %d  +    %d is  %d", a,b,a+b);
```

```
                        printf("\n %d   -      %d is   %d", a,b,a-b);
                        printf("\n %d   *      %d is   %d", a,b,a*b);
                        printf("\n %d   /      %d is   %d", a,b,a/b);
                        printf("\n %d   mod    %d is   %d", a,b,a%b);
                        }
          }
```

2. Experiment with the code in Exercise 1 by making the following changes and then recompile and run the program again (particular attention should be paid to the values being input):

   a. Change int to short and run it with input of 32000 and 32000. Any problems?

   b. Change int to char and run it with input of 127 and 127. Also try 127 and 1 as well as 128 and 128. Any problems?

   c. Change int to float, %d to %f, omit the last printf, and then try some decimal arithmetic. Experiment with very large and very small positive quantities.

## 5.7 | DATA TYPES

The fundamental data types (those from which all others can be derived) are listed here. Each is a keyword and thus may not be used as the name of a variable. In the cases where a word appears in brackets for part of the name of the data type, it is customary to omit that word; however, it does no harm to leave it in.

### Integral Data Types

---

| integral data types |
|---|

| | |
|---|---|
| `char` | /*always one byte*/ |
| `short [int]` | /*may be shorter than an integer*/ |
| `int` | /*32 bits on some machines such as a 3B-2 and an IBM 370*/ |
| `long [int]` | /*may be longer than an integer—it is on an IBM 370*/ |
| `unsigned char` | /*always one byte*/ |
| `unsigned short [int]` | /*may be shorter than an integer*/ |
| `unsigned [int]` | /*cannot represent negative integers*/ |
| `unsigned long [int]` | /*cannot represent negative integers*/ |

### Floating Data Types

> floating data types

```
float              /*single precision reals*/
long float         /*double precision reals*/
```

The arithmetic data types are now defined to be the set of integral data types and floating data types.

When arithmetic operators are mentioned, we mean those operators used with arithmetic data types (integral or floating).

## EXERCISES 5.7

1. Find the number of bytes each integral data type occupies on your machine.

2. On the DEC PDP-11, characters occupy 8 bits, integers 16, shorts 16, longs 32, floats 32, and doubles 64. What is the largest integer that can be stored? The largest short? The largest long? The largest unsigned short int? The largest unsigned int? The largest unsigned long int?

## 5.8  EXPRESSIONS, STATEMENTS, AND ASSIGNMENT

Expressions are comprised of any valid combination of constants, variables, operators, and function calls. If an expression is terminated with a semicolon (;) it becomes a statement.

Be sure to think of = as an operator—the assignment operator. The = is a binary operator with its operands the variable name (left-hand side) and the expression (right-hand side). Expressions have values at any given point in time, and in the case of an assignment expression, the value is the current value of the variable on the left-hand side.

■ **Example 5.8.1:**

| | |
|---|---|
| `x + y` | is an expression. |
| `x + y;` | is a statement. |
| `A=1+(x=2)` | is an expression because it does not end with a semicolon. The value of this expression will be 1 plus the value of x, hence 3. |
| `x=x - y` | is an expression because it does not end with a semicolon. The value of this expression will be the new value of x. |
| `x=sqrt(y);` | is a statement. The square root function is called with argument y.   ■ |

■ **Example 5.8.2** Consider the following declaration and sequence of assignments and note the values of each expression:

```
int a,b,c;
a=3;          /*the expression a=3 has value 3*/
b=5;          /*the expression b=5 has value 5*/
c=a+b*a;      /*this expression now has value 18, the current
                value of c */
c=b=a-b;      /*a-b has value -2, which gives b the value -2,
                which in turn gives c the value -2. The fully par-
                enthesized expression is c=(b=(a-b)). Note the
                rules of precedence and associativity.*/   ■
```

## EXERCISES 5.8

1. What is the essential difference between an expression and a statement?

2. Fill in the blank with the value of each of the expressions on the left side assuming that the statements given are executed sequentially.

   int x,y,z;

   | /*Expressions*/ | /*Values*/ |
   |---|---|
   | x = 7; | _____ |
   | y = x + 2 * x; | _____ |
   | z = x -y; | _____ |
   | z = x = y = x -y; | _____ |

## 5.9 THE DATA TYPES INT AND FLOAT

### The Data Type Int

Integer constants represented in decimal rorm consist of a finite sequence of digits that begin with a positive digit (can begin with a 0), which represents an octal (base 8) integer, or a 0x, which represents a hexadecimal (base 16) integer, and followed by zero or more ordinary digits (0 through 9). The reader is assumed to be somewhat familiar with the essentials of base n numbering systems (clearly bases 2, 8, 10, and 16 are most important).

■ **Example 5.9.1**

39

30

1234567890

Each of these is an ordinary base 10 integer. ■

When the unary operator "-" appears before an integer constant, a negative integer is obtained (also an expression).

■ **Example 5.9.2**

```
037        /*has the value 3 * 8 + 7 * 1 which is 31 */
0x37       /*has the value 3 * 16+ 7 * 1 which is 55 */
−39        /*constant expression*/
```
                                                                      ■

One must also be sure that the integer constant in question does not exceed the storage size allocated to that quantity. For example, on one particular UNIX-based microcomputer the following sizes are in force:

```
short 2 bytes      /*is sometimes shorter than an int */
int 4 bytes        /*always the same length as an unsigned*/
long 4 bytes       /*is sometimes longer than an int */
```

These sizes imply that there is a maximum integer that can be stored. For example, in the case of a short (2 bytes or 16 bits), the maximum short int is

```
0111 1111 1111 1111     /* 2**14 + . . . + 2 + 1 */
                        /* which equals 2**15−1 */
                        /*recall that the leading 0 is the sign
                        bit; 0 indicating positive*/
```

Can the negative of this number be stored? It would be the two's complement, which is obtained by changing every 0 to 1, every 1 to 0, and then adding 1 to that result:

```
  1000 0000 0000 0000     /*one's complement*/
+                    1     /*plus one*/
  ───────────────────     /*final result—a negative number*/
= 1000 0000 0000 0001
```

So the answer is affirmative. Thus, the number of integers that can be stored consists of:

```
(2**15−1)     positive numbers and
(2**15−1)     negative numbers and
1             number with a value of 0
```

Tallying yields $2**16 -2 + 1 = 2**16 -1$ numbers that can be stored. Hence, one can store one more number because in 16 bits there are $2**16$ possibilities. The "last" bit representation is 1000 0000 0000 0000, which is taken to represent $(-)(2**15)$.

To summarize, the numbers in the range from $(-)(2**15)$ to $(2**15)-1$, for example, can be represented as short integers on a machine using 16 bits for short integers. This is a range from $-32768$ to $32767$. Any number outside this range *cannot* be represented as a short int. Hence, the following declaration and assignment will cause overflow at run-time:

```
short int i;
i=32768;
```

Looking at the earlier table in Section 5.3, note that the unary operators $-$, $++$, $--$ have a higher priority than $*,/$, and %, which in turn have a higher priority than $+$ and $-$ (binary), which are higher than $=$ (assignment).

The definitions of $++,--$, , and % for int data follows:

$++$ is called an increment operator and $--$ is called a decrement operator. Both can be either a prefix or postfix operator for a variable of type int. Now, $++x$ (or $--x$) means increment (decrement) x by 1 and then use the new value of x in the expression. But $x++$ (or $x--$) means use x in the expression and then increment (decrement) by 1.

■ **Example 5.9.3**  Follow the sequence of assignments given below:

```
int x,y,z;
x=3;
y=4;
z=5;
x= y * z          /* x is now 20 */
x= ++y *z         /* y is incremented to 5 (and then used), and
                     x becomes 5* 5 =25 */
x= y-- *z         /* y value of 5 is used (and then decremented
                     back to 4), and x becomes 5* 5 =25) */
x= y-- + ++z      /* z is incremented to 6 (and then used), y is
                     used at 4 (and then decremented to 3), and
                     finally x becomes 4*6=24 */.              ■
```

■ **Example 5.9.4**  Be especially careful to avoid ambiguous expressions. For example what is the meaning of

```
y = ++x - x++;
```

On the one hand, the compiler is instructed to increment x (and then use it), while in the same expression the compiler is instructed to use x (and then decrement it). If x starts with the value of 5 and ++x is done before x++, then ultimately y will get the value of 6 − 6= 0, with x finishing at 7. If, on the other hand, x++ is performed before ++x, then y gets the value of 7 − 5= 2, with x finishing at 7 again. Be careful! A few words of advice concerning the int data types:

1. Use the data type *short* when storage is a primary consideration and the integer is relatively small. Keep in mind that a particular implementation may store a short and an int in the same amount of space.

2. Similarly, use the data type *long* when the integer might be relatively large. Again, the implementation is not required to provide more storage space for a long than an int.

3. Use space efficiently by declaring *unsigned,* if no negative values will be encountered. An unsigned is guaranteed to be the same length as an int in all implementations.

4. To find the amount of storage required for a particular object x, such as a variable v, expression e, or data type d, use the *sizeof* operator in the following way:

```
printf("\n the number of bytes used is %d",
sizeof(x));
```

### The Data Type Float

Real numbers (those that are not of any int type and have a decimal point) are of two types, *float* or *double.* The sizeof a float is less than or equal to that of a double, and on the 3B-2 machine, these sizes are four and eight bytes, respectively. Floats and doubles may be written in exponential notation. All real constants are treated as type double.

■ **Example 5.9.5** The following are examples of real numbers: 53.35, 0.32, −31.14, 3.07e+3, and 3.07e−3. The rules for the form of real numbers are:

1. The decimal point or the exponential part must be present. Hence, 3 is not real.

2. If the decimal point is used, then the integer part or the fractional part must be used. Thus, .e2 is not real.

3. If the decimal point is not used, then both the integer part and the exponential part must be used. ■

Values for real numbers can be described in terms of range and precision. Range indicates the smallest to the largest possible *positive* values that can be stored, while precision indicates the number of significant decimal places. Hence, not all real numbers can be stored, and, furthermore, operations involving real numbers might not yield mathematically exact answers on "the machine." There may be overflow that is lost. On a 3B-2, the range for a float (precision of 6 significant digits) or a double (precision of 16 significant digits) is from about $(10)**(-38)$ to $(10)**38$ and these numbers will be represented in the machine as

```
+- .dddddd * 10P (float-6 decimal digits)
+- .dddddddddddddddd *10P (double-16 decimal digits)
```

where p is in the interval from $-38$ to $+38$.

■ **Example 5.9.6**

```
float a;
double aa;
a = 12.3456789;
```
/\*stored as 0.123456\*10\*\*2=12.3456 with an error of .0000789 \*/

```
aa=12.34567890123456789;
```
/\*stored as 0.1234567890123456\*10\*\*2 =12.34567890123456 with an error of .00000000000000789 \*/

```
a=123456789012
```
/\*stored as 0.123456\*10\*\*12=123456789000 with an error of 12 \*/                    ■

## EXERCISES 5.9

1. Identify the base 10 equivalents of 026, 0x26, 0xAB, and 073 (bingo!).
2. Show the 16-bit integer equivalent of 82 and $-82$.
3. What is the range of integers that can be represented in a 32-bit integer?
4. Specify the value for each expression listed below executed immediately after the following declarations and initializations:

   ```
   int a,b,c;
   a=5;b=10;c=12;
   ```

   a. ++a
   b. ++b
   c. c++

    d.  a + (++b)

    e.  (a++) +b

    f.  (−a) + b++

**5.** Find the size of char, short, int, long, unsigned, float, and double on your machine by writing a C program using statements such as:

```
printf("\n a char is %d bytes long," sizeof(char));
```

## 5.10 | *ASSIGNMENT OPERATORS*

The assignment operators have the syntax of variable operator = expression, which is equivalent to variable = variable operator (expression) except in the case where variable is an expression—in this case it is evaluated only once.

The complete list of assignment operators is illustrated below. But first assume that the following declarations and assignments have been made:

```
int a,x,y;
a=2;
x=14;
y=5;
```

Now, suppose each of the following statements is executed immediately after those three assignments:

■ **Example 5.10.1.** "=":    `a =x+y;`    /*a is assigned 19*/    ■

■ **Example 5.10.2.** "·=":    `a *=x+y;`    /* a is assigned 2* (14+5)=38 shorthand for a=a*(x+y) */    ■

■ **Example 5.10.3.** "/=":    `x /=y;`    /* x is assigned 14/5 =2 shorthand for x = x/y      */    ■

■ **Example 5.10.4.** "%=":    `x %=y;`    /* x is assigned remainder of 14/5 =4 */    ■

■ **Example 5.10.5.** "+=":    `x +=y+1;`    /*x is assigned 14 + (5+1) =20 shorthand for x= x + (y+1)     */    ■

■ **Example 5.10.6.** "−=":    `x −=y+1;`    /* x is assigned 14 − (5+1) =8 shorthand for x = x − (y+1)     */    ■

■ **Example 5.10.7. ">>=":**

`x>>=2;`

/* The operator is >> and is defined as a right shift equal to the number of bit positions given by the right operand—and, at least in the case of unsigned quantities, filling the vacated bits with zeros. Thus, this is shorthand for x = x >> 2, which means x is assigned x >> 2. The value of x is 0000 1110 (14). Now shift right two digits to get 00 0011. Now fill in two left digits with zeros or ones (depends on machine) except if x is unsigned in which case always zeros. Obtain 0000 0011, which is 3 (equivalent to dividing by 2 twice and discarding remainder) or obtain 1100 0011 (99) on some machines when manipulating signed quantities. */ ■

■ **Example 5.10.8. "<<=":**

`x<<=2;`

/* The operator is << and is defined as a left shift equal to the number of bit positions given by the right operand. This is shorthand for x = x << 2, which means x is assigned x << 2. The value of x is 0000 1110 (14). Now left shift two digits to get 0011 10. Now fill in two right digits with zeros on all machines to get 0011 1000, which is 56 (equivalent to multiplying by 2 twice). */ ■

■ **Example 5.10.9. "&=":**

`x&=y;`

/* This is shorthand for x = x & y, which means x is assigned x & y (bitwise "and")
   0000 1110 (14)
& 0000 0101 (5)
is 0000 0100 (4)    */ ■

■ **Example 5.10.10. "^=":**

`x ^ =y;`

/* This is shorthand for x = x ^ y, which means x is assigned x^y (bitwise "exclusive or")
   0000 1110 (14)
^ 0000 0101 (5)
is 0000 1011 (11)    */ ■

■ **Example 5.10.11. "|=":**

`x|=y;`

/* This is shorthand for x = x|y, which means x is assigned x|y (bitwise "or")
   0000 1110 (14)
| 0000 0101 (5)
is 0000 1111 (15)    */ ■

<u>EXERCISES    **5.10**</u>

**1.** Perform each of the calculations in Examples 5.10.1 through 5.10.11 with the following declarations and initial assignments:

```
int a,x,y;
a=7;
x=4;
y=13;
```

**2.** Find out how your machine treats right shifting of a signed quantity.

**3.** Suppose the following declarations and initializations are made:

```
int a,b,c,d;
a=3;b=4;c=5;d=6;
```

Calculate the value of each of the following expressions:

a. $a -= --b * 5$

b. $c = 3 - d *3$

c. $3 - a * (b -=4) * 6$

## 5.11 | CONVERSIONS AND CASTS

First note that all floats in an expression are converted to doubles because floating point arithmetic in C is performed with double precision.

When data types are mixed in an expression, such as x + y, where x and y are not of the same type, then "implicit conversion" takes place, sometimes called widening, promotion, or coercion. This coercion will be denoted by the symbol "$\rightarrow$" in this text. The basic idea is that an operator dealing with certain data types (namely, char, short, unsigned char, and unsigned short) will coerce them, and then, if mixed modes are present, coerce the lower type to the higher type—with the resultant expression having the higher type. Coercion will not change the data type of the stored expressions, but will temporarily make the change during the evaluation of the expression. There are two basic rules for the evaluation of x op y where op is any operator:

**1.** Char and short are always converted to int:

```
char    →    int
short   →    int
```

and unsigned char and unsigned short are always converted to unsigned:

$$unsigned\ char \quad \rightarrow \quad unsigned$$
$$unsigned\ short \quad \rightarrow \quad unsigned$$

Note that these conversions occur even if operands are of same data type.

2. If the data types are still mixed, then the lesser one is promoted to the higher one (which will be the type of the expression) according to the following range:

$$int\ <\ unsigned\ <\ long\ <\ unsigned\ long\ <\ float\ <\ double$$

Do not use these rules across an equal sign.

Because of rule 1 on previous page, chars and ints may be mixed in expressions with each char being converted to an int. However, the question of whether the conversion of a char to an int can produce a negative integer depends upon the machine itself. On some machines sign extension is used. That is, if the left most bit of the char is a 1, a negative integer is produced; but on other machines, zeros are padded at the left end, producing a positive integer. The reader can take some assurance from the fact that all characters in the machine's standard character set are guaranteed to be converted to positive integers.

■ **Example 5.11.1**   Suppose a short is added to an int:

`short + int → int + int`        /\*resultant is of data type int\*/

Suppose an unsigned char is added to a double:

`unsigned char+double →unsigned+double`
`→double +double`
/\*resultant is of data type double \*/        ■

When converting across an equal sign, widening is generally no problem, but narrowing can have serious ramifications. For example, an int assigned to a float will cause no problems, but a float assigned to an int will be machine dependent and is risky. It is generally wise to use *explicit* conversions, called casts, when there is any doubt as to the validity of a result. A cast expression is of the form

`(type) expression`

and can be used anywhere an expression can. It is a unary operator with right to left associativity and with the same precedence as the other unary operators.

■ **Example 5.11.2**

```
int i;
float f;
char c;
i =3;
f = (float) i;
```
/*the value of i in storage is not changed*/
/*but f now has the float value corresponding to 3*/

```
c = i;
```
/* i =0000 0000 0000 0000 0000 0000 0000 0011
c = 0000 0011 truncate high-order bits*/

```
i = c;
```
/* i is returned to original value*/
/*however, if c had been negative to begin with (leading 1) then on some machines i=c causes padding with zeros while on others it causes padding with ones on the high end. In both cases the sequence i =c;c=i; leaves c unchanged*/ ■

One of the functions in the standard library is getchar(). This retrieves the next character from the terminal, and its return value (every function returns a value) is the integer equivalent of the char, unless an end-of-file is encountered (often entered by depressing ctrl-d followed by a return) or there is an error—in which case it returns EOF. EOF is often defined to be -1 by using the following statement in a C program:

```
#define EOF (-1)
```

■ **Example 5.11.3** The following code will cause trouble if the machine does not use sign extension (the if condition will always fail because c will always be positive and EOF is negative):

```
#define EOF (-1)
/* 1111 1111 1111 1111 1111 1111 1111 1111 */
char c;
c = getchar();
if (c ==EOF)
...
```

This problem can be remedied by changing the declaration to:

```
int c;
```

Furthermore, with the int declaration, getchar() can be used to read arbitrary input (all possible characters) and an EOF value that is distinct. The value of EOF, in this case, cannot be represented as a char, but rather must be stored as an int.

## EXERCISES 5.11

1. On your machine write and run a program with the following declarations and assignment:

   `float x; double y; x= 3000.0;`

   Have the program print the size of x, 3000.0, and x/y. Do x and 3000.0 have the same size?

2. The square root function "sqrt" requires an argument of type double. If n is an integer, show how to cast it so that its square root can be taken.

3. Show that the octal equivalent of 63 is 077. Now show that the assignment x = x & 077 will set to zero all but the low-order six bits of x (independent of size of x).

4. Determine what effect x = x ¦ mask will have on x in general.

5. The unary operator "~" converts each one-bit to a zero-bit and vice versa. Show that x = x & ~077 leaves the last six bits of x at zeros.

## 5.12 CONSTANTS

Generally speaking, constants of type short, unsigned, and float do not exist. Thus, the typical data types that admit constants are int, long, double, char, and string. Note:

1. If an integer is too long to fit into an int, it will be of type long.

2. An integer can be forced to be long by appending L or l, as in 53l or 53L.

3. Constant expressions are evaluated at compile time, not at runtime. Thus, in the statement

`pay = 40 * 3.35 * months_worked ;`    /*40*3.35 will be evaluated during compilation*/

## 5.13 PRECEDENCE

It is clear that there is a definite scheme for precedence of operators. Associativity is also an issue. However, certain commutative operators may be reordered at compile time even across parentheses. These operators are *, +, &, ^, and ¦. Thus, if

`x = a + (b+c);`

the programmer can't be sure whether x is assigned $(a+b) + c$ or the original. When dealing with very large or small quantities, the order of evaluation (even in theoretically commutative operations) may be important. If there is any doubt, one can save the results of an intermediate computation in a temporary variable and force the evaluation to the desired preference.

## 5.14 | *THE C PREPROCESSOR*

The power of the language C is enhanced with the preprocessor, which is invoked by placing the symbol "#" in column 1 of a control line followed by other code. Any effects that are caused continue from that point to the end of the file. There are several ways the preprocessor can assist the programmer—examples are given here to illustrate these.

**■ Example 5.14.1.
Inclusion of other
files in user's
source file:**

Quite often a user will want to include prewritten code in a source file. This can be accomplished with the preprocessor. Suppose myfile needs to be included at a certain point. At that point insert the line:

```
#include "myfile"
```

This will cause a search to be made in the current directory and, if not found, in standard places specified by the UNIX shell variable called PATH. On the other hand, if the search should be made only in standard places, but not in the current directory, then the statement should be (to decrease search time)

```
#include <myfile>
```

The definition of EOF is often included in the file called *stdio.h* found in the directory /usr/include. Hence, the following preprocessor code could be used:

```
#include "/usr/include/stdio.h"
```
■

**■ Example 5.14.2.
Definition of
constants in the
program:**

The programmer can improve readability and maintenance problems by defining symbolic constants at the beginning of a program. Suppose the user wishes the constant e to be 2.718281828 throughout and MINUTESPERDAY to be (24 *60). The appropriate statements are:

```
#define e  2.718281828
#define MINUTESPERDAY (24*60)
```

The programmer can see the effects of these preprocessor commands in program.c by using the compiler option -E (for expand) as follows:

```
$ cc -E program.c
```
■

■ **Example 5.14.3.**
**Redefinition of C**
**syntax:**

A programmer can change C syntax by using the preprocessor to redefine words. (Generally this should be avoided unless the change substantially improves code and the documentation can be measurably enhanced.) For example, if the programmer wishes to use when instead of if, write

```
#define when if
```

Obviously this example is concocted, but it is quite easy to use the preprocessor to make C look more like other languages, such as Pascal. ■

■ **Example 5.14.4.**
**Definition of macros**
**with arguments:**

A programmer can obtain the effect of a function call by an appropriate use of a macro definition with the preprocessor. Suppose the programmer wants to use the symbolism CUBE(X) for x to the third power throughout the program. Simply write

```
#define CUBE(x) ((x) * (x) * (x))
```

If within the program the code 4 / CUBE(x) appears, it will be expanded to read

```
4/((x) * (x) * (x))
```

A common mistake would be to write

```
#define CUBE(x) x*x*x
```

which would then expand the code 4 / CUBE(x) to read 4/ x∗x∗x, which is not what was intended.

In addition to the advantage of more readable and concise code, macros also permit in-line expansion without regard to the type of identifier. This can achieve significant savings if, for example, the CUBE macro needed to be used several times with different data types. The alternative would be to code several CUBE functions with different parameter types. Note also that the effect of the macro CUBE can be undone with the following preprocessor command:

```
#undef CUBE(x)
```
■

■ **Example 5.14.5.**
**Conditional**
**compilation:**

Sometimes it is useful to compile one chunk of code or another on the basis of a particular value. This can be accomplished with the use of the if else statement of the preprocessor. Suppose the programmer wants to compile chunk1 if x is defined and chunk2 if x is not defined. This would be done as follows: /∗interactive code to specify either #define x or #undef x ∗/

```
#ifdef x
```

```
/*chunk1 inserted here*/

    #else

/*chunk2 inserted here*/

    #endif
```
■

One of the most important tools in UNIX available to the C programmer is the *standard I/O package* that permits easy transfer of information between files and programs. It includes all the standard I/O functions written in C and file-related C functions that allow the user to open and close files. The description of these particular functions can be located in the UNIX manual under the 3S group. The 3S group is actually part of the 3C group, which is automatically loaded by the C compiler. However, the user should insert the following preprocessor code in any C program that uses the 3S group:

```
#include <stdio.h>
```

(Other groups available in C include the 3C group—standard C library, the 3F group—Fortran library, the 3M group—mathematics library, and the 3X group—specialized library, such as plotting routines.)

The file *stdio.h* will usually be found in the directory /usr/include and includes a set of variable definitions and macros to provide a specific way of handling files. Here is a complete list of the functions in the standard I/O package that use stdio.h:

```
fopen(); fclose(); getc(); getchar();putc();
putchar(); fgets(); gets(); fgetw(); getw();
putw(); fputs(); puts(); fprintf(); printf();
fscanf(); scanf(); fread(); fwrite(); fflush();
ungetc(); setbuf(); popen(); pclose();feof();
ferror(); clearerr(); fileno().
```

Because these functions are declared in the header file, stdio.h, they do not need to be declared in the program itself. Here is a brief example showing how to open a file for reading, echo its contents back to the screen, and then close it.

■ **Example 5.14.6**    Open a file, get a character, and print it on the screen until end of file (EOF) is reached, and then close the file.

```
/***********************/
/* CHAPTER 5  5.14.6.C */
/***********************/

#include <stdio.h>

main()
{
  int ch;
  FILE *fp;
  fp = fopen("myfile","r");
  while ((ch = getc(fp)) != EOF)
    putc(ch,stdout);
  fclose(fp);
}


/**********/
/* OUTPUT */
/**********/
The details including error checking are skipped at this point.
but at least the reader now has the ability to work with a file.
```

Note that stdio.h uses a buffer so that the reading and writing can be accomplished more efficiently. Thus, the kernel first fills the buffer (usually of size 512 or 1,024 bytes) in main memory. Then getc transfers one character at a time from the buffer to the program, not from the disk to the program. When the characters in the buffer have all been read, the I/O system refills the buffer with the next block of data. Similarly, putc fills an output buffer but does not write directly to the screen (stdout). When the buffer is filled, actual output to the screen takes place. ∎

To run the program above (program.c), compile with

$ **cc program.c**

and then execute with the command

$ **a.out**

## EXERCISES 5.14

1. Set your UNIX PATH variable to be efficient for C programming.
2. Use the preprocessor to define HOURSPERDAY, PI, and MILESTOTHESUN to be appropriate constants.
3. Redefine at least one C construct so that it now has the syntax of one of your favorite languages.
4. Use appropriate macros to define x**2, x**3. Then define x**5 using the previous macros.
5. Print the contents of stdio.h to find the value of EOF.
6. What is the purpose of the E option for the cc compiler? Try it.
7. List all the I/O functions included in stdio.h.

## 5.15  *CHAPTER SUMMARY*

1. Identifiers can be used as keywords, names of library and user-defined functions, names of variables, and names of constants.

2. There are 15 different levels of precedence for operators in C, most of which associate from left to right.

3. ASCII code is often used to represent characters, some of which must be escaped.

4. The printf function can be used to format output.

5. A string in C is a sequence of characters surrounded by double quotation marks.

6. Comments are used to document programs and begin with a /* and end with a */.

7. Variables in C must be declared and they can be initialized at that time.

8. C uses integral and floating data types, collectively known as arithmetic data types.

9. An expression followed by a semicolon (;) is a statement.

10. An assignment expression has a value equal to the value of its right-hand side.

11. Octal integers begin with 0 and hexadecimal with 0x.

12. Increment and decrement operators are available to increase or decrease the value of a variable.

13. All real constants are of type double.

14. Real numbers can be stored with a certain accuracy (precision) and for only in a certain range.

15. C has a number of specialized assignment operators.

16. C has shift operators that can be applied to bit configurations, as well as logical "and," "or," exclusive "or," and "ones complement."

17. Conversions and casts are used to change data types, often to force compatibility.

18. The C preprocessor can be used to include other files, define constants, redefine C syntax, define macros with arguments, and do conditional compilation.

19. One of the most important tools in UNIX available to the C programmer is the standard I/O package, which permits easy transfer of information between files and programs. It includes all the

standard I/O functions written in C and file-related C functions that allow the user to open and close files. The description of these particular functions can be located in the UNIX manual under the 3S group. The 3S group is actually part of the 3C group, which is automatically loaded by the C compiler. However, the user should insert the following preprocessor code in any C program that uses the 3S group: #include <stido.h>. *(Other groups available in C include the 3C group—standard C library, the 3F group—Fortran library, the 3M group—mathematics library, and the 3X group—specialized library such as plotting routines).*

# CHAPTER 6

# *Control Flow in C*

A programmer typically needs to solve a problem with computer code that is substantially more complex than simply having the computer execute one statement after another until the end of the program is reached (sequential processing). Only the very simplest problems will have code that can be designed in that fashion.

The computer programming statements used to modify the top-to-bottom (sequential) execution of code are called *control statements* and these do vary among languages—both in syntax and even as to what types of statements are available. Only those statements available in the C language will be considered here.

## 6.1 | *INTRODUCTION TO CONTROL*

Control might be achieved by testing an expression for truth or falsity and then executing alternative chunks of code based on the truth value of that expression (the if statement or the if else statement).

A more powerful statement called the *switch statement* provides for multiway branching by testing an expression for any number of constant values and then executing separate chunks of code based on any one of the possible values of the expression.

The *while statement* permits the programmer to repeatedly test whether a user-defined expression is true and as long as it is so, execute a chunk of code. Thus, for example, a while statement could be used to test whether data values satisfy a certain condition, and then the processing of data values could proceed for as long as the answer is affirmative. It is important to note that the test occurs at the top of the loop before the chunk is executed. Hence, if the test fails immediately, the chunk of code is *never* executed.

The *do statement,* on the other hand, permits the programmer to execute a chunk of code before testing whether a user-defined expression is true. As long as it is true, the chunk is executed repeatedly. Thus, this construct is similar to the while statement, except here the testing occurs *after* the code is executed, not before. The chunk of code is always executed at least once.

The *for statement,* like the while statement, provides for looping through specified code repeatedly as long as a user-defined expression is true. It also provides for initialization prior to execution of the code and evaluation of another expression with each pass through the code. Any code expressed as a for statement can be shown to be equivalent to code expressed as a statement followed by a while statement.

The *break* and *continue statements* are used to alter the normal flow of execution. The break statement, when encountered in for, while, do, or switch control statements, provides for an immediate exit from that control statement *to the statement immediately following the control statement.* (Its syntax is the single word break.) On the other hand, the *continue statement* may occur only inside for, while, or do control statements, and it causes transfer of control to be passed to the end of the chunk being executed. (Its syntax is the single word continue.) It is quite possible that the chunk will then be executed again because the test condition is still true.

Prior to an in-depth analysis of any of the control structures, it will be necessary to provide the operating tools necessary to do the testing for the flow of control. First, refer to page 000 for a reminder of the complete set of operators available in C.

The operators generally used to control flow include:

1. relational operators (level 6): $<$ less than, $>$ greater than, $<=$ less than or equal to, and $>=$ greater than or equal to

2. equality operators (level 7): $==$ equal, $!=$ not equal

3. logical operators (levels 2, 11, and 12): ! unary negation, && logical and, || logical or

Other operators still to be explored include the comma operator (,) (level 7).

So, after all of these operators are studied here, coupled with the introduction given in Chapter 5, there will just be a few remaining operators to explore in later chapters. They are:

4. conditional operator (level 13): exp1 ?: exp2 : exp3

5. pointer (to filed) operator (level 1): $->$

6. index operator (level 1): [ ]

7. addressing operator (level 2): &

8. indirection operator (level 2): *

9. function call (level 1): ()

### Relational Operators

The relational operators are binary (need two expressions) and yield either 0 (the int 0 and the double 0.0 both represent false) or 1 (all values other than 0 and 0.0 represent true). Note that this is just the opposite of UNIX where zero represents true and nonzero represents false. Note also that the data type of the resultant expression is int.

Each of the relational operators, designated in general as relop, compares two expressions, say exp1 relop exp2, and returns a value of 0 (false) or 1 (true) according to whether the value of exp1 − exp2 is positive, zero, or negative as specified in the following table:

| exp1-exp2 (value) | exp1<exp2 | exp1>exp2 | exp1<=exp2 | exp1>=exp2 |
|---|---|---|---|---|
| | | Value Returned | | |
| positive | 0 | 1 | 0 | 1 |
| zero | 0 | 0 | 1 | 1 |
| negative | 1 | 0 | 1 | 0 |

■ **Example 6.1.1**   Let relop designate any one of these relational operators, $<$, $<=$, $>$, or $>=$. Then (exp1 − exp2) relop 0 is the same as exp1 − exp2 relop 0 because the latter is parenthesized in the following sequence:

```
(exp1 − exp2)              level 4 operator
(exp1 − exp2) relop 0      level 6 operator
```

Hence, there is no danger of misinterpretation to use expressions such as x −y > 0, x −y <= 0, and such. They mean

$$(x-y) > 0, \qquad (x - y) <= 0, \text{ etc.}$$    ■

■ **Example 6.1.2**   Consider the following program and be sure you understand the output as shown.

```
main()
{
  int i=4, j=4, k=9;
  double a=3.0e+100, b=1.0e-40;
  char c='r';
  printf("\nThe value of c='q'+1 is %d",(c='q'+1));
  printf("\nThe value of i+j*k <= k+30 is %d",i+j*k<=k+30);
  printf("\nThe value of j<4<k is %d",j<4<k);
  printf("\nThe value of a<a+b is %f\n",a<a+b);
}

/**********/
/* OUTPUT */
/**********/
The value of c='q'+1 is 114
The value of i+j*k <= k+30 is 0
The value of j<4<k is 1
The value of a<a+b is 0.000000
```
                                                                ■

### Equality Operators

Both of the equality operators, designated in general by eqop, compare two expressions, say exp1 eqop exp2, and return a value of 0 (false) or 1 (true) according to whether the value of exp1 $-$ exp2 is zero or nonzero as specified in the following table:

| exp1-exp2 (value) | exp1==exp2 | exp1 != exp2 |
|---|---|---|
| zero | 1 | 0 |
| nonzero | 0 | 1 |

■ **Example 6.1.3**  Let eqop designate either of the two equality operators. Then (exp1 $-$ exp2) eqop 0 is the same as exp1 $-$ exp2 eqop 0 because the latter is parenthesized in the following sequence:

```
(exp1 - exp2)              level 4 operator
(exp1 - exp2) eqop 0       level 7 operator
```

Hence, there is no danger of misinterpretation to use expressions such as x $-$y $==$ 0 and x $-$y $!=$ 0, and so on. They mean (x$-$y) $==$ 0 and (x $-$ y) $!=$ 0 respectively. ■

Recall that the value of an assignment statement is the value of the left-hand side. So, the value of a$=$2 is 2 (which represents true) while the value of a$==$2 depends upon the current value of a. If a is 2 then the value of a$==$2 is 1 (which represents true), otherwise its value is 0. The moral of the story is that a programmer typically does *not* want to check for a flag of, say, $-$1 by writing

```
while (a=-1)
```
/*the value of a$=-$1 is $-$1 (true) because "a$=-$1" is an assignment statement and hence the condition is always satisfied*/

but rather would use
```
while (a==-1)
```
/*the value of a$==-$1 is dependent upon the current value of a */  ■

■ **Example 6.1.4**  The following program illustrates some examples using equality operators:

```
main()
{
   int i=4, j=4, k=9;
   double a=3.0e+100, b=1.0e-40;
   char c='r';
   printf("\nThe value of 'q'+1 == c is %d",'q'+1==c);
   printf("\nThe value of j*k-72/j*2 == k-2*i*4-1 is %d",j*k-72/j*2==k-2*i*4-1);
   printf("\nThe value of k == j+5 == i is %d",k == j+5 == i);
   printf("\nThe value of a*b != a+a is %d\n",a*b != a+a);
}

/**********/
/* OUTPUT */
/**********/
The value of 'q'+1 == c is 1
The value of j*k-72/j*2 == k-2*i*4-1 is 0
The value of k == j+5 == i is 0
The value of a*b != a+a is 1
```

### Logical Operators

The logical operators, designated in general logop, are either unary, in the case of negation !, or binary, in the case of the logical and (&&) and the logical or ($||$). They return a value of 0 (false) or 1 (true) according to the value of !exp1, exp1 && exp2, and exp1 $||$ exp2 negative as specified in the following table:

| exp1 | exp2 | !exp1 | exp1 && exp2 | exp1 $||$ exp2 |
|---------|---------|-------|--------------|-----------|
| zero    |         | 1     | NA           | NA        |
| nonzero |         | 0     | NA           | NA        |
| zero    | zero    | 1     | 0            | 0         |
| zero    | nonzero | 1     | 0            | 1         |
| nonzero | zero    | 0     | 0            | 1         |
| nonzero | nonzero | 0     | 1            | 1         |

Note carefully that zero designates false and can have an actual value of 0 (int) or 0.0 (double), while nonzero designates true and can have any nonzero value, either of type int or double. Recall the conversion rules of Chapter 5 for mixed mode expressions (p. 137). For example a char type combined with an int type in an expression forces the char type to be converted to int type; similarly, if a double type appears, the entire expression will be of type double.

It is instructive to note that the logical and (&&) of two expressions is 1 (true) only when both expressions are true, and that the logical or ($||$) is 0 (false) only when both expressions are false. This agrees with intuitive notions of combining English statements into compound statements. This phenomenon is especially important because for both the && and the $||$ operators, the evaluation of the expressions stops when the final outcome is determined. Thus, if exp1 && exp2 appears, and exp1 is false (0 or 0.0), then exp2 will not be evaluated. Similarly, if exp1 ┊┊ exp2 appears, and exp1 is true (nonzero), then exp2 will not be evaluated.

■ **Example 6.1.5**　The value of ! ! 2 is that of (! (! 2)) is that of (! 0) is that of 1. Similarly, the value of ! − ! −3 is that of ! (− ! (−3)) because negation associates right to left. The expression now evaluates to ! ( − 0 ), which is 1. ■

■ **Example 6.1.6**　Consider the following program and be sure to check that the output is as specified. Recall that the value of an assignment expression is the value assigned to the variable on the left-hand side.

```
main()
{
    int i,j,k;
    (i=0) && (k=1);
    printf("i= %d k = %d\n",i,k);
    (k=1) && (j=1);
    printf("k = %d j = %d\n",k,j);
    (i=1) && (k=1);
    printf("i = %d k = %d\n",i,k);
    (k=0) ┊┊ (j=0);
    printf("k = %d j = %d\n",k,j);
}

/**********/
/* OUTPUT */
/**********/
i= 0 k = 0
k = 1 j = 1
i = 1 k = 1
k = 0 j = 0
```

■ **Example 6.1.7**　The while loop is used to evaluate an expression, and if it is true, then perform some processing. A typical construct might be as follows:

```
i=0;
while( i++ < 2 && (c =getchar()) != EOF)    /*process something—code re-
                                              places this comment*/
```

The parenthesized equivalent of the expression behind the while is generated in the following sequence:

| | |
|---|---|
| `i++` | level 2 |
| `i++ < 2` | level 6 |
| `(c = getchar()) != EOF` | level 7 |
| `(i++ < 2) && ((c = getchar()) !=EOF)` | level 11 |

Now note carefully again: on the first evaluation of the expression, i (value 0) is compared to 2 (true), a character is fetched from the terminal, and then i is incremented to 1. On the second evaluation of the expression, i (value 1) is compared to 2 (true), a character is fetched from the terminal again, and again i is incremented (now to 2). On the third evaluation of the expression, i (value 2) is compared to 2 (false) and evaluation of the remaining part of the expression is *not* done. So in this example two characters are read from the terminal. ∎

## *EXERCISES*  **6.1**

1. In each of the examples that follow, give an expression that is equivalent but does not use negation:

   a. !(a <=b)
   b. ! (a >=b || x < y)
   c. ! (a >=b && x < y)
   d. ! (a == b)
   e. !(a >=b) || x < y
   f. ! (a>=b) && x < y

2. What does the following program print?

```
main() {
    int a,b;
    double x;
    a= 1; b=4; x =2.0;
    printf("\n the value of a < b is %d", a <b);
    printf("\n the value of (a < b) || a=1000 is %d",(a <b) || a=0);
    printf("\n the value of (a > b && a=1000) is %d", (a > b && a=
                                                1000);
    printf("\n the value of (!!! x) is %f", (!!!x));
}
```

## **6.2** | *STATEMENTS AND BLOCKS*

To quote from Section 5.8: "Expressions are comprised of any valid combination of constants, variables, operators, and function calls. If an expression is terminated with a semicolon (;) it becomes a statement." Statements are defined recursively (in terms of themselves) and fall into two categories: (1) simple statements (a single expression terminated with a semicolon); and (2) compound statements, or blocks, which consist of a left brace {, followed by zero or more declarations, followed by zero or more statements (recursion), terminated by a right brace }.

Note carefully that a C program consists of main( ) followed by a block, a block (compound statement) ends with a right brace, not a semicolon; and blocks may appear in programs anywhere (simple) statements can appear.

The concept of a block is very useful when combined with control flow statements within a program simply because the entire block can be treated as a single statement to be executed repeatedly as long as a condition holds, or to be executed only when a particular condition holds—there are many possibilities. From now on the term *statement* will be taken to mean either a simple statement or a block.

■ **Example 6.2.1** The following program has two blocks within the main block that are unrelated to each other:

```
main()
{
  {
    int a;
    a = 1;
    printf("\nThe value of a is %d",a);
  }
  {
    double a;
    a = 1.0;
    printf("\nThe value of a is %f\n",a);
  }
}

/**********/
/* OUTPUT */
/**********/
The value of a is 1
The value of a is 1.000000
```
■

The reader is encouraged to run this program and note the results. The central point (to be explored further in a later chapter) is that these *parallel* blocks with their own declarations, such as those above, permit the programmer to use variables and then dispose of them, literally freeing their memory space for other uses. In this example, int a is declared but then its existence terminates when the block with double a declaration is entered. Obviously, this idea of blocks with their own private variables is an important and powerful tool. Programmers can encase simple statements in a block designated to perform a certain task without worry that the (local) variables declared there will collide in any fashion with variables declared in other parallel blocks.

Before leaving the concept of statements, one final note: there is available an empty statement whose syntax is a single semicolon (;). It should be inserted in code anywhere the syntax requires a statement but no action is required to be taken.

### EXERCISES   6.1

1.  Is the following code a block?

```
{ a = b < 3;
    { printf("\nthis is a printf
statement");
        ;
    }
}
```

2.  True or false:

    a.  Every statement is terminated with a semicolon.
    b.  { } is a statement.
    c.  { ;;;;} is a statement.
    d.  { { {
    
    ```
              { a=1;}
    } } } is a statement.
    ```

3.  Is the following code a block?

```
{ a = b < 3;
    { printf("\nthis is a printf statement");
        ;
    } ;
}
```

## 6.3 | THE if STATEMENTS

The if statements (which are themselves statements) can have either of
the following syntaxes:

1.  `if (expression) statement`     /* if is the only keyword*/

2.  `if (expression)`               /* if and else are the only
    `statement1`                    keywords*/
    `else statement2`

■ **Example 6.3.1**   The if else version can get fairly complicated as evidenced by the following construction with a box around each if else statement shown to
set off code:

```
if (a >b)
    max = a;

    else    if ( a==b)  {
                  max =a ;
               printf("\nThere is a tie") ;
                  }

            else   if ( a < b && x < y)
                      { max = b;
                         printf("\n x < y") ;
                         }

                   else printf("\n x >=y") ;
```

printf("\n finished with the if else") ;

Notice that

1. Each else is associated with the closest previous if keyword that hasn't used an else. Indentation has no bearing whatsoever on this association—the association is simple and invoked no matter how clear the code might appear from the formatting—BE VERY CAREFUL!

2. Following each else keyword there must be a statement which can be the empty statement if desired. Hence, the printf statement following the last else is optional. That printf statement serves as the default case here in case the condition following each if is false ( 0 or 0.0).

3. If an expression is true then the statement immediately following it is executed and the execution of the entire if else statement is over.

4. The last printf statement is always executed.

This code would usually be indented as follows:

```
if (a>b)
      max = a;
else if (a ==b) {
        max =a;
        printf("\nThere is a tie");
        }
```

```
else if (a < b && x < y) {
               max = b;
               printf("\n x < y");
               }
else printf("\n x >=y");
printf("\nfinished with the if else");
```

So, the outcome is as follows (with each possibility ending with the print "finished with the if else").

1. If (a> b), then max =a.
2. Otherwise, if (a ==b), then max = a and print "there is a tie".
3. Otherwise, if (a < b && x < y), then max = b and print "x < y".
4. Otherwise print "x >=y". ■

■ **Example 6.3.2**   An alternative is to leave off the last else statement, making the consequent of the innermost else an if statement. There is no default case in the circumstances and control continues to the last printf statement. The example is now rewritten with this change:

```
if (a >b)
  max = a;

else   if ( a==b)  {
             max =a ;
          printf("\nThere is a tie") ;
             }

       else   if ( a < b && x < y)
                 { max = b;
                   printf("\n x < y") ;
                     }

printf("\n finished with the if else") ;
```

This would usually be indented as follows:

```
if (a>b)
      max = a;
else if (a ==b) {
         max =a;
         printf("\nThere is a tie");
         }
else if (a < b && x < y) {
            max = b;
            printf("\n x < y");
            }
printf("\n finished with the if else");
```

So, the outcome here is as follows, with each possibility ending with the print "finished with the if else".

1. If ( a> b), then max =a.

2. Otherwise, if (a ==b), then max = a and print "there is a tie".

3. Otherwise, if (a < b && x < y), then max = b and print "x < y". ∎

## EXERCISES 6.3

1. Distinguish clearly between the following codes:

   a. ```
      if (a = 1)
            printf("\nthe value of a is %d",a);
      ```

   b. ```
      if (a==1)
            printf("\nthe value of a is %d",a);
      ```

2. Correct the syntax of the following code segments:

   a. `if a == b {}`

   b. `if a = b printf("\n the value of a is %d",b)`

   c. ```
      if a = b /*do nothing here*/
        else printf("\nthe value of a is %d",a)
      ```

   d. ```
      if (a==b) {
              a =1;
              b= 2;
              };
        else printf("\na is not equal to b");
      ```

**3.** Predict the outcome of the following program segment:

```
int a,b,;
a=1;
b=2;
if (a==1)
      if (b=1)
         printf("\n %d %d %d", a,b,a*7*b % 3);
   else
         printf("\n %d %d %d", a+b,a-b,a*b);
```

**4.** Complete the following program (fill in the underlined portions) that permits a single character from the keyboard to be input and then increments appropriate variables in case it is a blank, a digit, an alphabetic character, or anything else. This will be modified shortly to count the number of characters of each type for an arbitrary stream of input from the keyboard:

```
#include <stdio.h>                        /*to use getchar*/
main()
{ int blanks=0,
      digits=0,
      letters=0,
    anythingelse=0;
int holdchar;
    holdchar=                             /*fetch the character here*/
    if (holdchar== _)                     /*check for a blank*/
         ++blanks;
else if (_____ && _____ )                 /*check for a digit here*/
    ++digits;
else if ((_____ ) || (_____ ))            /*check for lowercase and
                                          uppercase letter here*/
else                                      /*it's something else*/
         _____ ;
printf("blanks %d digits %d letters %d
        anything else %d", blanks,
    digits,letters,
    anythingelse);
}
```

## 6.4 | *THE SWITCH STATEMENT*

The switch statement provides for multiway branching, specified by the keywords case and/or default, depending upon which of one or more values an integral expression matches. Cases and the default may appear in any order with the default being executed if none of the other cases match.

If a case matches the integral expression, then that code associated with it (a block or a sequence of statements) is executed as is *all the code for later cases unless the keyword "break" is used to cause immediate exit from the switch.* It is thus normally a grand idea to insert a break in each chunk of code associated with each value to stop *falling* through the remaining code and executing it regardless of whether any more matches occur. Note also that the expression evaluated must at least convert to data type int. Furthermore, cases must not be repeated.

The syntax of the switch statement is:

```
switch(integralexpression) {
case integralvalue1: block1 or statements1
case integralvalue2: block2 or statements2
...
[default]           : blockn or statementsn
}
```

where the default is optional, and the integral expression, blocks, and statements are user chosen. It is executed as follows:

1. Evaluate the integral expression.
2. Find the case matching the value of the integral expression and execute that code associated with it *and all code for later cases;* if no match is found execute the default case, or if there is no default, terminate the switch.
3. An executed break statement always forces termination of the switch statement.

■ **Example 6.4.1**   The following code illustrates how to increment variables that count the number of ones, twos, threes, white space (blanks, newlines, and tabs), and other characters (it will later be expanded to count these for arbitrary keyboard input):

```
#include <stdio.h>
main()
{
  int getit, smalldigit, whitespace, others;
  switch(getit = getchar())
  {
    case '1':
    case '2':
    case '3':
      ++smalldigit;
      break;
    case ' ':
    case '\t':
    case '\n':
      ++whitespace;
      break;
    default:
      ++others;
      break;
  }
  printf("\nThe number of small digits is %d",smalldigit);
  printf("\nThe number of white space characters is %d",whitespace);
  printf("\nThe number of other characters is %d",others);
}

/*********/
/* INPUT */
/*********/
2

/***********/
/* OUTPUT */
/***********/
The number of small digits is 1
The number of white space characters is 0
The number of other characters is 0                             ■
```

## EXERCISES 6.3

1. Rewrite Example 6.4.1 so that each small digit and each white space character is counted separately.

2. What is the purpose of a break statement in a switch statement?

3. Write a program using a switch statement that allows the user to input two integers, compare them, and print which is larger (or if there is a tie).

4. Write a program using a switch statement that permits the user to enter three characters and then prints the result back to the terminal with the newline character printed as \n and the tab printed as \t.

## 6.5 | THE WHILE STATEMENT

Syntax: `while (expression)`
          `statement`

The while statement with this syntax provides for testing an expression for true or false; if the expression is true, a statement is executed and control passes back to testing the expression. This process is repeated as long as the expression is true. Whenever the expression is false, control passes to the next statement following the while statement. Note that it is possible that the statement within the while statement is executed forever (if expression is always true such as in a=1) or never (if the expression is false upon entry).

The while statement is powerful—it permits indefinite repetition to process the same code over and over again. Coupled with the if statement many problems can be solved with a minimum of coding.

■ **Example 6.5.1**    The following code segment counts the number of digits entered at the terminal:

```
#include <stdio.h>

int c;
int digits;
c=0;
main()
{
  while ((c = getchar()) != '\n')
  {
    if (c >= '0' && c <= '9')
      digits++;
  }
  printf("total = %d\n",digits);
}

/*********/
/* INPUT */
/*********/
1 2 3 a b c 4 5 6 d e f 7 8 9 g h i

/***********/
/* OUTPUT */
/***********/
total = 9
```

Notice that the statement following the testing of the expression is an if statement. Notice also that the value of c=getchar( ) is the int value of the character itself. ■

■ **Example 6.5.2**    The next code segment causes problems in that an infinite loop is encountered because n starts out negative and gets decremented each time through the loop (remember that 0 or 0.0 is false and anything else is true, hence, the condition n--is always true here):

```
int k, n;
n =-100;
k = 0;
while (n--) {
    k = n + k;
}
```

■

### *EXERCISES* **6.5**

1. Modify Exercise 6.3.4 that permits a single character from the keyboard to be input and then increments appropriate variables in case it is a blank, a digit, an alphabetic character, or anything else. It should be modified to count the number of characters of each type for an arbitrary stream of input from the keyboard.

2. Modify Example 6.4.1 to permit any number of characters to be input and the number of each type to be printed.

3. Rewrite the expression n—in Example 6.5.2 so that positive values assigned to n yield the same value of true or false, but negative values terminate the loop.

4. Write a while loop that simply fetches characters from the keyboard and skips them until a nonblank character is encountered.

5. Write a program using a while statement that reads an integer n from the terminal and then:

```
if n is positive sums the even integers from n to 2*n;
if n is negative sums the even integers from n to 2*n;
if n is zero prints 0.
```

## **6.6** | *THE FOR STATEMENT*

Syntax:  `for    (expression1;expression2;expression3)`
         `statement`

The for statement with this syntax executes by:

1. evaluating expression1 (expression1 is optional)

2. evaluating expression2 (expression2 is optional)

3. if expression2 is false then the for statement terminates with control passing to the next statement following the for statement. If, on the other hand, expression2 is true (if it does not appear it is assumed to always be true), then statement is executed and expression3 (optional) is evaluated

4. returning to step 2

Note that it is possible that the statement within the for statement is executed forever (if expression2 is always true such as in a=1) or never (if expression2 is false upon entry).

The for statement is powerful. It permits initialization and indefinite repetition to process over and over again the same code. It is extremely useful for processing members of an array where expression1 is the initialization step, expression2 checks to see whether the end of the array has been reached, and expression3 increments a counter.

Note also that a for statement is itself a statement. As such it can appear anywhere a statement can. Thus, the following with asterisks (∗) enclosing each for statement is a perfectly valid construction, which can easily be exploited for multiple looping. Notice that the innermost for statement is processed first as many times as the middle for statement permits, and then the middle for statement is processed as many times as the outermost for statement permits. This construction can be extended to any desired depth (three is not sacred).

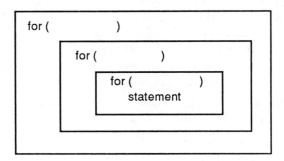

■ **Example 6.6.1**   The following program adds the integers from one to one hundred:

```
#include <stdio.h>

main()
{
  int i, sum;
  sum = 0;
  for (i=1; i <= 100; ++i)
    sum += i;
  printf("\nsum = %d\n",sum);
}

/**********/
/* OUTPUT */
/**********/
sum = 5050
```

■

■ **Example 6.6.2**   The following program prints the first integer greater than or equal to 10,001 that is divisible by 39:

```
#include <stdio.h>

main()
{
  int i;
  for (i=10001;i%39 !=0;i++);
  printf("\n%d is divisible by 39\n",i);
}

/**********/
/* OUTPUT */
/**********/
10023 is divisible by 39
```

■

### Comma Operator

The comma operator (,) has the lowest precedence in the language C, but it is extremely useful in for statements to perform several initializations and/or several iterations through indices. Its syntax is:

*expression1, expression2*

Expression1 is evaluated followed by expression2 and the value of the whole comma expression is the value of the right operand; its type is also that of the right operand. Note that most commas used in programs are not comma operators; in particular, commas used in initialization lists and commas used to separate argument lists in functions are not comma operators.

■ **Example 6.6.3**    The next program adds the integers from one to one hundred (another version of Example 6.6.1):

```
#include <stdio.h>

main()
{
  int i, sum;
  for (sum=0, i=1; i <= 100; ++i)
    sum += i;
  printf("\nsum = %d\n",sum);
}

/**********/
/* OUTPUT */
/**********/
sum = 5050
```

■

## EXERCISES  6.6

1. The for statement (if it has a nonempty expression2 and no continue statement in the statement itself) is equivalent to a single statement followed by a while statement. Write the while equivalent of the following for statement:

   ```
   for(i=1; i < n; i++)
       i= i + n;
   ```

2. Trace the contents of each memory variable:

   ```
   sum =0;
   n =12;
   for (i=0;i < n; i += 2)
       sum += i;
   ```

3. Trace the contents of each memory variable:

```
sum = 0;
n = 12;
i = 0;
for (i==2; i < n; i += 2)
        sum += i;
```

4. Trace the contents of each memory variable:

```
sum = 0;
n = 12;
i = 0;
for ( ; i < n; i += 2)
sum += i;
```

5. Trace the contents of each memory variable:

```
sum = 0;
n = 12;
i = 0;
for ( ;      ; i += 2)
        sum += i;
```

6. Trace the contents of each memory variable:

```
sum = 0;
n = 12;
i = 2;
for ( ; sum < 12      ; )
        sum += i;
```

7. Write a program using nested for statements that uses the int (but only with values 0 or 1) variables called b1 and b2, and for all possible combinations of their truth values (0 or 1) prints the values of b1 && b2, b1 || b2, and ! b1 in a table.

8. Write two programs, one using a for statement and the other a while statement, that read a positive integer n and print the sum of the squares of the first n even integers and the sum of the cubes of the first n odd integers.

9. Use a single for statement with the comma operator to solve Exercise 8.

**10.** Will the statement in the body of the following be executed?

```
int i,j,k ;
for ( i = 0 , j=1 , k=0; i++ ; (++k ) +1)
        /*statement goes here*/
```

**11.** The Fibonacci numbers are defined recursively as f0 = 0 and f1 = 1 (initializations) and after that each Fibonacci number is the sum of the previous two. Write a program that prints the first 50 Fibonacci numbers.

## 6.7 | *THE DO STATEMENT*

*Syntax:* `do statement while (expression);`

The do statement with this syntax executes statement and then tests an expression for true or false; if true, the statement is executed again and control passes back to testing the expression. This process is repeated as long as the expression is true. Whenever it is false, control simply passes to the next statement following the do statement. Note that it is possible that the statement within the while statement is executed forever (if the expression is always true such as in a=1), and it will always be executed at least once.

The do statement, as opposed to the while and the for statement, tests at the bottom of the loop. In all such statements, one principle holds uniformly—it is a good idea to test a relational expression rather than an equality expression. Two expressions may be equal mathematically, but fail a computer equality test due to machine limitations.

It is a good idea to enclose the statement with the body of the loop in the do statement inside braces. For one thing it makes it clearer that the keyword while is not the beginning of a while statement.

■ **Example 6.7.1**  This program results in an infinite loop on many machines because of the test for nonequality. It would be better to test for greater-than-or-equal-to instead.

/*try to multiply the numbers ranging from ".01" to ".99" incremented by ".001" each time*/

```
/* CHAPTER 6    6.6.1.C  */

#include <stdio.h>

main()
{
  double product, increment;
  for (increment=.01, product = 1.0; increment != .99; increment+=.001)
  {
    product *= increment;
    printf("\nstill looping");
  }
}
```

&#9632;

## EXERCISES 6.7

1. A positive integer is defined to be prime if its only positive divisors are the number 1 and itself. Write a program that prints all prime numbers less than one thousand. An outer loop to progress from one to one thousand can be done with a for statement. At each step along the way, say at k, testing can be done to determine if k has any positive divisors other than one and itself.

## 6.8 | THE BREAK AND CONTINUE STATEMENTS

The break statement was introduced as a statement to be used within a switch statement to provide an early exit. In general, the break statement can also be used within for, while, do while, and switch statements to provide immediate exits, as opposed to exiting via the testing of an expression. Control simply passes to the next statement after the loop itself. This is an abrupt way to leave a loop, but it can be effective in certain circumstances.

On the other hand, the continue statement (syntax: continue), used only in a for, while, or do while statement, causes the current iteration to end and (1) in the case of the for and while statements, the expression is immediately tested (to determine if more iterations are to be done); and (2) in the case of the for statement, control passes to the initialization expression.

&#9632; **Example 6.8.1** The following program is used to exit from the loop upon encountering a withdrawal larger than $2,000:

```
/*  CHAPTER 6  6.7.1.c   */

#include <stdio.h>

main()
{
  int error=0;
  float w;

  while (1)
  {
    scanf("%f",&w);
    if (w > 2000.0)
    {
      error = -1;
      break;
    }
  }
  if (error == -1)
    printf("\nlarger withdrawal attempted.\n");
}


/* INPUT */
2001


/* OUTPUT */
larger withdrawal attempted.
```

■

■ **Example 6.8.2**    The following program is used to do special processing only for withdrawals greater than $2,000 (skipping all other withdrawals):

```
/*  CHAPTER 6   6.7.2.C   */

#include <stdio.h>

main()
{
  long float w;
  while (1)
  {
    scanf("%lf",&w);
    if (w <= 2000.0)
      continue;
    else
    {
      printf("Processing large withdrawals\n");
      break;
    }
  }
}

/* INPUT */
1000
20003

/* OUTPUT */
Processing large withdrawals
```

■

1. The following segment of code counts the number of characters entered before the first x is entered and also counts the number of lowercase letters entered up to that point. Rewrite it without using either a break or a continue statement.

```
while(c= getchar()) {
    if ( c == 'x')
        break;
    ++number;
    if ( c >= 'a' && c <= 'z')
        ++lowercase;
}
```

2. The following segment of code does not process negative numbers. Rewrite it without using either a break or a continue statement.

```
i = -10;
n = 100;
while ( i < n) {
    i = i + 1;
    if ( i < 0)
        continue;
    sum += i;
}
```

## 6.9 CHAPTER SUMMARY

1. The relational operators are used to compare two expressions.
2. The equality operator (==) is not to be confused with the assignment operator (=).
3. The logical operators, and (&&) and or (||) are used to combine expressions.
4. A block, sometimes called a compound statement, begins and ends with brackets ({ and }) and may have its own set of declarations.
5. The if statements are used to branch depending upon the truth value of expressions.

6. The switch statement provides for multiway branching based on values of an integral expression.

7. The while statement is used to test an expression and then executes a loop as long as the expression is true.

8. The for statement is used to initialize, test an expression, and then execute a loop and evaluate another expression as long as the first expression is true.

9. The comma operator has as its value and data type that of its right operand.

10. The do statement executes a statement, then as long as an expression is true, repeatedly executes the initial statement.

11. The break statement provides for early exit from loops and the switch statement.

12. The continue statement ends the current iteration of a loop and passes control to the test expression or initialization.

# Functions and Program Structure in C

A programmer typically must break down the solution to a problem into smaller pieces that solve smaller, and thus more manageable problems. In the programming language C, the solution to each of these smaller problems often corresponds to a function written in C, and occasionally to a UNIX shell script, which can be called from C function. These functions perform the same role as do subroutines, functions, and procedures in other languages, such as Pascal and FORTRAN.

Recall from Chapter 1 that the tools that can be used in a C program fall into three categories:

1. *Built-in functions,* called *UNIX C functions,* that cannot stand alone but rather must be part of a C program. UNIX C functions are of two types:

    a. Type I: *system calls.* These are part of UNIX itself. There are about 60 and they should be standard on every UNIX, or UNIX look-alike, system. As part of the "kernel" of UNIX, the low-level interface with the hardware, they are available to C programs automatically and without the necessity of declaring them in the C program.

    b. Type II: *library functions.* These are add-ons to the operating system and use system calls to perform their tasks. They may not be standard, although they often are, across UNIX systems. Some of the library functions must be declared in the C program to make them available.

2. *UNIX commands,* or sequences of UNIX commands stored in a file called a shell script, that can stand alone in UNIX itself, and can also be called from a C program. In fact, they are called via one of the library functions, "system."

3. *User-written C functions* that should be thought of as the task-oriented modules of the C program.

The built-in functions are "on the shelf" already (and perhaps already compiled) and, hence, do not need to be coded by the user. They will be studied later. The concept of shell scripts has already been discussed in Chapter 4 and the method of calling them from within C programs will be discussed later. In this chapter, the primary emphasis will be on user-written functions.

Several key points need mentioning:

1. Every C program begins by executing the function called main ( ).

2. Functions often serve as black boxes in that the details of their internal manipulations need not be of concern.

3. The *types* of data (but not the actual values of that data) that are passed to functions, as well as the types of data that functions return to the main program must usually be specified by the programmer.

4. An actual C program may have the code for its built-in functions, shell scripts, and user-written functions scattered across several files on disk (but an individual function cannot be split among several files). The user may then choose to compile these source code segments separately and then load them along with the previously compiled functions stored in libraries.

## 7.1 | FUNCTIONS AND THEIR ARGUMENTS

A function consists of two parts, the body and the header.

1. The header, is of the form:

```
data_type function_name(arg1,arg2,...,argn)
data_type arg1;...; data_type argn;
```

The arguments arg1, arg2,..., argn (also called formal parameters) and declarations are optional, but if args do appear, it is sometimes necessary (and always a good idea) to declare them, otherwise they default to data type int. Furthermore, the data type of the function itself is the data type to which the expression returned by the function is converted. This data type also defaults to int.

2. The body, is simply a block or compound statement, and is of the form:

```
{ declarations /*optional*/
  statements /*optional*/
}
```

A C program is a set of functions with execution beginning at the function called main. The individual functions can appear in any sequence whatsoever on the source file (even main itself *can* appear anywhere in that sequence).

One of the most important statements that can appear in the body of the function is the return statement whose syntax is:

```
return    or    return(expression)
```

which obeys two rules:

1. Execution of a return statement terminates the execution of the function in which it occurs and causes control to be passed back to the calling environment. Several return statements may appear in the same function.

2. If an expression is included in the return statement (*the latter syntax*), the value of the expression is passed back to the calling environment *and* converted to the data type preceding the name of the function.

■ **Example 7.1.1**    The following function named worthless has no arguments, defaults to a data type specifier of int (even though it has no return statement), and has no declarations and no statements (*it does absolutely nothing*):

```
worthless() {}
```
■

■ **Example 7.1.2**    The following function named print_prompt prints a menu for the user but receives no values from the main function (print_prompt has no arguments, returns no value of an expression to the main function, has no return statement):

```
print_prompt()
{
        printf("\n Choose your option now");
        printf("\n 1) return to UNIX" );
        printf("\n 2) edit a file");
        printf("\n 3) compile a C program");
        printf("\n 4) execute a C program");
        printf("\n 5) return to the database");
}
```

This menu could be called five times as in the following C program:

```
main()
{
      int j;
      for (j=0 ; j < 5; j++)
            print_prompt();
}
print_prompt()
{
      printf("\n Choose your option now");
      printf("\n 1) return to UNIX" );
      printf("\n 2) edit a file");
      printf("\n 3) compile a C program");
      printf("\n 4) execute a C program");
      printf("\n 5) return to the database");
}
```

Here is the complete program and the output.

```
/*    CHAPTER 7  7.1.2.C   */
#include <stdio.h>

main()
{
  int j;
  for (j = 0; j < 5; j++)
    print_prompt();
}
print_prompt()
{
  printf("\nChoose your option now");
  printf("\n1) return to UNIX");
  printf("\n2) edit a file");
  printf("\n3) compile a C program");
  printf("\n4) execute a C program");
  printf("\n5) return to the database\n");
}



/**********/
/* OUTPUT */
/**********/
Choose your option now
1) return to UNIX
2) edit a file
3) compile a C program
4) execute a C program
5) return to the database
```

```
Choose your option now
1) return to UNIX
2) edit a file
3) compile a C program
4) execute a C program
5) return to the database

Choose your option now
1) return to UNIX
2) edit a file
3) compile a C program
4) execute a C program
5) return to the database

Choose your option now
1) return to UNIX
2) edit a file
3) compile a C program
4) execute a C program
5) return to the database

Choose your option now
1) return to UNIX
2) edit a file
3) compile a C program
4) execute a C program
5) return to the database
```

Variables declared within the body of a C function are called *local variables* (with respect to that function), exist only for the use of the function itself and only during its execution. Variables that are neither formal parameters nor locally declared are called *global variables*. They must be declared outside the functions. (One function cannot be nested inside another, but blocks can be nested.)

■ **Example 7.1.3**    The purpose of the following program is to use a function to average five integer valued test scores (provided each is greater than or equal to zero) and have the function return the average as a double:

```
/*    CHAPTER 7    7.1.3.C    */

#include <stdio.h>

double average();

main()
{
  int test1, test2, test3, test4, test5;
  scanf("%d %d %d %d %d",&test1, &test2, &test3, &test4, &test5);
  printf("Average = %.2f\n",average(test1,test2,test3,test4,test5));
}

double average(a,b,c,d,e)
int a,b,c,d,e;
{
  double ave;
  int valid_data;
  valid_data = (a>=0 && b>=0 && c>=0 && d>=0 && e>=0);
  if (valid_data)
  {
```

```
      ave = (a + b + c + d + e) / 5;
      return(ave);
    }
  else
    return;
}


/*********/
/* INPUT */
/*********/
100 95 90 85 80


/**********/
/* OUTPUT */
/**********/
Average = 90.00
```

    ■

■ **Example 7.1.4**     The previous function does not return a useful value to the calling environment if an argument is negative. This can be remedied by changing the last statement to return $(-1.0)$. The following complete program will average any set of five nonnegative integers entered at the terminal:

```
/*     CHAPTER 7    7.1.4.C    */

main()
{
  int x,y,z,w,u;
  double answer;
  double average();
  printf("\nEnter five integers ");
  scanf("%d %d %d %d %d",&x,&y,&z,&w,&u);
  answer = average(x,y,z,w,u);
  if (answer < 0.0)
    printf("a negative value was entered\n");
  else
    printf("\nthe average is %f\n",answer);
}

double average(a,b,c,d,e)
int a,b,c,d,e;
{
  double ave;
  int valid_data;
  valid_data = (a>=0 && b>=0 && c>=0 && d>=0 && e>=0);
  if (valid_data)
  {
    ave = (a + b + c + d + e) / 5;
    return(ave);
  }
  else
    return(-1.0);
}


/*********/
/* INPUT */
/*********/
Enter five integers 1 2 3 4 5


/**********/
/* OUTPUT */
/**********/
the average is 3.000000
```

    ■

In the previous example, the function average is built to operate only on five values of data type int. If the programmer accidentally, by the value of an expression, passes other data types to the function average, the system will *not* balk—it will simply return nonsense. For example, the square root function expects an argument of type double, hence, sqrt(9) while not illegal will not yield 3. Note also that the function average was declared in the main function precisely because its purpose was to return a value whose data type was not int. A function that returns a value of data type int need not be declared in the function that calls it—though it does no harm to do so, and might be a useful habit for documentation purposes.

A function name (with any appropriate arguments), which returns a value of a certain data type, can legally appear in any other function anywhere that an expression of the same data type may occur. Arguments are passed "by value"—each argument is evaluated and its value is passed to become the value of the corresponding formal parameter. The value of a variable that is passed to a function thus has absolutely no effect on the variable itself in the calling environment.

■ **Example 7.1.5**  The following example illustrates call by value in that the value of the variable x cannot be changed in the function called harmless:

```
/*  CHAPTER 7    7.1.5.C    */

main()
{
  int x,y;
  x = 1;
  y = harmless(x);
  printf("the value of x is %d while y is %d\n ",x,y);
}
int harmless(a)
int a;
{
  printf("\n the value of a is %d ",a);
  a = a + 5;
  printf("\n the value of a is %d\n ",a);
  return(a*a);
}


/**********/
/* OUTPUT */
/**********/
 the value of a is 1
 the value of a is 6
 the value of x is 1 while y is 36                            ■
```

■ **Example 7.1.6**  The technique of storing C functions in different files can be very helpful when it comes to compilation. Suppose in Example 7.1.4 that the main function is stored under prog1.c and that the average function is stored under average.c. To compile, use:

```
$ cc -o a.out prog1.c average.c
$
```

This yields the relocatable object code in files saved under the names prog1.o and average.o, with the executable file saved under a.out. If average.c did not yield an error-free compile, correct that source code, recompile average.c, and load it with the other object code. This technique can save a significant amount of compile time if there are many functions. Proceed as follows:

```
$ cc -o a.out prog1.o average.c
$
```
■

When a name is followed by a left parenthesis and that name has not been previously declared, it automatically becomes a function name. For example, suppose one had a function called convert whose job was to take a small positive integer and return a value of data type char (say, the ASCII equivalent of the integer) as follows:

```
char convert(a)
int a;
{...
    char c;
    ...
    return (c);
}
```

In this case, any expression involving convert(a) is going to have convert(a) promoted to data type int. Therefore, there is no need to specify the data type char for the function convert(a). One may as well omit the type specifier because the default is int.

Similarly, because float is converted to double in expressions, there is no reason to specify a function as returning a value of data type float.

All arguments in C are passed "call by value," but it is possible to pass the address of a variable, which effectively enables "call by reference"— that is, it is possible by passing addresses to have a function change the values of the variables in the calling environment. The method to do this will be discussed later.

A function returns a value to the calling environment by the return (expression) statement. This value is then stored in the name of the function. However, if the purpose of the function is simply to perform a task and not return a value, then the function should just be invoked as the statement. (Remember that a function can be used anywhere an expression of the same data type can and that an expression followed by a semicolon is a statement.)

*f(arg1,arg2,...,argn);*

The programmer can provide a bit of protection against the calling environment's misuse of a function that was not intended to return a value by declaring its type specifier "void." A function declared to have type specifier void will (1) cause a warning to be issued by the compiler if that functions name is used in an expression that dictates a value; and (2) never return a value back to the environment. (*Some* value is generally returned to the calling environment by a function even if no return statement is used.)

■ **Example 7.1.7**    The following code will not run because the function ascii_equiv has a type specifier of void: /*this C program trys to print out the characters associated with each ASCII value from 32 to 42 */

```
main()
{
    int i;                       /*loop variable */
    int j;                       /* designed to hold value
                                    returned*/

    void ascii_equiv();          /* remember that functions
                                    returning non int values must
                                    be declared in the calling
                                    environment*/


    for (i=32; i < 43; i++) {
        j = ascii_equiv(i);      /*illegal—the function was
                                    declared void*/

        }
}
void ascii_equiv(k)
int k;
{
    printf("\n the ASCII character
    associated with the integer %d is
    %c",k,k);
}
```
■

■ **Example 7.1.8**    The following code revises that of Example 7.1.7 and solves the problem
properly:

```
main()
{
  int i;
  for (i=32; i<43; i++)
    printf("\nthe value returned is %d\n",ascii_equiv(i));
}
int ascii_equiv(k)
int k;
{
  printf("the ASCII character associated with the integer %d is %c\n",k,k);
}


/**********/
/* OUTPUT */
/**********/
the ASCII character associated with the integer 32 is

the value returned is 56
the ASCII character associated with the integer 33 is !

the value returned is 56
the ASCII character associated with the integer 34 is "

the value returned is 56
the ASCII character associated with the integer 35 is #

the value returned is 56
the ASCII character associated with the integer 36 is $

the value returned is 56
the ASCII character associated with the integer 37 is %

the value returned is 56
the ASCII character associated with the integer 38 is &

the value returned is 56
the ASCII character associated with the integer 39 is '

the value returned is 56
the ASCII character associated with the integer 40 is (

the value returned is 56
the ASCII character associated with the integer 41 is )

the value returned is 56
the ASCII character associated with the integer 42 is *
```

## EXERCISES   7.1

1. Modify Example 7.1.4 so that any number of data sets of five integers can be entered and either averaged or have the same message printed as before.

**2.** Write a function called exp(m,n), where m,n >0, that has arguments of type int and that returns m raised to the nth power (this function is not built into C). Store this function under the name exp.c.

**3.** Write a function called add_powers(k,n), where k,n > 0, that calls the function in Exercise 7.1.2 and whose purpose is to return the following sum:

$$exp(1,k) + exp(2,k) + \ldots + exp(n,k)$$

Store this function under the name powers.c.

**4.** Write a C program whose purpose is to permit the user to input values of k and n and print out the table with k rows and n columns whose entry in row k, column n, is the value returned by add_powers(k,n) (Exercise 7.1.3). Store this function under the name main.c. Test it with k=3 and n =4.

**5.** Use the technique of Example 7.1.6 to compile Exercises 7.1.2, 7.1.3, and 7.1.4.

**6.** Write an interactive program that prompts the user as to how many floating point numbers are to be entered and what they are. The program should then print a table showing the minimum, maximum, and average of these numbers. The program should include at least the following functions:

    a. a function that accepts two floating point numbers and returns their minimum

    b. a function that accepts two floating point numbers and returns their maximum

    c. a function that does the prompting

    d. a function that does the printing

**7.** Write a function that returns the 16th root (type double) of its argument k of type int. The sqrt( ) function will be useful.

**8.** Write a function f( ) that returns the next to the largest prime number less than or equal to a specified positive integer >=2 (its argument). For example f(3) = 2, f(4) =2, f(5)=3, f(6)=3, f(7) =5,etc.

**9.** Write a function whose input is the number of hours worked and which returns the wages (based on $9.80 per hour up to 40 hours and time and a half for that time exceeding 40 hours).

## 7.2 | *SCOPE AND STORAGE CLASSES*

The scope of a name is that portion of a program over which the name is defined. This can get rather complicated in that source text for a program may have been saved in several files, and moreover, functions may have been previously compiled and thus need to be loaded from libraries. Examples will be given ranging from the simple to the complex to illustrate the three rules of scope.

1. Variables are only known within the block in which they are declared. Variables with the same name, but declared in different blocks, are thus *different* variables.

2. If a variable name has already been declared in a block, but is declared again within a block inside the first one, then the original variable name is temporarily hidden (and hence unavailable) until the inner block is exited.

3. The name of a variable (and its associated space) is unavailable after the block in which it is defined is left.

■ **Example 7.2.1**   The two declarations of i in this code are totally unrelated to each other:

```
{
        int i;                /* outer i */
i = 10;
    {
                              /*any reference to i in this block will
                              be to the "outer" i with a current value
                              of 10 unless the variable name i is
                              declared again here in the "inner"
                              block */

                              int i;   /*the original i with value 10 is
                              now hidden by the new declaration*/

        i = 20;
    }

                              /*in this part of the code the i with the
                              value 20 has just died—its memory
                              space is freed because the inner block
                              has been left*/

                              /*the only i in existence here has a
                              value of 10—execution is still in the
                              outer block */

}                                                              ■
```

Blocks can be nested to several depths (the actual limit is system dependent) as the following example illustrates.

■ **Example 7.2.2**

```
/*    CHAPTER 7  7.2.2.C   */

main()
{
  char i,j,k,l;
  i = 'i'; j = 'j'; k = 'k'; l = 'l';
  printf("%c %c %c %c\n",i,j,k,l);
  {
    int j,k;
    j = 5; k = 6;
    printf("%c %d %d %c\n",i,j,k,l);
    {
      float j;
      j = 7.8;
      printf("%c %.1f %d %c\n",i,j,k,l);
    }
    j = k;
    printf("%c %d %d %c\n",i,j,k,l);
  }
  printf("%c %c %c %c\n",i,j,k,l);
}


/**********/
/* OUTPUT */
/**********/
i j k l
i 5 6 l
i 7.8 6 l
i 6 6 l
i j k l
```

In addition to being able to nest blocks inside one another, the programmer may choose to have *parallel blocks,* two or more blocks whose outer brackets are at the same depth level, as shown here:

```
{
        /* this is inside block 1 */
}
{
        /* this is inside block 2 */
}
```

It is possible that parallel blocks will be nested (perhaps deeply) inside other blocks. Rules 1 and 3 apply to blocks independent of their relative position to other blocks, thus, they apply to parallel blocks in particular. Programmers often choose to use parallel blocks to preserve memory. (Remember that memory allocated within a block is freed when that block is left.) Moreover, parallel blocks are useful for algorithms that have many tasks to be performed at the same level.

It is useful to think of a function as simply a header followed by a block, satisfying the following provisos:

1. Functions can only be declared in parallel at the outermost level. They cannot be nested.

2. The block of a return statement may use return statements to pass data to the calling environment and parameters to receive data from the calling environment.

The following example illustrates parallel blocks and the scope of variables.

■ **Example 7.2.3**

```
{
    char c1,c2,c3;        /*these variables are available
                          within the whole block unless they
                          are hidden by an inner
                          declaration*/

    {
        int c1;
        float c3;
        char c4;

                          /*the original char c1 and c3 are
                          hidden; the original char c2 is
                          available; a new char c4 is
                          available*/
    }
    {
        int c1,c2;

                          /*the original char c1 and c2 are
                          hidden; the original char c3 is
                          available; new int c1 and c2 are
                          available*/
    }
}
```

■

Every variable and function in the language C has an attribute called its *type*. The type of a variable indicates the kind of data that is expected to be stored in the memory location associated with the name of the variable. For example, int x simply means that memory associated with x is assumed to be an integer. The type (or type specifier) of a function indicates the type of data that is expected to be returned by the function (stored in the memory location associated with the name of the function) via the return statement. The default type of a function is that of int.

Each function and variable has, in addition to its type, an associated *storage class* that enables the user to determine the scope of the function or variable. Storage classes available are auto (automatic), extern (external), register, and static.

## Auto and Extern

The storage class, if explicitly specified, is named immediately prior to its data type. Auto is the most frequently used storage class and is, in fact, the default for variables declared within the body of a function, including those declared in any block inside that function. The word "auto" is used in languages other than C and usually means that the variable automatically comes into existence when the function is called and automatically is freed (losing its value) when the function is exited. Hence, if a function is called several times, the programmer using variables of storage class auto must be careful to set the values of such variables with each function call. If the auto variable is initialized in its declaration within a function, then it will be reinitialized to that value each time the function is entered.

**■ Example 7.2.4**   The code given here illustrates several important points.

```
if (n > 0)        {
    int i;                         /*equivalent to auto int i; */
                                   /* i is declared for the private use of the
                                      condition "n > 0") */

    for (i = 0; i <= n; i++)          {
                                   /*do processing here*/
                                  }
                 }
```
■

The storage class of a function is always that of extern, meaning that its return value is external or global to all other functions. Hence, it is globally available in the entire program, or at least globally available within the source file where it resides. Variables defined outside a function are by default of storage class extern. (*Defined* in this context uses the same syntax as declarations have used; the variable is created and assigned storage, and this definition serves as the declaration for the rest of the source file, though not necessarily the entire program.)

There must be only one definition of a single external variable in the entire source program. Initialization can take place in this definition, but if an external variable is not explicitly initialized, it defaults to an initial value of zero. These defined variables and their storage locations are then available to any function declared after the variables' definitions.

For example, if

```
int i;   /* or extern int i */
```

appears outside of functions, we say it only defines i, causes storage to be allocated, and serves as the implicit declaration of i for the remaining source file, not necessarily the entire program. It also makes i global to all functions declared after it in the program.

However, if

```
extern int i;
```

is declared inside a function, it means that i must have been defined outside the function, perhaps even in another file. Remember there can be only one definition of a particular external variable in an entire program, therefore in any of the files that make up the program. Other source files must have extern declarations to enable them to access an external variable that is defined in a different source file. Similarly, external variables that are used before they are defined must also have extern declarations. The usual way of avoiding problems such as these is to put external definitions at the beginning of the source file.

Any function that wishes to use an extern variable can do so only if one of two things is true (1) the function has that variable declared within it, for example, extern int i, so that i is known to the function; or (2) the external definition of the variable occurs in the source file before it is used in the function that needs it. No declaration of that variable within the function that uses it is needed in this situation. It can, however, be declared, for example, extern int i, if this improves the clarity of the code.

The most important thing is that variables of storage class extern do not lose their values upon function exit. It thus is not necessary to reset their values when a function is called. Their scope is by default global—they are available to all functions declared after them. However, it is still possible to hide the external variable by declaring a variable with the same name within a function or just a block.

Because variables of storage class extern do not lose their values upon function exit and because they default to global, they can be used to pass information back and forth between functions. This technique can be used in addition to, or instead of, formal parameters and return expressions. However, the program (and thus the programmer) is at risk if variables are routinely declared storage class extern when no real need exists for functions to share their data. It is quite possible that functions will inadvertently change the value of a variable of storage class extern (a so-called side effect) and destroy the modularity of the code. It is generally better to permit functions access only to data they truly need and to force them to pass back only data desired. Thus, the use of parameters and the return expression is generally preferred over global variables.

On the other hand, one can imagine situations in which functions share data and neither function ever calls the other. In these cases, it might be convenient to share the data in external variables, particularly if this data is stored in a number of variables and would make the parameter list inordinately long.

The following examples illustrate some of these points:

### ■ Example 7.2.5

```
int a =1,b=2, c=3,d;
```
/*global variables with storage allocated—this is a definition—could have also used extern int instead of just int */

```
main()
{
    extern int a,b,c,d;
```
/*main will use these variables—but this declaration is not really necessary because they appear in the same source file as their definition and thus have already been implicitly declared—see comments about declaring external variables within functions*/

```
    d= g();
    printf("%d %d %d %d", a,b,c,d);
```
/* prints 1 2 3 60 */

```
}
int g()
```
/*functions are always external*/

```
{
    extern int c;
```
/*permits g( ) to use the global variable c—but again not necessary because of its definition in the same source file */

```
    int a,b;
```
/*the external a and b are now hidden, but the external c is still available*/

```
   a= 4;                                      /* local a* /
   b= 5;                                      /* local b */
   return(a*b*c);                             /*returns 4*5*3=60 */
}
```

Here is the program and output without all the comments.

```
/*      CHAPTER 7  7.2.5.C     */
int a=1, b=2, c=3, d;

main()
{
  extern int a,b,c,d;
  d = g();
  printf("%d %d %d %d\n",a,b,c,d);
}
int g()
{
  extern int c;
  int a,b;
  a=4;
  b=5;
  return(a*b*c);
}


/**********/
/* OUTPUT */
/**********/
1 2 3 60
```

■ **Example 7.2.6**

```
int a=1,b=2,  c=3,d;
```
/*global variables with storage allocated—this is a definition*/

```
main()
{
    d= g();
    printf("%d %d %d %d", a,b,c,d);
```
/* prints 4 5 3 60 */

```
}
int g()
```
/*functions are always external*/

```
{
    a= 4;
```
/* global a */

```
    b= 5;
```
/* global b */

```
    return(a*b*c);
```
/*returns 4*5*3=60 */

```
}
```

Here is the program and output without the comments.

```
/*    CHAPTER 7  7.2.6.C    */

int a=1, b=2, c=3, d;

main()
{
  d = g();
  printf("%d %d %d %d\n",a,b,c,d);
}
int g()
{
  a=4;
  b=5;
  return(a*b*c);
}


/**********/
/* OUTPUT */
/**********/
4 5 3 60
```

■ **Example 7.2.7**   This example shows source code scattered across three files called prog1a.c, prog1b.c, and prog1c.c.

In prog1a.c:

```
int i;                          /* i is external—this is its
                                   definition*/

main()
{
    int i;                      /* hides the global i in main */

    ...

}
```

In prog1b.c:

```
int g(x)
int x;
{
    extern int i;               /* this extern declaration is necessary
                                   if the purpose is for g() to use the ex-
                                   ternal i defined in prog1a.c—this is be-
                                   cause the definition appears in a
                                   different source file from the place
                                   where the variable is to be used—re-
                                   member there can be only one defini-
                                   tion for an external variable */

    ...

}
```

In prog1c.c:

```
int h(x)
int x;
}
```

/*there is no declaration of i here—in this case if i is referred to in this function there will be a compile error because the external i in prog1a.c is in another source file*/

∎

### Register

The storage class *register* should be used in a declaration of a variable when it appears that the variable will be used often and that it would thus be advisable to attempt to store its value in a machine register. If the compiler is unable to locate a register to do this, because the data type requested to be stored doesn't fit the computer's registers or perhaps too many variables are already stored in registers, then the word register is ignored and the default storage class auto takes over. No harm has been done. The advice to the compiler was simply ignored. In addition to choosing the variables wisely for possible storage in registers, it is also wise to make such declarations close to the use of such variables in the code.

∎ **Example 7.2.8** Looping through while statements is a good place to use register storage for the control variable:

```
{       register int i;
        while ( i > 0) {
            . . .
            i--;
        }
}
```

∎

### Static

The last storage class to be discussed is static. This storage class can apply to either external variables or internal variables or even functions themselves. In any case, the usual declaration is only changed by beginning it with the keyword static.

The scope of internal static variables is the same as if they are declared auto. They are local to the block or function in which they are declared. However, unlike auto variables, internal static variables do not die when the function is exited, but rather keep their existence and their current value. They can thus be used to provide a function or block with storage that is accessible only from within that function or block but is also permanent storage that keeps its value from one entry of the function or block to the next.

■ **Example 7.2.9**

```
int a =1,b=2, c=3,d;                    /*global variables with storage
                                        allocated—this is a definition*/

main()
{
    int i;
    d = g();
    for (i =0; i < 2; i++)    {
    printf("%d %d %d %d", a,b,c,d);
                                        /*prints 1 2 3 2400 the first time */
                                        /* prints 1 2 3 2400 the second
                                        time*/



            }
}
int g()                                 /*functions are always external*/
{
    static int c =6;                    /*local c, but retains its last value
                                        when function is exited*/

    int a,b;                            /*the external a,b, and c are now
                                        hidden*/

    a= 4;                               /* local a* /
    b= 5;                               /* local b */
    c= a*b*c;                           /*c is 120 the first time*/
                                        /*c is 4*5*120=2400 the second
                                        time*/

    return(a*b*c);                      /*returns 4*5*6= 120 the first
                                        time*/
                                        /*returns 4*5* 2400=48000 the
                                        second time*/
```
■

Here is the program and output without the comments.

```
/*    CHAPTER 7   7.2.9.C    */
int a = 1, b = 2, c = 3, d;

main()
{
  int i;
  d = g();
  for (i=0; i<2; i++)
  {
    printf("%d %d %d %d\n",a,b,c,d);
  }
}
int g()
{
  static int c = 6;
  int a,b;
  a = 4;
  b = 5;
  c = a*b*c;
  return(a*b*c);
}


/**********/
/* OUTPUT */
/**********/
1 2 3 2400
1 2 3 2400
```

The default storage class for a function is extern, which means that its name is known globally, so any other function can call it. A function, however, can be declared of storage class static, which makes its name known only within the file in which it is declared. This technique can be useful to provide privacy for a particular function—simply declare it static in a source file different from another source file from which it is to be hidden.

■ **Example 7.2.10**   In prog1a.c:

```
int i;                    /* i is external—this is its
                             definition*/

main()
{
        int i;            /* hides the global i in main*/

        ...

}
```

In prog1b.c:

```
static int g(x)           /*the function g can call h if h is not
                            of storage class static */
```

```
int x;
{
        extern int i;
        ...
}
```

In prog1c.c:

```
int h(x)
```
/*the function h cannot call g—g is of storage class static—known only in the file prog1b.c */

```
int x;
{
```
/* there is no declaration of i here—in this case if i is then referred to it will cause a compile error because the external i in prog1a.c is in another source file*/

```
}
```
■

Finally, *static external* variables are just like external variables in one sense—they both keep their values when a block or function is exited. However, just like static functions, static external variables have as their scope only the remainder of the source file in which they are defined. (Remember that such variables need not also be declared in functions in the same source file.) Again, note that such variables can be used as a privacy mechanism to protect their values from being inadvertently changed by other functions in other source files.

■ **Example 7.2.11**    In prog1a.c:

```
static int i;
```
/* i is external—this is its definition but it is only known in this source file*/

```
main()
{
```
/*the static external i can be used here without an explicit declaration*/

...

```
}
```

In prog1b.c:

```
static int g(x)
```
/*the function g can call h if h is not of storage class static */

```
int x;
{
    extern int i;
```
/*illegal because i is defined as static and appears in another file*/

```
    ...
}
```

In prog1c.c:

```
int h(x)
```
/*the function h cannot call g—g is of storage class static—known only in the file prog1b.c */

```
int x;
{
    int i;
```
/*this is a local variable i */

```
}
```

■

One final note: if the name of a defined external variable is also used as a formal parameter for a function, then within the function itself, any references to that name are references to the formal parameter. The external variable has again been essentially hidden while in the function.

## EXERCISES 7.2

1. Suppose the following program all appears in one file. What will be printed?

```
int a;
int f(b)
int b;
{
    b = b +3;
    a = b -3;
    return ( a + b);
}
main()
{
```

```
        extern int a;
        a = 20;
        printf(" %d %d", a, f(a*a));
}
```

2. Assume the following code appears in one source file. What is printed?

```
int i;
main()
{
        int i, a,b;
        for (i=0; i < 3; i++)    {
                a = f(i + i);
                b = g( i + 3);
                printf("\n %d %d" , a,b);
        }
}
int g(i)
int i;
{
        static int j = 2;
        while ( j > 0 )    {
                i = i + 5;
                j = j -1;
        }
        return ( i);
}
int f(i)
int i;
{
        int j = 5;
        do { i = i-6; j = j -3;}
                while (j > 0);
}
```

3. In UNIX the program called time will time an executable program. Make several of the variables in Exercise 2 of register storage class and run the program time to see if there is a speed up in execution time:

```
$ time a.out
```

**4.** Distinguish clearly among the storage classes auto, extern, register, and static.

**5.** Write a function that has as its input any integer n between one and one hundred and has as its output the factorization of the integers (into primes) between one and n inclusive. Be sure to break the code into functions and make the variables chosen solve the problem using storage classes that insure privacy of information where appropriate.

**6.** Distinguish clearly between the definition and possible declarations of an external variable.

## 7.3 | *INITIALIZATION AND RECURSION*

This section will summarize the various rules on initialization and provide an introduction to the important concepts of recursion, the capability of a function to call itself. All functions in C have recursion, which can greatly improve the readability of code. It is unlikely, however, that storage and speed both will be improved by using code consisting of functions that call themselves.

Variables that use storage classes static or external default to an initialization of zero (done once at compile time), while variables that use storage classes automatic or register default to undefined initializations done each time the function or block is entered.

Variables other than arrays and structures (not yet discussed) may be initialized when they are declared or defined to a constant expression. Examples are:

```
int i = 2;
char c = 'c';
double factor = .07 * .03;
```

Automatic and register variables permit even greater freedom in initializations. They can be initialized to any expression that has previously defined values including the name of a function call. The initializations of arrays and structures will be discussed later.

As noted, recursion is the capability of a function to call itself, that is, to invoke another instance of itself. For example, the problem of multiplying the first n positive integers can easily be solved by recursion. The idea is that the answer to the problem with, say, n =10 is "10 times the answer to the problem with n =9." But the answer to the problem with n=9 is "9 times the answer to the problem with n =8," and so on. Eventually the problem to be solved comes down to a case in which it can generally be done almost by inspection. In this problem, n=1 is the last case and the answer is 1. The algorithm and code are:

| ALGORITHM | CODE |
|---|---|
| **1.** Input n, a positive integer | ```product(n)``` <br> ```int n;``` |
| **2.** If n=1 then ans=1 | ```{``` <br> ```if (n==1)``` <br> ```return(1);``` |
| **3.** Otherwise ans=n*ans(n−1) | ```else``` <br> ```return(n *product(n−1));``` <br> ```}``` |

Here is the code reproduced:

```
product(n)
int n;
{
    if (n==1)
        return(1);
    else
        return(n* product(n−1));
}
```

The tracing of the code is as follows (with n=3):

|  | return value |  |
|---|---|---|
| n=3 | 3* product (2) | suspend execution with n=3 to call the function with n=2 |
| n=2 | 2* product (1) | suspend execution with n=2 to call the function with n=1 |
| n=1 | 1 | the function with n=1 is finished |

Hence, n=2 returns 2*1 and the case n=2 is finished. Hence, n=3 returns 3*(2*1) and the case n=3 is finished. The answer is 6. Be careful running this program with large n—the product grows very quickly!

The product function can easily be rewritten to avoid recursion as follows:

```
product(n)
int n;
{
        int answer=n;       /*build up the answer starting with n */
            for ( ; n > 1; n--)
                    answer = answer * (n-1);
                    return(answer);
    }
```

It is easy to find examples where recursion can get out of hand because of an excessive number of function calls. Each and every time a function calls itself the following must be saved: the addresses of the local variables the function uses, the return address needed to continue execution at the point left off, and the addresses of the parameters. These entities taken together are called a *stack frame* and are stored in a stack. A stack has the fundamental property that the last in (stored) must be the first out. The function product's execution (above) can be visualized with the following stack frames on the stack. (Each time a function is invoked its stack frame gets pushed on the stack—each time a function is exited its stack frame gets popped from the stack—when the stack is empty the original function has been exited.):

Time ⟶

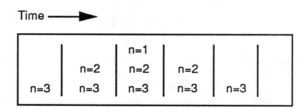

■ **Example 7.3.1** This illustrates how quickly the number of function calls can grow and, hence, cause inefficiencies. Imagine a function f() whose job is to accept a positive integer ($n >= 1$) and return the following:

| | |
|---|---|
| n=1 | return 1 |
| n=2 | return 1 |
| n=3 | return 2 |
| n=4 | return sum of previous 3 terms= $1 + 1 + 2$ |
| n=5 | return sum of previous 3 terms= $1 + 2 + 4$ |
| ... | ... |

Its recursive code is as follows:

```
f(n)
int n;
{
        if (n <=2)
                return(1);
        else if (n=3)
                return(2);
        else
                return( f(n-1) + f(n-2) + f(n-3));
}
```

The number of calls to f necessary to compute f(n) is as follows:

| n | number of calls | |
|---|---|---|
| 1 | 1 | |
| 2 | 1 | |
| 3 | 1 | |
| 4 | 4 | (f(4),f(3),f(2), and f(1)) |
| 5 | 1+4+1+1=7 | (f(5),f(4),f(3), and f(2)) |
| 6 | 1+7+4+1=13 | (f(6),f(5),f(4), and f(3)) |
| 7 | 25 | |
| 8 | 46 | |
| 9 | 85 | |
| 10 | 157 | |
| 11 | 289 | |
| etc. | | |

Here is the code that will actually count the number of function calls necessary to compute f(n):

```
countf(n)
int n;
{
    if (n <=3)
        return(1);
    else
        return( countf(n-1) + countf(n-2) + countf(n-3)+1);
}
```

## **7.4** | *CHAPTER SUMMARY*

1. Functions are the building blocks in the language C that permit a programmer to divide the solution to a problem into smaller, more manageable pieces.

2. The return statement is used to terminate the execution of a function and to possibly pass values of expressions back to the calling environment.

3. Arguments to functions are passed by value to formal parameters in the header of the function.

4. A function by default returns data of type int and the storage class associated with the function is extern.

5. The type specifier void prohibits a function from returning a value.

6. Separate compilation of functions can be done in C.

7. Variables of storage class automatic come into existence when the block or function in which they are declared is entered, and die when exit takes place. Such variables can be hidden when the same names are used to declare variables in a block nested inside the original one.

8. Variables in parallel blocks are private to each block and unrelated to each other.

9. External variables should be defined only once, but they should be declared as often as the context dictates. Particular attention needs to be paid to whether the use of an external variable occurs in the same source file as its definition.

10. Functions that share information via external variables lose some of the desirable properties of modularity and increase the chance of undesirable side effects.

11. The storage class register can be used to achieve increases in speed by storing values of certain types of variables in high-speed registers.

12. Static variables can be used to preserve values of variables after exit from blocks or functions. Static external variables and functions also permit the names of variables and functions to be known only within a particular source file.

13. A formal parameter name that is the same as an external variable name essentially hides the external variable during execution of the function with that parameter.

**14.** Variables that use storage classes static or external default to an initialization of zero (at compile time) while variables that use storage classes automatic or register default to undefined initializations.

**15.** All functions in C can call themselves (recursion), but sometimes the number of calls necessary to solve a problem creates inefficiencies in execution. When a function calls itself, a stack frame of data is pushed onto a stack, and execution of that instance of the function is temporarily suspended. When execution of a function is completed, a stack frame of data is popped from a stack. When the stack is empty, the execution of the function is complete.

# CHAPTER 8

# Pointers and Arrays in C

In the previous chapters some of the best examples of the concepts could not be given until the concepts of arrays and pointers were discussed. The material in this chapter will therefore allow the reader to significantly extend his or her arsenal of practical examples.

As do many other modern languages, the language C permits the declaration and use of pointer variables. A *pointer variable* (or simply a pointer) is a variable whose value is the address of another variable. An important use of pointers is as an argument for a function. In fact, the name of an array *is* an example of a pointer, but its value cannot be changed.

Pointers can point to (hold the address of) characters for the purpose of keeping track of strings. C permits multidimensional arrays and elements of these are easily found with pointers. Pointers can also point to (hold the address of) an array of pointers for ease of storage management. Pointers can also be declared to point to a function. Since the function main() can accept arguments from the command line, this provides a strong connection with UNIX.

## 8.1 | POINTERS: ADDRESSES, FUNCTION ARGUMENTS, ARRAYS

### Addresses

The value assigned to a variable of, say, data type int, float, char, or whatever, is stored in a certain number of contiguous bytes beginning at a particular memory location, or address, in the machine. For example, the declaration and subsequent assignment:

```
int i;
i = 10;
```

might allocate four bytes of storage to hold the value assigned to variable i, say, beginning at address 230, and visualized in the following way:

| Variable | Address | Value at Address |
|----------|---------|------------------|
| i | 230 | 10 |

This same address of i can actually be found with the aid of the unary address operator (&), which is a level 2 operator, applied to i associating right to left. Hence, the value of &i is 230 in this case. So, one way to find addresses is to apply the operator & to an ordinary variable.

Another way to find addresses is to declare pointer variables that point to (hold the address of) an ordinary variable or even a pointer variable. These declarations are accomplished by using the level 2 indirection operator (*) with the following syntax:

```
type *var_name;
```

where type is a user-chosen data type, and var_name is a user-chosen variable name. For example,

```
int *p1;
```

declares p1 to be a pointer variable that holds the address of an integer variable. In this case, *p1 is the actual integer value stored at the address pointed to by p1. The value of *p1 is an ordinary integer, so *p1 can be used anywhere a variable of type int can be.

■ **Example 8.1.1**   Consider the following six statements, numbered so that tracing of their effects can be done:

```
1. int i = 10;
2. int j = 20;
3. int *p1;
4. int *p2;
5. p1 = &i;
6. j = *p1 + 1;
```

The following schematic shows the possible effects (memory locations chosen arbitrarily) of the six statements above:

| Variable | Associated Address | Value at Address |
|----------|--------------------|------------------|
| **1.** i  | 230 | 10 |
| **2.** j  | 234 | 20 |
| **3.** p1 | 900 | ? |
| **4.** p2 | 904 | ? |
| **5.** p1 | 900 | 230 |

/* *p1 is now the value stored at 230 which is 10, i.e. *p1 == 10 */

| | | |
|----------|--------------------|------------------|
| **6.** j | 234 | 11 |

This could also have been accomplished with:

```
int i = 10;
int j = 20;
j = i + 1;
```

Here is the program and output:

```
/*    CHAPTER 8   8.1.1.C    */

main()
{
  int i=10;
  int j=20;
  int *p1;
  int *p2;
  p1 = &i;
  j = *p1+1;
  printf("i = %d j = %d p1 = %d\n",i,j,*p1);
}


/**********/
/* OUTPUT */
/**********/
i = 10 j = 11 p1 = 10
```

■ **Example 8.1.2**   Each of the following three sets of instructions cause the same values in i and j at the end:

1. `int i,j, *p;`

2. `p = &i;`

3. `j = *p;`

Trace:

| Variable | Associated Address | Value at Address |
|---|---|---|
| **1.** i | 230 | ? |
| **1.** j | 234 | ? |
| **1.** p | 900 | ? |
| **2.** p | 900 | 230 |
| **3.** j | 234 | contents of 230 |

**1'.** *int i,j, \*p;*
**2'.** *j = \*&i; /\* same as \*(&i) \*/*

Trace:

| Variable | Associated Address | Value at Address |
|---|---|---|
| **1'.** i | 230 | ? |
| **1'.** j | 234 | ? |
| **1'.** p | 900 | ? |
| **2'.** j | 234 | contents of 230 |

**1''.** *int i,j;*
**2''.** *j=i;*

Trace:

| Variable | Associated Address | Value at Address |
|---|---|---|
| **1''.** i | 230 | ? |
| **1''.** j | 234 | ? |
| **2''.** j | 234 | contents of 230 ∎ |

Remember that a declaration like

```
int *p;
```

declares p to be a pointer variable, hence, like any other variable it is associated with an address in memory. However, the content of that address is itself another address, and *p is what is stored at *that other address*.

Pointers can also be initialized at the time of declaration. For example:

```
int a=10, *p = &a;
```

declares a to be of type int and initializes a at 10, and also declares p to be a pointer to an integer (could be expressed p is of type int *) and initializes p to the address of a (p is assigned &a), visualized in memory as follows:

| Variable | Associated Address | Value at Address |
|----------|--------------------|--------------------|
| a | 100 | 10 |
| p | 900 | 100 |

There are several rules that must be observed:

1. It does not make sense to compute the address of a constant. Hence, **&5** is illegal.

2. It does not make sense to compute the address of an expression that is not a variable. Hence, **&( i + j )** is illegal.

3. It does not make sense to compute the address of a register variable. Hence,

```
register r; int *p; p = &r;
```

   is illegal.

■ **Example 8.1.3**   Assume that p1 and p2 are declared as pointers to integers and that i is declared as an integer. The following statements are executed sequentially as follows:

```
int *p1, *p2, i;
i =20;
p1 = &i;
i = *p1 + 3;
*p1 = 0;
*p1 = *p1 + 1;
(*p1)--;
i = *p1--;        /* same as i = *(p1--) p1 points to an
                  integer and hence p1-- should point to the
                  preceding memory location holding an
                  integer—might be four bytes less */

p2 = p1;
```

This sequence of declarations and statements might produce the following results in memory:

| Variable | Associated Address | Value at Address |
|---|---|---|
| i | 100 | |
| p1 | 900 | |
| p2 | 904 | |
| i | 100 | 20 |
| p1 | 904 | 100 |
| i | 100 | 20+3 |
| i | 100 | 0 |
| i | 100 | 0+1 |
| i | 100 | 1−1 |
| i | 100 | contents of 96 |
| p2 | 904 | 100 |

Here is the program and output:

```
/*    CHAPTER 8   8.1.3.C    */

main()
{
    int *p1, *p2, i;
    i = 20;
    p1 = &i;
    printf("i = %d p1 = %d\n",i,*p1);
    i = *p1 + 3;
    printf("i = %d\n",i);
    *p1 = 0;
    printf("p1 = %d\n",*p1);
    *p1 = *p1 + 1;
    printf("p1 = %d\n",*p1);
    (*p1)--;
    printf("p1 = %d\n",*p1);
    i = *p1--;
    printf("i = %d p1 = %d\n",i,*p1);
    p2 = &i;
    printf("p2 = %d\n",*p2);
}


/**********/
/* OUTPUT */
/**********/
i = 20 p1 = 20
i = 23
p1 = 0
p1 = 1
p1 = 0
i = 0 p1 = 0
p2 = 0
```

### Function Arguments

This section will show how to accomplish the equivalent of call by reference by using pointers as the formal parameters in functions. Remember that all arguments to functions are passed call by value, which simply means that when a variable name is passed to a function as a formal parameter, the called function creates its own local copy of that variable with its associated initial value, but the called function cannot alter the value of the variable back in the calling environment.

Remember also that the methods used so far to return values to the calling environment are via global variables or the return statement as the following example illustrates.

■ **Example 8.1.4**   This code shows how to use a return statement to return the average of two integers back to the calling environment:

```
average(a,b)
int a,b;
float ans;
ans=(a+b)/2;
{
       return ( ans);
}
```

This function could be called from main() with the statement:

```
ave= average(c,d);
```
/*where ave, c, and d are declared in main() */   ■

Here is the complete program and output:

```
main()
{
  int c, d;
  float ave;
  c = 10;
  d = 5;
  ave = average(c,d);
  printf("average = %2f\n",ave);
}
average(a,b)
int a,b;
{
  float ans;
  ans = (a+b)/2;
  return(ans);
}


/**********/
/* OUTPUT */
/**********/
average = 7.000000
```

Another way to accomplish the same objective, although usually less desirable, is to use an external variable to store the average computed by the function:

```
double ave;                    /*ave is global or external*/
average(a,b)
int a,b;
{
      ave = (a + b) /2;
}
```

This function could be called from main() with the statement:

```
average(c,d);      /*where c and d are declared in main()   */
```

A third way to accomplish the same objective is to (1) use pointer variables as one or more of the formal parameters in the function, (2) use the *deferenced* pointer in the body of the function, and (3) pass addresses to one or more of the function's formal parameters.

The function itself cannot change the values (addresses) assigned to the pointer variables, but the function can change the dereferenced value or values.

Here is the previous example rewritten to use this technique:

■ **Example 8.1.5**

```
average(a,b,p1)
int a,b, *p1;
{
      *p1 = ( a + b)/2;
}
```

This function could be called from main() with the statement:

```
average(c,d, &ave);      /*where int c, d, ave are declared in
                           main() */
```

Trace:

| Variable | Associated Address | Value at Address |
|----------|-------------------|------------------|
| c | 100 | say 10 |
| /* c is declared and receives a value somewhere*/ | | |
| d | 104 | say 20 |
| /* d is declared and receives a value somewhere*/ | | |
| ave | 108 | garbage |
| /* ave is declared, but is not assigned a value*/ | | |

| Variable | Associated Address | Value at Address |
|---|---|---|
| a | 200 | 10 |

/* a receives the value of c in the function call */

| b | 204 | 20 |

/* b receives the value of d in the function call */

| p1 | 900 | 108 |

/* p1 (pointer) receives the value &ave (an address) */

| ave | 108 | 15 |

/* *p1 (the value stored at 108) receives the average of a and b */

Here is the function embedded in a program along with the output (no comments):

```
/*    CHAPTER 8   8.1.5.C    */

main()
{
  int c,d, *ave;
  c = 5;
  d = 10;
  average(c,d,&ave);
}
average(a,b,p1)
int a,b,*p1;
{
  *p1 = (a+b)/2;
  printf("average = %d\n",*p1);
}


/**********/
/* OUTPUT */
/**********/
average = 7
```

■ **Example 8.1.6**  This is a classic example of using a function to interchange the contents of two memory locations. The function must be passed memory addresses, that is, the formal parameters of the function must be pointer variables. Notice that, in effect, *two* values (the values of i and j) are returned to the calling environment.

```
/*   CHAPTER 8   8.1.6.C    */

main()
{
  int i, j;
  i = 4;
  j = 8;
  printf("before interchange i= %d j = %d\n",i,j);
  interchange(&i,&j);
  printf("after interchange i= %d j= %d\n",i,j);
}
interchange(a,b)
int *a, *b;
```

```
{
    int temp;
    temp = *a;
    *a = *b;
    *b = temp;
}


/**********/
/* OUTPUT */
/**********/
before interchange i= 4 j = 8
after interchange i= 8 j= 4
```

And here is the analysis of the program:

| Variable | Associated Address | Value at Address |
|---|---|---|
| i | 100 | 4 |
| j | 104 | 8 |
| a | 900 | 100 |
| b | 904 | 104 |
| temp | 908 | 4 |
| i | 100 | 8 |
| j | 104 | 4 |

Now that the reader has been introduced to pointers and addresses, and pointers and function arguments, it is time to establish the relationship between pointers and arrays.

## Arrays

Typically, a programmer needs a number of variables and associated memory locations to hold data of the same data type. For example, a program may need 365 variables of type int to store the highest temperatures for each day of a particular year. Variables named

> *temp[0], temp[1],...,temp[364]*

can have memory allocated for them by declaring the following array:

> *int temp[365];*

The *indexing* (or subscripting) for arrays in C always begins with zero and the number or expression appearing in the declaration is the number of variables declared. Thus, to declare only 10 int memory locations with an array named x one would write:

> *int x[9];*

Arrays, such as those shown above having only a single index, are called *one-dimensional arrays*. Rules for declaring them are very simple:

1. The variable name of the array is subject to the same restrictions as ordinary variable declarations.

2. The number of memory locations (the size of the array) must be positive.

Finally, it is nice to know that when a one-dimensional array is declared, the memory locations are allocated sequentially in the computer. Furthermore, if x is the name of the declared array, then x is identical to &x[0]. Hence, an array name is an address or equivalently a pointer that is fixed. Repeat—the following Boolean expression is true:

```
x == &x[0]
```

Arrays can be of any storage class except register. Except for those of storage class automatic, which begin their life with unknown values, they may be initialized by enclosing the sequential list of values, separated by commas, within brackets. Thus,

```
static int x[4] = {0,2,4,6};
```

declares x to be an array of data type int, with four members, initialized as x[0]=0, x[1]=2, x[2]=4, and x[3]=6. If not enough values are initialized, the leftover variables are automatically set to zero. Thus,

```
static int x[4] = {0,2};
```

declares x to be an array of data type int, with four members, initialized as x[0]=0, x[1]=2, x[2]=0, and x[3]=0. By the same token, if no values are initialized, then all variables are considered leftover and automatically set to zero. Thus,

```
static int x[4];
```

declares x again to be an array of data type int, with four members, initialized as x[0]=0, x[1]=0, x[2]=0, and x[3]=0. So, external and static arrays always get initialized to zeros or specified values. On the other hand, external and static arrays may also have their size determined implicitly by the number of initializers. Thus,

```
static int x[] = {0,3,6,9};
```

and

```
static int x[4] = {0,3,6,9}
```

are identical declarations. The following are equivalent declarations:

```
static char text[5] = { 'i',' ', 'a','m','\0'};
static char text[ ] = "i am";
```

Note that an array of chars initialized as a string automatically has the null char denoted \0 appended to its end. The programmer must be careful to allocate room for this trailing char by choosing an appropriate size for the array.

The following example illustrates some of the basic principles of arrays.

■ **Example 8.1.7**

```
static int x[4]= {3,6,9};
int *p1,a;
p1 = &x[0];
a=*p1;
a = *(p1+2);                    /* an int address plus two
                                   more ints */

p1 =x + 1;
x[3] == *(x+3);                 /* this is true (1) because x
                                   + 3 is 100 + 3(offset) =112,
                                   while *112 is 0; so is x[3] */

&x[2] == x +2;                  /* this is true (1) because x
                                   + 2 is 108; so is the address
                                   of x[2] */

p1 = x;
x = p1;                         /* illegal because x is the
                                   address of x[0], and is
                                   therefore a constant and
                                   cannot be changed*/

p1 = &x;                        /* illegal because x is the
                                   address of x[0], and is
                                   therefore a constant, and one
                                   cannot take the address of a
                                   constant */
```

Trace:

| Variable | Associated Address | Value at Address |
|----------|--------------------|------------------|
| x[0]     | 100                | 3                |
| x[1]     | 104                | 6                |
| x[2]     | 108                | 9                |
| x[3]     | 112                | 0                |
| a        | 116                | unknown          |
| p1       | 900                | 100              |

| Variable | Associated Address | Value at Address |
|----------|-------------------|------------------|
| a | 116 | 3 |
| a | 116 | 9 |
| p1 | 900 | 104 |
| p1 | 900 | 100 |

Here is the example slightly rewritten so that it works.

```
/*    CHAPTER 8  8.1.7.C   */

main()
{
  static int x[4] = {3,6,9};
  int *p1, a;
  printf("x[0] = %d x[1] = %d x[2] = %d x[3] = %d\n",x[0],x[1],x[2],x[3]);
  p1 = &x[0];
  a = *p1;
  a = *(p1 + 2);
  p1 = x + 1;
  x[3] == *(x + 3);
  &x[2] == x + 2;
  p1 = x;
  x[0] = *p1;
}



/**********/
/* OUTPUT */
/**********/
x[0] = 3 x[1] = 6 x[2] = 9 x[3] = 0
```

Notice in the example just completed that pointer arithmetic is a bit unusual, to say the least. If, for example, the value of the pointer variable p is 100 (points to location 100), then p + 1 points to the next possible location able to hold the same data type. This may or may not be 101. If an int occupies four bytes, then p + 1 in this case would be 104. Similarly, p + i would be 100 + 4*i, while p − i would be 100 − 4*i (i is an integer). Chars normally occupy exactly one byte and, hence, if p points to a char then p + i would be the value of p plus i.

Another point (pardon the pun) needs to be addressed (this is too much). When printing the value of pointers, use the printf function with the %d format, but cast the value into an int. For example,

```
int *p;
printf("the value of p is %d", (int)p);
```

will declare and print the value of p.

Three additional points need to be emphasized:

**1.** Within the body of a function, char *s and char s[] *are* different (char *s creates a pointer variable, while char s[] creates a constant pointer, no storage allocated, and cannot be incremented or decremented).

**2.** Pointers to the members of the same array can be compared with $<$, $<=$, $>$, and $>=$. In addition, tests for equality, $==$ and $!=$, can be done, including comparing the value of the pointer with NULL.

**3.** Pointer addition or subtraction of a pointer and an integer can be done as has been illustrated previously. However, it is exceedingly important to remember that the integer always refers to the size of the object being pointed to. Thus, if p is a pointer to an int, say, with value 900, then p + 3 will be 912 if an int occupies four bytes. On the other hand, if p is a pointer to a double, which occupies, say, eight bytes, then p + 3 will be 924.

The last topic to be discussed in this section is that of using arrays as formal parameters in functions.

```
f(s)
char *s;
{
    . . .
}
is equivalent to
f(s)
char s[];
{
    . . .
}
```

In these cases, the function f() is passed an array name and the function can act as if it has been passed either an array or a pointer. (Remember that the name of an array *is* a constant pointer to the first element in the array.) In these cases, it *is* legal to increment or even decrement s because it is simply a local variable. The following example illustrates this idea.

```
/*    CHAPTER 8  8.1.8.C    */
main()
{
  char *t;
  t = "yes";
  printf("the length of the string is %d\n",length(t));
}
length(s)
char *s;
```

```
{
  int k = 0;
  for ( ; *s!='\0'; ++s)
     ++k;
  return(k);
}


/**********/
/* OUTPUT */
/**********/
the length of the string is 3
```

■

■ **Example 8.1.8**

The trace:

| Variable | Associated Address | Value at Address |
|---|---|---|
| t (constant) | 100 | 900 |
| | 900 | 'y' |
| | 901 | 'e' |
| | 902 | 's' |
| | 903 | '\0' |
| s | 200 | 900 |
| k | 101 | 0 |
| /* *s == 'y' so ++k ; ++s */ | | |
| k | 101 | 1 |
| s | 200 | 901 |
| /* *s == 'e' so ++k ; ++s */ | | |
| k | 101 | 2 |
| s | 200 | 902 |
| /* *s == 's' so ++k ; ++s */ | | |
| k | 101 | 3 |
| s | 200 | 903 |
| /* *s == '\0' so stop loop and return (3) to length() */ | | |

■

The following example redoes Example 8.1.8 using pointer arithmetic.

■ **Example 8.1.9**

```
main()
{
      char *t;
      t="yes";
      printf("the length of the string is %d",length(t));
}
```

/*compute length of a string*/

```
length(s)
char s[];
{
      char *p = s;            /*p is initialized to s */
      for( ; *p; p++)         /*the test condition can also be written as *p != '\0' */
          ;                   /* each time do nothing in the loop, but then advance p one
                                 more unit as long as *p is true */
      return(p−s);            /*units p has advanced */
}
```

The trace:

| Variable | Associated Address | Value at Address |
|---|---|---|
| t (constant) | 100 | 900 |
| | 900 | 'y' |
| | 901 | 'e' |
| | 902 | 's' |
| | 903 | '\0' |
| s | 200 | 900 |
| p | 300 | 900 |

/* *p has value 'y'—nonzero so true; hence p++ */

| | | |
|---|---|---|
| p | 300 | 901 |

/* *p has value 'e'—nonzero so true; hence p++ */

| | | |
|---|---|---|
| p | 300 | 902 |

/* *p has value 's'—nonzero so true; hence p++ */

| | | |
|---|---|---|
| p | 300 | 903 |

/* *p has value '\0'—zero so false; hence end loop */

/* return (3)—the value of p − s */

Here is the example without all the comments.

```
/*    CHAPTER 8  8.1.9.C    */

main()
{
  char *t;
  t = "yes";
  printf("the length of the string is %d\n",length(t));
}
length(s)
char s[];
{
  char *p = s;
  for ( ; *p; p++)
    ;
  return(p-s);
}


/**********/
/* OUTPUT */
/**********/
the length of the string is 3
```
■

## EXERCISES  8.1

1. Trace the following program and compare the results with Example 8.1.6.

```
main()
{
      int i,j ;    /*the variables whose values will be in-
                     terchanged */

      i = 4;
      j = 8;
      interchange( i, j);
}
interchange(a,b)
int a, b;
{
      int temp;
      temp = a;
      a    = b;
      b    = temp;
}
```

2. Write a complete program that uses pointer declarations and pointer arithmetic to print the number of bytes used to store a char, an int, a short, a long, a float, and a double on your system.

**3.** Write a function f() that accepts any array of integers as a parameter and whose sole purpose is to average the numbers stored in the array. Now write a complete C program that permits the user to interactively enter 10 integers into an array, pass the "subarray" of the last six integers only to the function f(), and then print the average of those six integers. Give at least two alternative notations that could be used to pass the subarray.

## 8.2 | *CHARACTER POINTERS*

The last two examples in Section 8.1 provided an initial glimpse into the idea of pointers to characters. This section will provide greater detail and illustrate the functions available in the standard library for manipulating strings. The first order of business will be to reinforce the idea that character pointers can easily be initialized as can arrays of characters.

■ **Example 8.2.1**

```
/*    CHAPTER 8   8.2.1.C    */

char u[] = "unix";
char *d = "dos";
main()
{
   char *c = "c";
   printf("%s %s %s\n",u,d,c);
   d = c;
   while (*c != '\0')
   {
      *c += 2;
      c++;
   }
   printf("%s\n",d);
}


/**********/
/* OUTPUT */
/**********/
unix dos c
e
```

Trace:

| Variable | Associated Address | Value at Address |
|---|---|---|
| u[0] | 100 | 'u' |
| u[1] | 101 | 'n' |
| u[2] | 102 | 'i' |
| u[3] | 103 | 'x' |
| u[4] | 104 | '\0' |
| d | 200 | 900 |
|  | 900 | 'd' |
|  | 901 | 'o' |
|  | 902 | 's' |
|  | 903 | '\0' |
| c | 300 | 1000 |
|  | 1000 | 'c' |
|  | 1001 | '\0' |

/* d = c */

| d | 200 | 1000 |

/* *c != '\0' thus *c +=2; c++ */

|  | 1000 | 'e' |
| c | 300 | 1001 |

/* *c == '\0' thus end loop */  ■

■ **Example 8.2.2**   Copy string pointed to by s2 into the space occupied by the string pointed to by s1. The method is to copy the deferenced value of s2 to the deferenced value of s1 and as long as the value of this assignment is true (not '\0') increment each pointer by 1 and repeat process.

```
strcopy(s1,s2);                          /* s1←s2 */
char *s1,*s2;
{
    char c;                              /*hold value of assignment*/
    c = ( *s1 = *s2);
    while ( c != '\0') {
            ++s1;
            ++s2;
            c = ( * s1 = *s2);
    }
}
```
■

■ **Example 8.2.3**  This is another version of strcpy() with a trace done to facilitate understanding:

```
strcpy(s1,s2);
char *s1, *s2;
{
        while ((*s1++ = *s2++) != '\0')
            ;

}
```

Analysis: suppose the following memory locations store the data as indicated, prior to the execution of the while statement. (Remember that * and ++ associate right to left with same priority. Hence, the incrementing applies to s1 and s2, but they do not get incremented until *after* they have been deferenced.) So the loop condition really tests for the value of (*s1 = *s2) != '\0' and then computes s1++ and s2++:

| Variable | Associated Memory Location | Value |
|----------|---------------------------|-------|
| s1 | 900 | 100 |
| | 100 | 'a' |
| | 101 | 'b' |
| | 102 | '\0' |
| s2 | 902 | 200 |
| | 200 | 'x' |
| | 201 | 'y' |
| | 202 | 'z' |
| | 203 | '\0' |

/*s1 = *s2 has value 'x'; this and the incrementations cause */

| | 100 | 'x' |
|----------|------|-----|
| s1 | 900 | 101 |
| s2 | 902 | 201 |

*/s1 = *s2 has value 'y'; this and the incrementations cause */

| | 101 | 'y' |
|----------|------|-----|
| s1 | 900 | 102 |
| s2 | 902 | 202 |

/*s1 = *s2 has value 'z'; this and the incrementations cause */

| Variable | Associated Memory Location | Value |
|---|---|---|
|  | 102 | 'z' |
| s1 | 900 | 103 |
| s2 | 902 | 203 |

/*s1 = *s2 has value '\0'; this and the incrementations cause (and the loop to end) */

| | 103 | '\0' |
| s1 | 900 | 104 |
| s2 | 902 | 204 | ∎ |

There are various functions that manipulate strings found in the standard library, which can usually be accessed in C programs by including the following line. (Descriptions of these functions are found in the UNIX manual, sections 3C and 3S.)

```
#include <string.h>
```

## String Handling Functions

Here are nine examples of string handling functions with comments replacing the actual code.

```
1.  int strcmp(s1,s2)
    char *s1, *s2;
    {
```
/* if s1 is lexicographically less than (greater than) s2, return an int less than (greater than) 0; if s1 equals s2, return(0) */
```
    }
2.  int strncmp(s1,s2,k)
    char *s1, *s2;
    int k;
    {
```
/* same as strcmp() except that no more than k characters are to be compared*/
```
    }
```

```
3.    int strlen(s)
      char *s;
      {
```
/* counts the number of characters in the string pointed to by s, not including the char '\0' */
```

      }
4.    *char index(s1,c)
      char *s1;
      char c;
      {
```
/* if the char c is included in the string s then it returns a pointer to the first occurrence of c in s; otherwise it returns NULL */
```

      }
5.    *char rindex(s1,c)
      char *s1;
      char c;
      {
```
/* same function as index() except that the search for c starts at the right end of s instead of the left */
```

      }
6.    *char strcat(s1,s2)
      *char s1,s2;
      {
```
/* s1 and s2 are concatenated in the space occupied by s1; the pointer returned points to the first char of s1 and the new string (as usual) still ends with '\0' */
```

      }
```

```
7.   *char strncat(s1,s2,k)
     *char s1,s2;
     int k;
     {



     }
```

/* same as strcat() except
that a maximum of k
characters preceding '\0'
of s2 are appended to s1 */

```
8.   *char strcpy(s1,s2)
     *char s1,s2;
     {



     }
```

/* s2 is written into the
space occupied by s1—the
new string, as always, ends
in '\0' and the return value
is the value of s1 */

```
9.   *char strncpy(s1,s2,k)
     *char s1,s2;
     int k;
     {



     }
```

/* same as strcpy() except
that exactly k characters
are moved; if s2 has less
than k characters then the
new string will have
trailing '\0' 's; if s2 has k
characters or more then
the new string may or may
not end with a null
character*/

## EXERCISES 8.2

1. Write a version of Example 8.2.2 using arrays rather than pointers as formal parameters, and indexing within the function itself.

2. Write your own versions of the string handling functions in the standard library and test them.

3. Assume the following declarations and assignments have been made:

```
char *s1,*s2,*s3,*s4, a[10];
s1="a good language to use is C";
s2="an example of an operating system is
UNIX";
s3="cobol";
s4="pascal";
*a ='\0';
```

Now show what each of the following printf statements will print:

a. `printf("%d",strlen(s2));`

b. `printf("%d",strlen(s2+2));`

c. `printf("%d",strcmp(s1,s2));`

d. `printf("%d",strcmp(s3+5,a));`

e. `printf("%d",strncmp(s1,s2,1));`

f. `strncmp(s4+4,s2+5,7));`

g. `printf("%s", strcpy(s2,s1+10));`

h. `printf("%s",strcpy(s3,s4));`

i. `printf("%s",index(s4,'s'));`

j. `printf("%s", index(index(s2,'o'),'b'));`

4. Write the following function in C so that it counts the number of words in an arbitrary '\0' terminated string. Words are separated by ' ', '\n', or '\t'.

```
int count(s)
char *s;
{
    int counter;
    while (not pointing at '\0') {
        while(pointing at white space)          /*skip white space*/
            increment pointer
        if (not pointing at '\0') {
            increment counter                   /*another word*/
            while(not pointing at white space
                  or '\0')
                increment pointer
```

```
        }                                           /*end if*/
    }                                               /*end while*/

    return(counter);
}
```

**5.** Predict the output for the following program segment:

```
int k =20;
int *p = &k;
printf("%d %d %d", p, *p -20, p + 3);
```

**6.** Predict the output for the following program:

```
#include <stdio.h>
main()
{
    int *i = NULL;
    char *c = NULL;
    double *d = NULL;
    printf("%d %d %d %d", (int)(&i+4),(int)(&c+1),
                (int)(&d-5),&c+1==&d);
}
```

**7.** Identify the errors in the following program:

```
#define SIZE = 3;
main()
{
    char s[SIZE] ="123";
    int t[SIZE] = {1,2,3};
    double d[SIZE - 6];
    char u[3.0];
}
```

**8.** Predict the output for the following program:

```
main()
{
    char a[3], *p =a;
    printf("%d %d", (int)p, (int)&a[0])
    silly(&a[1]);
    p = &a[2];
    printf("%d ",(int)p);
```

```
        }
        silly(b)
        char *b;
        {
                char k ='k', *q = &k;
                b= q;
        }
```

9. Find the purpose of the following function mystery(), which returns a pointer to a char:

```
        char *mystery(s)
        char *s;
        {
                char *hold = s;
                char c;
                char *j ;
                for ( j = s + strlen(s) −1; s < j;
                        s++,j--){
                        c = *s;
                        *s = *j;
                        *j = c;
                }
                return(hold);
        }
```

10. A palindrome is a string that when reversed is identical to itself. Write a function that receives a pointer to a string and returns the int value one if the string is a palindrome and zero otherwise (see previous exercise).

11. The following function expects to receive a pointer to a string of digits, such as 2345. What does it return?

```
        convert(s)
        char *s;
        {
                int n=0;
                for ( ; *s >='0' && *s <='9'; ++s)
                        n= 10 * n + *s −'0';
                return(n);
        }
```

**12.** Write a function that accepts a single ASCII character and returns its uppercase equivalent. Hence, if a is received, A is returned.

**13.** Find the purpose of the following function extract(), which returns a pointer to a char:

```
char *extract(s,c)
char *s;
char c;
{
    char *temp= s;
    char *hold;
    for(hold =s ; *s !='\0'; s++)
        if ( *s != c)
            *temp++ = *s;
    *temp = '\0';
    return(hold)
}
```

## 8.3 | *MULTIDIMENSIONAL ARRAYS*

The language C permits arrays to have several dimensions, including two, three, and so on. A two-dimensional array s of char, with three rows and five columns, would be declared as

```
char s[3][5];
```

This array s cannot be declared as char s[3,5]; s is, in reality, an array of arrays, that is, it is an array with five components, each of which is itself an array with three components. Its contents can be visualized as a rectangular matrix of chars as follows:

| s[0][0] | s[0][1] | s[0][2] | s[0][3] | s[0][4] |
| s[1][0] | s[1][1] | s[1][2] | s[1][3] | s[1][4] |
| s[2][0] | s[2][1] | s[2][2] | s[2][3] | s[2][4] |

Thus, there are five components (columns), each consisting of a one-dimensional array (a column) of three chars. Similarly, a three-dimensional array t of char with three rows, five columns, and, say, 10 "height" can be declared by simply writing

```
char t[3][5][10];
```

The array t is also an array of arrays and should be visualized as the following plane of locations at height 0:

| | | | | |
|---|---|---|---|---|
| t[0][0][0] | t[0][1][0] | t[0][2][0] | t[0][3][0] | t[0][4][0] |
| t[1][0][0] | t[1][1][0] | t[1][2][0] | t[1][3][0] | t[1][4][0] |
| t[2][0][0] | t[2][1][0] | t[2][2][0] | t[2][3][0] | t[2][4][0] |

and then similar planes stacked on top of this plane, all the way to height 9. Thus, the declaration char t[3][5][10] sets aside $3 * 5 * 10 = 150$ memory locations, each capable of storing a single char.

Inside the computer, the actual storage of the elements is done by row, that is, storage is allocated in a contiguous fashion with the rightmost subscript varying most quickly. In the case of two dimensions this means that storage for the following array is allocated beginning in the northwest corner, and moving to the right, then through each successive row, finally ending with the southeast corner.

| | | | | |
|---|---|---|---|---|
| s[0][0] | s[0][1] | s[0][2] | s[0][3] | s[0][4] |
| s[1][0] | s[1][1] | s[1][2] | s[1][3] | s[1][4] |
| s[2][0] | s[2][1] | s[2][2] | s[2][3] | s[2][4] |

In the case of three dimensions, this means that storage for the array above is allocated beginning in the northwest corner (on plane 0 and sweeping through all entries directly above that entry), and then moving to the right (through all entries again beginning on plane 0), repeating this for each successive entry, row by row (on plane 0), finally ending with the southeast corner. Each time a new entry on plane 0 is encountered all entries above it are then sequentially allocated.

■ **Example 8.3.1**

Consider the declaration:

```
double s[3][5];
```

| | | | | |
|---|---|---|---|---|
| s[0][0] | s[0][1] | s[0][2] | s[0][3] | s[0][4] |
| s[1][0] | s[1][1] | s[1][2] | s[1][3] | s[1][4] |
| s[2][0] | s[2][1] | s[2][2] | s[2][3] | s[2][4] |

Let $0 <= i <= 2$ and $0 <= j <= 4$. There are many ways to refer to the same element of an array. Assume the following storage locations are used. Let c = # of columns, r = # of rows. (It is very important to be able to determine s[0], s[1], s[2], and also s itself. Pointer arithmetic will then be used for some of the computations.)

| Variable Name | Associated Storage Location |
|---|---|
| s[0][0] | 100 = &s[0][0] = s[0] |
| s[0][1] | 108 = &s[0][0] + 5 * 0 + 1 |
| s[0][2] | 116 |
| s[0][3] | 124 |
| s[0][4] | 132 |
| s[1][0] | 140 = s[1] |
| s[1][1] | 148 |
| s[1][2] | 156 = &s[0][0] + 5 * 1 + 2 = ( s[1]+ 2) |
| s[1][3] | 164 |
| s[1][4] | 172 |
| s[2][0] | 180 = s[2] |
| s[2][1] | 188 |
| s[2][2] | 196 |
| s[2][3] | 204 = &s[0][0] + (5 * 2 + 3)(8's) = (s[2] +3)= 180 + 3(8's) = (*s + 2) + 3=(100+ 2(40's)) + 3(8's) |
| s[2][4] | 212 |

Note carefully that s[0] =100, s[1]=140, and s[2]=180:

| Variable | Associated Memory Location | Value |
|---|---|---|
| s[0] | s | 100 |
| s[1] | s+1 | 140 |
| s[2] | s+2 | 180 |

Hence, s is the address of s[0], and when an integer is added to s, the scale factor is 40.

In general,

**1.** s[i][j]= * ( &s[0][0] + c * i + j)
**2.** s[i][j]= *(s[i] + j)
**3.** s[i][j]= * ((*s + i) + j)
**4.** s[i][j]= (s(i))[j] = (*(s + i))[j]

Any one of these four notations can be used to refer to the value of s[i][j]. ∎

Just as one-dimensional arrays may be used as formal parameters for functions, so may two-dimensional arrays. Recall that in the header of a function, pointers and arrays are interchangeable. Thus, the following are equivalent:

total(s)       total(s)

int *s;        int s[];

Similarly, in two dimensions the following are equivalent:

total(s)       total(s)

int s[][3];    int (*s)[3];

and in three dimensions:

total(s)       total(s)

int s[][3][2]; int (*s)[3][2];

The point here is that only those constants need to be specified that are necessary to generate the correct storage-mapping function.

■ **Example 8.3.2**   The following program uses a function to sum only those integers stored in a two-dimensional array (with 10 rows and 5 columns) that are positive:

```
/*    CHAPTER 8   8.3.2.C    */
main()
{
  int k[10][5];
  k[5][1] = 5;
  possum(k);
}
possum(s)
int s[][5];
{
  int i,j,total;
  total = 0;
  for (i=0;i<10;++i)
  {
    for (j=0;j<5;++j)
    {
      if (s[i][j] >= 0)
        total +=s[i][j];
    }
  }
  printf("total = %d\n",total);
  return(total);
}


/**********/
/* OUTPUT */
/**********/
total = 5
```

This program could also use the function written as follows (using alternative notations for s[i][j] and the function's parameter—clearer ? NO!—but possible to be cryptic, yes!):

```
/*    CHAPTER 8  8.3.2A.C    */

main()
{
  int k[10][5];
  k[5][1] = 5;
  possum(k);
}
possum(s)
int (*s)[5];
{
  int i,j,total;
  total = 0;
  for (i=0;i<10;++i)
  {
    for (j=0;j<5;++j)
    {
      if (*((*s+i)+j) >= 0)
        total += (*(s+i))[j];
    }
  }
  printf("total = %d\n",total);
  return(total);
}



/**********/
/* OUTPUT */
/**********/
total = 5
```

■

■ **Example 8.3.3**  The following program uses a function to sum only those integers stored in a three-dimensional array (with five or fewer rows, columns, and heights) that are positive:

```
/*    CHAPTER 8  8.3.3.C    */

main()
{
  int k[5][5][5];
  k[3][3][3] = 5;
  possum(k,5,5,5);
}
possum(s,rows,columns,heights)
int rows,columns, heights;
int s[][5][5];
{
  int i,j,k,total;
  total = 0;
  for (i=0;i<rows;++i)
  {
    for (j=0;j<columns;++j)
    {
      for (k=0;k<heights;++k)
      {
        if (s[i][j][k] >= 0)
          total += s[i][j][k];
```

```
        }
      }
    }
    printf("total = %d\n",total);
    return(total);
}


/**********/
/* OUTPUT */
/**********/
total = 5
```

■

■ **Example 8.3.4** The next program illustrates a function that shows how to pass a function the number of minutes elapsed in the day and convert it to actual time in hours and minutes:

```
main()
{
   time(180);
}
time(minutes)
int minutes;
{
   int hours;
   hours = minutes/60;
   minutes = minutes%60;
   printf("hours = %d minutes = %d\n",hours,minutes);
}


/**********/
/* OUTPUT */
/**********/
hours = 3 minutes = 0
```

■

*Multidimensional arrays,* like single-dimensional arrays, can be of any storage class except register. Multidimensional arrays (except for those of storage class automatic, which begin their life with unknown values) may be initialized by enclosing the values of each of the single-dimensional arrays that make up the multidimensional array in braces separated by commas. In the case of two-dimensional arrays, this means initialization is accomplished row by row, while in the case of three-dimensional arrays, initialization is done "height by height." Thus,

> *static int x[2][4] = {{0,2,4,6},{1,3,5,7}};*

declares and initializes x to be an array of data type int, initialized as x[0][0]=0, x[0][1]=2, x[0][2]=4, x[0][3]=6, x[1][0]=1, x[1][1]=3, x[1][2]=5, and x[1][3]=7. If not enough values are initialized, the leftover variables are automatically set to zero. Thus,

> *static int x[2][4] = {{0,2}, {1,3,5}};*

declares and initializes x to be an array of data type int initialized as
x[0][0]=0, x[0][1]=2, x[0][2]=0, x[0][3]=0, x[1][0]=1, x[1][1]=3, x[1][2]=5,
and x[1][3]=0. By the same token, if no values are initialized, then all
variables are considered leftover and automatically set to zero. Thus,

```
static int x[2][4];
```

declares x again to be an array of data type int, initialized to all zeros.
So, external and static arrays always get initialized to zeros or specified
values. On the other hand, external and static arrays may also have their
size determined implicitly by the number of initializers. Thus,

```
static int x[2][] = {{0,3,6,9}};
```

and

```
static int x[2][4] = {{0,3,6,9}};
```

are identical declarations.

## EXERCISES  8.3

1. Extend the analysis of Example 8.3.1 to three-dimensional arrays.
   In particular, complete all the alternative representations for the
   array declared as follows:

   ```
   int s[3][5][2];
   ```

2. Extend Example 8.3.3 to make it a complete program with input
   coming from the terminal (or from initialization) and output going
   to the terminal.

3. A leap year is defined as any that is divisible by 4 and is not divisible by 100, or is divisible by 400. The following table is useful in
   dealing with the number of days in a month (note the second
   month):

   ```
   static int day[2][12] = {
        {31,28,31,30,31,30,31,31,30,31,30,31},
        {31,29,31,30,31,30,31,31,30,31,30,31}
   } .
   ```

   Now, write a function that has three parameters: year of type int,
   month of type int, and monthday of type int, and returns the day
   of the year corresponding to the parameters. For example, if the
   function is called count(), then count(1988,3,20) should return
   31+29+20=80, while count(1989,3,20) should return
   31+28+20=79.

**4.** This problem is the inverse of Exercise 8.3.3. Write a function that accepts four parameters, year of type int, yearday of type int, monthpointer that points to an int, and daypointer that points to an int. The function should leave with monthpointer and daypointer set correctly. For example, if the function is called calendar(), and the main function uses

```
int *m, *d;
```

then calendar(1988,79,&m,&d) should leave with m pointing to a location holding 3 and d pointing to a location holding 20, as should calendar(1989,80,&m,&d).

## 8.4 | *POINTERS TO POINTERS*

This section will be devoted to developing a nice program that uses an array of pointers. (Remember that a pointer is a variable that can hold the address of a specified data type.) Each of the pointers will point to the first character of a string. These strings need to be sorted. For example, the following picture depicts the situation in which five strings have been read into consecutive memory locations. (Remember each string ends with the character \0.) In order to keep the picture simple, the memory locations associated with the pointer variables pointing to the strings are not shown. The first column of pointer variables is housed in an array called p. The words themselves are housed in an array called w, with each word ending with the terminating character \0. The idea is to read the strings that need to be sorted into consecutive memory locations so that no fixed length need be allocated for varying length strings. Each time a string is read in, the next p[i] has as its value the address of the first character of that string. Hence, at input time the following would be true:

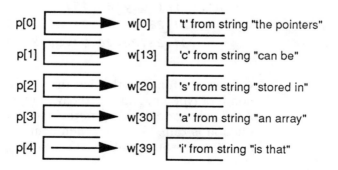

Now suppose an algorithm can make p[0]==&w[30] as shown below; hence, *p[0]==*&w[30]==w[30]. Now imagine that the algorithm could also be constructed so that p[1]==&w[13], p[2]==&w[39], p[3]==&w[20], and p[4]==&w[0]. The picture is now as follows (each p[i] holds an address):

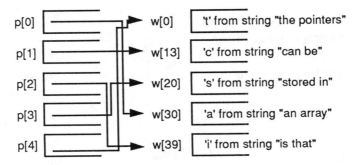

Then the following loop will produce the desired output:

```
for (i=0; i < 5; i++)
    printf("%s\n", p[i]);
```

Output:

```
an array
can be
is that
stored in
the pointers
```

A SORTED LIST!!

Using this method, sorting will have been accomplished without moving the strings themselves, just adjusting the pointers to the strings, and without having to reserve a uniform amount of storage to accommodate the longest string. The null character \0 terminates each string for the purpose of printing its value, and the pointer from the array p addresses the beginning of each string so that a particular string can be found. It almost seems too good to be true—no data movement, no excess storage!

Now that the basics are understood the full scale problem will be attacked. Read in the number of strings and the strings themselves from the terminal, sort them in ascending order, and print the sorted list back to the terminal. The sort that will be used will be the shell sort, which is very efficient.

```
                                          /*sort a list of strings that are
                                          entered at the terminal*/
#define NUMBEROFSTRINGS 1000              /*maximum number of strings
                                          to be entered*/

#define TOTALLENGTH 24000                /*maximum number of
                                          characters for the combined
                                          strings—permitting an average
                                          of 24 chars per string*/

main()
{
    char *p[NUMBEROFSTRINGS];            /*an array of pointers, each of
                                          which will be an address of the
                                          first character of a string*/

    char w[TOTALLENGTH];                 /*an array of characters
                                          holding the words as they are
                                          read in*/

    char *trackit;                       /*trackit will be a pointer
                                          moving through (with each
                                          read) the array w */

int i, n;                                /* i is a loop variable and n is
                                          the number of words to be
                                          sorted*/

printf("\n how many words do you want sorted ? ");
scanf("%d", &n);
if (n <= NUMBEROFSTRINGS) {
    scanf("%s",w);                       /*get the initial word and store
                                          at address w */

    printf("\n input the words now");    /*prompt the user*/
    trackit = w;                         /*initialize trackit */
                                         /* read in the words now */

    for(i=0;i<n; ++i)    {
        p[i]=trackit;
        scanf("%s",p[i]);                /* recall p[i] is an address*/
        trackit = trackit + strlen(trackit) +1;
}
```

/* sort the words now by passing shellsort the address of the first string and the number of strings*/

shellsort(p,n);

/*now print them back in sorted order */

```
        printf("\n%20s","the sorted list is:");
        for (i=0, i < n ; i++)
            printf("%s\n%20s, p[i], "");
        printf("\n");
        }
        else printf("\n stop--there are too many words");
}
shellsort(s,n)
```

/*this function sorts strings whose first characters are stored in s[0], s[1],...,s[n − 1], it will be passed the address of p[0], namely p itself, and the number of strings to be sorted*/

```
char *s[];
int n;
```

/*The basic idea of the shell sort is to compare elements that are far apart early in the process and then to decrease the interval between compared elements gradually to one. There are three loops that will be needed:

1. control the size of the gap eventually shrinking it to zero
2. compare each element that is separated by gap
3. reverse those that are out of order*/

```
{
        int gap, i,j;
        char *temp;
        gap = n/2;
        for( ; gap > 0; gap = gap/2)
```

/*the gap between compared elements will be repeatedly halved */

```
        for (i = gap; i < n; i++)
```
/*this is the loop to repeatedly increase the indices for a particular gap*/

/*the following loop does a single comparison if the initial compared elements are in order—otherwise it interchanges them, and then repeatedly backs up both indices by the gap until it finds pairs of elements in order (if they are out of order it simply interchanges them)*/

```
for (j = i-gap; j>=0; j = j -gap)  {
        if(strcmp(s[j],s[j+gap]) <=0) break;
        temp =s[j];
        s[j]=s[j+gap];
        s[j+gap]=temp;                 /*they are interchanged*/
    }
}
```

Suppose n = 10, and the words are

| now | is | the | time | for | all | good | men | to | their | party |
|-----|----|-----|------|-----|-----|------|-----|----|-------|-------|
| 0   | 1  | 2   | 3    | 4   | 5   | 6    | 7   | 8  | 9     | 10    |

The gap is initially set to $10/2=5$, and beginning with 0 and 5, those elements 5 apart (up to 4 and 9) are compared and interchanged if necessary. However, if an interchange is made (say 2 and 7) then prior to comparing the next pair (3 and 8), the elements are decremented by 1 (back to 2 and 7) and compared as long as the subscripts make sense, but only until the pair compared is in order. Then the gap is set to $5/2=2$ (integer) and the process is repeated. This process is repeated again with a gap of 1, and thus ends (smallest possible gap). The elements are then in order.

**gap=5;** gap $>0$ so continue outer loop

**i=5;** i$<$ 10 so continue middle loop

**j=0;** **j>=0;** compare "now" and "all"; interchange;

| now | is | the | time | for | all | good | men | to | their | party |
|-----|----|-----|------|-----|-----|------|-----|----|-------|-------|
| 5   | 1  | 2   | 3    | 4   | 0   | 6    | 7   | 8  | 9     | 10    |

**j= −5;** stop inner loop; set i=6, i $<$ n and so continue middle loop

**j=1;** **j>=0;** so continue inner loop; compare "is" and "good"; interchange;

| now | is | the | time | for | all | good | men | to | their | party |
|-----|-----|-----|------|-----|-----|------|-----|-----|-------|-------|
| 5 | 6 | 2 | 3 | 4 | 0 | 1 | 7 | 8 | 9 | 10 |

0&5 should be checked now—do not interchange

**j= −4;** so stop inner loop; set i=7; i < n and so continue middle loop

**j=2; j>=0;** so continue inner loop; compare "the" and "men"; interchange;

| now | is | the | time | for | all | good | men | to | their | party |
|-----|-----|-----|------|-----|-----|------|-----|-----|-------|-------|
| 5 | 6 | 7 | 3 | 4 | 0 | 1 | 2 | 8 | 9 | 10 |

1&6 should be checked now—do not interchange

**j=−3;** so stop inner loop; set i=8; i < n and so continue middle loop

**j=3; j>=0;** so continue inner loop

compare "time" and "to"; do not interchange; break; set i=9;

continue middle loop;

**j=4; j>=0;** so continue inner loop

compare "for" and "their"; do not interchange; break; set i=10; stop inner loop; so comparisons with gap=5 have resulted in comparisons (and possible interchanges) of s[0] and s[5], s[1] and s[6], s[0] and s[5] again, s[2] and s[7], s[1] and s[6] again (because s[2] and s[7] were interchanged), s[3] and s[8], and s[4] and s[9].

Now set gap =2 and continue process with this gap followed by a gap of 1 and then 0 (stop): results are:

| | now | is | the | time | for | all | good | men | to | their | party |
|-----|-----|-----|-----|------|-----|-----|------|-----|-----|-------|-------|
| 0&2 | 5 | 6 | 7 | 3 | 4 | 0 | 1 | 2 | 8 | 9 | 10 |
| 1&3 | 5 | 6 | 7 | 3 | 4 | 0 | 1 | 2 | 8 | 9 | 10 |
| 2&4 | 5 | 6 | 7 | 3 | 2 | 0 | 1 | 4 | 8 | 9 | 10 |
| 1&3 no change |
| 3&5 | 3 | 6 | 7 | 5 | 2 | 0 | 1 | 4 | 8 | 9 | 10 |
| 2&4 no change |
| 4&6 | 3 | 4 | 7 | 5 | 2 | 0 | 1 | 6 | 8 | 9 | 10 |
| 3&5 no change |
| 5&7 | 3 | 4 | 5 | 7 | 2 | 0 | 1 | 6 | 8 | 9 | 10 |
| 4&6 no change |
| 6&8 | 3 | 4 | 5 | 7 | 2 | 0 | 1 | 6 | 8 | 9 | 10 |

| | | | | | | | | | | |
|---|---|---|---|---|---|---|---|---|---|---|
| 7&9 | 3 | 4 | 5 | 9 | 2 | 0 | 1 | 6 | 8 | 7 | 10 |
| 6&8 no change | | | | | | | | | | |
| | 3 | 4 | 5 | 9 | 2 | 0 | 1 | 6 | 8 | 7 | 10 |
| 0&1 | 3 | 4 | 5 | 9 | 2 | 0 | 1 | 6 | 8 | 7 | 10 |
| 1&2 | 3 | 4 | 5 | 9 | 1 | 0 | 2 | 6 | 8 | 7 | 10 |
| 0&1 no change | | | | | | | | | | |
| 2&3 | 3 | 4 | 5 | 9 | 1 | 0 | 2 | 6 | 8 | 7 | 10 |
| 3&4 | 4 | 3 | 5 | 9 | 1 | 0 | 2 | 6 | 8 | 7 | 10 |
| 2&3 no change | | | | | | | | | | |
| 4&5 | 4 | 3 | 5 | 9 | 1 | 0 | 2 | 6 | 8 | 7 | 10 |
| 5&6 | 4 | 3 | 6 | 9 | 1 | 0 | 2 | 5 | 8 | 7 | 10 |
| 4&5 | 5 | 3 | 6 | 9 | 1 | 0 | 2 | 4 | 8 | 7 | 10 |
| 6&7 | 5 | 3 | 6 | 9 | 1 | 0 | 2 | 4 | 8 | 7 | 10 |
| 7&8 | 5 | 3 | 6 | 9 | 1 | 0 | 2 | 4 | 8 | 7 | 10 |
| 8&9 | 5 | 3 | 6 | 8 | 1 | 0 | 2 | 4 | 9 | 7 | 10 |
| 7&8 no change | | | | | | | | | | |

now is the time for all good men to their party

Print out: `all for good is men now the their time to party`

The final example in this section will provide the reader with a firm understanding of the differences between an array of pointers to char (each pointing to a char) and a two-dimensional array of type char. The former array can be visualized as yielding an array of non-right justified chars, while the latter is a rectangular array (left and right justified) of chars.

■ **Example 8.4.1**

```
main()
{

    static char message[2][100] =
        {"four score", "and seven"};

        /*  1.  can be initialized because its storage class is
                static—space for 2*100=200 characters is
                allocated. This is equivalent to the initial-
                ization {{'f','o','u','r',' ','s','c','o','r','e','\0'},
                {'a','n','d',' ','s','e','v','e','n','\0'}}
```

2. note that message itself is an array with two components, message[0] and message[1]— these in turn are each arrays of 100 chars— i.e., each component, message[0] and message[1], is a string. This explains why the initializations for each component end with the char '\0'. Note also that chars not initialized default to the blank char ' '.

3. the access to each char of message[i][j] is accomplished by the compiler with a storage mapping function requiring one multiplication and one addition (see the section on two-dimensional arrays).

4. message uses space for 400 bytes */

```
static char *p[2] =
{"four score","and seven"};
```

/* 1. here p has two components, p[0] and p[1], each of which points to a char. Thus space for two pointers is allocated.

2. p[0] points to "four score" (11 chars—don't forget the char '\0') while p[1] points to "and seven" (10 chars)

3. so p uses space for two pointers (perhaps a total of 8 bytes) and 21 chars (21 more bytes). Thus p uses only 14.5% of the space that message does.

4. the compiler does not use a mapping function to access p[i][j]—hence access is faster also.

5. note that message[0][199] is valid while p[0][199] is invalid.*/

```
printf("\n%s%s\n",message[0],message[1]);
printf("\n%s%s\n",  p[0],p[1]);
```

/* prints:     four score and
                    seven
                    four score and
                    seven        */

```
printf("\n%c%c\n",  message[0][0],message[0][1]);
printf("%c%c\n",  p[0][0],p[0][1]);
```

/* prints:     fo
                    fo       */

```
}
```

Here is the same program and output without all the comments:

```
/*      CHAPTER 8    8.4.1.C    */

main()
{
  static char message[2][100] = {"four score", "and seven"};
  static char *p[2] = {"four score", "and seven"};
  printf("%s %s\n",message[0],message[1]);
  printf("%s %s\n",p[0],p[1]);
  printf("%c%c\n",message[0][0],message[0][1]);
  printf("%c%c\n",p[0][0],p[0][1]);
}


/**********/
/* OUTPUT */
/**********/
four score and seven
four score and seven
fo
fo
```
■

## EXERCISES 8.4

1. Use the ideas of the example in Section 8.4 to solve the following translation problem: A sentence is to be translated word for word from English to French. The user is to read in approximately 50 English words and their translations in French. These should be accessed through two arrays of pointers. Then a sentence is to be input in English and the output should be the French translation.

2. Trace the shell sort using the following integer data: 4,7,2,5,65,43,33,89,90,32,1

3. Try to modify the program given in Section 8.3 so that the user does not have to input the number of strings to be sorted.

4. Work through the calculations of message and p given in this section with message redefined as static char message[2][1000] and the same initializations. In particular, what percentage of space utilization is required for p with respect to message?

## 8.5 | ARGUMENTS TO MAIN()

C programs can receive information directly from the UNIX operating system by writing main with two arguments, conventionally called argc and argv. The argument *argc,* shorthand for *arg*ument *c*ount, is always at least one because it is the number of command-line arguments with which the program is invoked. For example, if prog.c is compiled and then run as follows, argc is one because the sole argument is a.out itself:

```
$ cc prog.c
$ a.out
```

The argument *argv,* shorthand for *arg*ument *v*alues, on the other hand, is an array of pointers to each of the command-line arguments. In the case above, argv[0] points to the character a of the string a.out.

■ **Example 8.5.1**    Suppose prog.c is to be run with files called file1, file2, and file3. The program would be compiled and run as follows:

```
$ cc prog.c
$ a.out file1 file2 file3
```

The following is the proper declaration of prog.c:

```
main(argc,argv)
```

```
int argc;              /*number of arguments*/
char *argv[];          /*array of pointers to each argument on the
                         command line*/
{
```

/* in this program argc will be 4 and argv[1] points to the first character of the string "file1" (just say argv[1] points to "file1", argv[2] points to "file2", and argv[3] points to "file3") */

```
}
```

■ **Example 8.5.2**    This example, called echoit.c, is a C program that uses command line arguments to do the same task as the UNIX utility echo. Hence, the following would take place:

```
$ cc echoit
$ a.out this is my message
this is my message
```

Here is echoit.c with input and output shown:

```
/*   CHAPTER 8  8.5.2.C   */
main(argc,argv)
int argc;
char *argv[];
{
  int i;
  i = 1;
  for( ;i < argc; i++)
    printf("%s%c",argv[i],(i<argc-1) ? ' ':'\n');
}
```

```
/*********/
/* INPUT */
/*********/
a.out 8.4.1

/**********/
/* OUTPUT */
/**********/
8.4.1
```
∎

∎ **Example 8.5.3** Here is another version of echo:

```
main(argc,argv)
int argc;
char *argv[];
{
    while (--argc > 0) /* after the comparison then decrement argc */
        printf("%s%c",*++argv,(argc > 1)?' ':'\n');
}
```

Picture the following

```
argv ──────→argv[0]──────→"a.out"
            argv[1]──────→"this"
            argv[2]──────→"is"
            argv[3]──────→"my"
            argv[4]──────→"message"
```

or

| Memory Location | Variable | Value | |
|---|---|---|---|
| | argv | 100 | |
| 100 | argv[0] | 200 | |
| 104 | argv[1] | 206 | |
| 108 | argv[2] | 211 | |
| 112 | argv[3] | 214 | |
| 116 | argv[4] | 217 | |
| 200 | | 'a' | "a.out" |
| 206 | | 't' | "this" |
| 211 | | 'i' | "is" |
| 214 | | 'm' | "my" |
| 217 | | 'm' | "message" |

argc==5; decrement argc before the comparison; still > 0; before argv is used, increment it (now points at argv[1]); deference argv and print it as a string ("this"); argc is still greater than 1, so print a blank. Repeat.

Here is the program with input and output (but no comments):

```
/*    CHAPTER 8  8.5.3.C   */

main(argc,argv)
int argc;
char *argv[];
{
  while (--argc > 0)
    printf("%s%c",*++argv,(argc > 1)?' ':'\n');
}


/*********/
/* INPUT */
/*********/
a.out 8.4.1


/**********/
/* OUTPUT */
/**********/
8.4.1
```
■

## EXERCISES 8.5

1. When a UNIX command is run it is often the case that an argument beginning with a minus sign is the second argument (argv[1]) signaling an optional flag or parameter. Modify echoit so that if the flag -r is present, each argument will be echoed in reverse order.

2. Repeat Example 8.5.1 but in this case have the arguments printed out in abbreviated fashion (only the first three characters) if the flag -a is present.

3. Modify Example 8.5.1 so that each argument is printed on separate numbered lines if the flag −n is present.

4. Modify Examples 8.5.1, 8.5.2, and 8.5.3 and write a single program that encompasses all three possibilities written in any order whatsoever, or with flags concatenated. Thus, −ras is legal as is −r −a, −s, or any combination of one or more flags.

## 8.6 | *POINTERS TO FUNCTIONS*

The reader has significantly extended his or her repertoire in this chapter by learning about pointers and arrays and their intimate connection. Despite the powerful features of these tools, C appears to be limited by the fact that all functions have external scope and are at the same level. That is to say, a function cannot be defined within another function. But just as C permits a variable to have as its value a pointer, a function can also have as its return value a pointer to a prescribed data type.

■ **Example 8.6.1**  The declaration

```
int *f();
```

tells the compiler that *f() is an int; i.e. f() points to an int; i.e., f is a function whose return value points to an int. Parentheses bind tighter than *, so fully parenthesized the same declaration would be

```
int *(f())
```
■

■ **Example 8.6.2**  The declaration

```
int (*f)();
```

on the other hand, informs the compiler that (*f)() is an int; i.e., *f is a function that returns an int; i.e. that f is a pointer to a function that returns an int. Thus, f points to a function, while *f is the function, and (*f)(x) is the call to the function. ■

■ **Example 8.6.3**  Now, suppose the problem is to compute all the deductions that must be taken from an employee's paycheck during the year. Define x to be the gross pay and

> f() returns the social security tax
>
> g() returns the state income tax
>
> h() returns the federal income tax.

Each of the functions f, g, and h will use x as an argument and can easily be defined using current tax tables. For example, f() might be as follows:

```
double f(x)
double x;
{
    if (x < 45000.00) return (.07 * x);
                      else return ( 45000 *
                      .07);
}
```

A simple definition of each of the functions f, g, and h followed by the function main() calling another function to add each of them will now do the task of adding f(x), g(x), and h(x). Remember that f, g, and h must also be declared in main because they do not return an int.

Here is the entire program with the bodies of f, g, and h omitted:

```
double f(x)
double x;
{
}
                                    /* body of f here */

}
double g(x)
double x;
{
}
                                    /* body of g here */
double h(x)
double x;
{                                   /* body of h here */
double addthem(f1,g1,h1,x)
double (*f1)(), (*g1)(), (*h1)(), x ;
```
/*for example: *f1 is a function that returns a double; i.e. f1 is a pointer to a function that returns a double. Thus f1 points to a function, while *f1 is the function, while (*f1)(x) is the call to the function. */

```
{
     return( ((*f1)(x) + (*g1)(x) + (*h1)(x) );
}
main()
{
     double f(), g(), h(), addthem(), x;
     printf("enter the salary now");
     scanf(%f,&x);
     printf("\n%.7f\n",addthem(f,g,h,x));
}
```

The real value of being able to pass a function other functions becomes even more impressive when used with recursion (Section 7.3).

## EXERCISES   8.6

1. Define clearly the difference between double (*f)() and double *f() as declarations.

2. Complete the code for the functions f, g, and h given in Section 8.6 and run the program.

3. Write a C program that will do the following calculation for any defined function f returning a double, given any integer values of m and n, m <= n:
   f(m)* f(m) * f(m) + f(m+1) * f(m+1) * f(m+1) + . . . + f(n) * f(n) * f(n).
   Test your code with the function f(x) = 1/ (x * x) and m = 1, n = 1000.

4. The function x to the fifth power plus three, written x**5 + 3 is a smooth function that is guaranteed to have a value x1 between a==−2.0 and b==0.0 for which x1 **5 +3 ==0; this is because ((−2.0) **5) +3 < 0 while (0.0 ** 5 ) + 3 > 0; hence, it must cross the x axis between these values. The method of bisection to find the approximate root of this function, accurate to error =.001, is as follows:
   a. Show that f(a) and f(b) have opposite signs.
   b. Find the midpoint m = (a+b)/2.
   c. Calculate f(m).
   d. If f(m)= 0 done.
   e. Use the appropriate interval [a,m] or [m,b] and return to step 1, repeating the process until the new interval is of length < .001; if that happens, use the midpoint of that interval as the approximate answer for the root.

   Write a function called root that calls itself if necessary to find the root of a function f on the interval [a,b] to within any prescribed error. Now write a C program that calls this function to find the approximate root of x**5 + 3 on the interval [−2,0] accurate to .0001.

5. The functions x**2 and cos x must meet for some x on the interval [0,6.28] because 0==0**2 < cos 0 and 6.28**2 > cos 6.28. Find this point accurate to .00001 by using the general root function of number 4 applied to the function x**2 − cos x.

6. The greatest common divisor of two positive integers p and q, p >=q, can be found by taking the integer division of p by q; if it is zero, the g.c.d. is q; otherwise, the g.c.d of p and q is the g.c.d. of q and the remainder when p is divided by q. For example,

g.c.d$(20,5)$=g.c.d$(5,4)$=g.c.d$(4,1)$=4. Write a recursive function that calculates the g.c.d of two positive integers and then write a program that tests your function.

## 8.7 | CHAPTER SUMMARY

1. A pointer variable is a variable that is declared with the * notation and whose value is either NULL or an address of another variable.

2. The address of a variable can be found with the address operator &. The * and & associate from right to left (with same precedence level) and are inverses of each other, (i.e., *&v and v are identical if v is a variable).

3. Pointers can be initialized at the time of declaration, but one cannot take the address & of either a constant, a register variable, or an expression that is not a variable.

4. The equivalent of call by reference can be accomplished by using pointers as the formal parameters in functions, passing addresses to these formal parameters, and then using the deferenced pointers in the function itself.

5. Arrays can be declared with the name of the array subject to the same restrictions as ordinary variable declarations.

6. Arrays always begin with subscript zero and the name of the array is identical to the address of the initial element of the array.

7. Arrays, except for those of storage class automatic, may be initialized either in whole or in part. The default values are zero.

8. External and static arrays may have their sizes determined implicitly by the number of initializers.

9. An array of chars initialized as a string automatically receives the char \0 as its last char.

10. An array is a constant address and cannot be changed; however, it can be used in expressions involving pointer arithmetic, which compensates for the size of the associated data type.

11. When printing the value of pointers using printf with the %d format, but then cast the value into an int.

12. Within the body of a function, char *s and char s[] are different.

13. Pointers to members of the same array can be compared including tests for equality.

14. As formal parameters in a function, char *s and char s[] are identical, that is, the function can act as if it has been passed either a pointer or an array, and s can be incremented or decremented in this case.

**15.** Various string handling functions can be accessed by including the following line:

> `#include <string.h>`

**16.** An array of arrays can be created by notation, such as char s[3][5], which declares s to be an array with five components, each of which is itself an array with three components. The base address is &s[0][0]. Three-dimensional arrays can similarly be declared.

**17.** There are several alternative notations to refer to s[i][j] as in number 16.

**18.** In the header of a function only those constants need to be specified for arrays that are necessary to generate the correct storage mapping function. All except the first size must be specified.

**19.** Multidimensional arrays, except for storage class automatic, can be initialized using the same principles as for single-dimensional arrays.

**20.** An array of pointers can be used to sort a list of strings without reserving a uniform amount of storage to accommodate the longest string, and without actually moving the strings themselves, just adjusting the pointers.

**21.** C programs accept two arguments called argc and argv in the function main that permit information to be passed directly from UNIX to a C program.

**22.** The value of argc is the number of command line arguments (always at least one) and argv is an array of pointers to char (strings).

**23.** The declaration int *f() defines f as a function whose return value points to an int.

**24.** The declaration int (*f)() defines f as a pointer to a function that returns an int.

**25.** The declaration in number 24 is appropriate in the header of a function when the programmer wants that function to use a value returned by that function.

# CHAPTER 9

# Structures in C

The limitation of an array is that all of the data items stored must be of the same data type; for example, integers, reals, chars, or any other values might be stored in each component. In real life, however, much of the time the data that needs to be grouped together is not homogeneous. The data for a particular student might include student identification (an integer), name (a pointer to a char), grade point average (a real), and perhaps other data. This chapter shows how diverse data elements such as these can be grouped together and associated with a single variable name called a *structure,* and how each data element can then be accessed by the structure member operator "." in a variable called a *member* of the structure—a structure typically has many members, depending on the application.

The collection of such data considered as an aggregate, for a single student, is called a record in some languages, such as Pascal, and a table in others, such as Cobol, but in C the nomenclature is that of a structure.

A structure can then be accessed in several ways, depending upon the type of members it has and the programming choices used by the programmer. One simple manner, but effective in certain situations, is to build an array of structures, thereby storing a structure as a component of an array. In this instance each component of the array is itself a structure (thus the array has homogeneous data values). The programmer can then access an individual structure by simply specifying the appropriate subscript (for example the ith record).

In some applications, it is not efficient in terms of access considerations to store structures as the elements of an array. An example of this would be a case in which the number of structures needed is highly variable, making it difficult to set an upper bound on the highest subscript needed for the array. Another problem case involves instances in which structures need to be appended to (or even deleted from) the existing set of structures (perhaps in the middle of an array) thereby causing much data movement to keep the structures in a predefined order. One might have a situation in which one thousand structures have been sorted into the components of an array, and then an additional structure needs to be stored somewhere near the middle. This would obviously be time consuming to accomplish because the elements following the one to be inserted would all have to be moved down one component each. Clearly, an array of structures would not be a time-effective solution.

Rather, the application might dictate that the structures be linked together with pointers so that the pointers themselves simply need be adjusted to accomplish insertion and/or deletion. The pointers can actually be defined as part of the individual structures and can be constrained to point to another structure. A set of such structures linked together by pointers is called a *linked list* and will be covered in this chapter.

While it is often the case that a member of a structure has a predefined bit length determined in fact by the data type of the member, it is also possible to assign bit lengths to the individual members of a structure. These members are then called fields and can be accessed just as any other member of a structure can. So, for example, if only one bit is needed to store a data value, perhaps a yes(y) or no(n) response, then storage for that single char can be set aside in the structure, permitting the programmer to use space efficiently.

A *union* has essentially the same syntax as a structure, but has the added benefit of permitting the programmer to have its members share common storage. This, too, can result in significant space savings. For example, a union might be used to effect space savings by using the same storage location to hold either a structure for a student living off campus or a structure for a student living on campus. These structures may be totally different in nature, but the union is used to simply set aside space for the largest structure.

## 9.1 | *STRUCTURES AND FUNCTIONS*

### Declaring Structures

There are several ways that structures may be declared. Suppose that the programmer wishes to have a structure with the following member components:

account_number which is an int;

name which is a pointer to a char;

balance which is a float;

and due_date which consists of a pointer to a char.

■ **Example 9.1.1**   The following declaration can be made:

```
struct account {
     int account_number;
     char *name;
     float balance;
     char *due_date;
} a1, a2;
```

The following statements then accurately describe the effect of the above declaration:

1. The a1 and a2 are structure variables of data type struct account.

2. The members of struct account are account_number, *name, balance, and *due_date.

3. The members of struct account can be accessed through either variable, a1 or a2.

4. The members of struct account are accessed by the name of the structure variable concatenated with the member structure operator ".", followed by the name of the member. Thus, the following would be a valid set of assignments:

```
a1.account_number=93485;
a1.name          ="Jones";
a1.balance       =93.45;
a1.due_date      ="9/20/88";
```

5. Members must always be accessed through the structure variable as noted in number 4; hence, if another structure variable a3 is declared with a member with the name account_number of data type int, then there can be no confusion between a1.account_number and a3.account_number.

6. The identifier account in this example is called a structure *tag name* and is optional; the programmer can use it in additional declarations of the same kind without repeating the detailed description of each member.

7. Struct is a keyword.

8. An additional variable a3 of type struct account can be declared by simply writing:

```
struct account a3;
```

To summarize the declarations and assignments of Example 9.1.1 as they might appear in a program:

```
struct account{
   int account_number;
   char *name;
   float balance;
   char *due_date;
}a1, a2;
struct account a3;
main()
{
   a1.account_number = 93485;
   a1.name           = "jones";
   a1.balance        = 93.45;
   a1.due_date       = "9/20/88";
}
```

■ **Example 9.1.2**   The following declaration could have been made:

```
struct account {

      int account_number;

      char *name;

      float balance;

      char *due_date;

};
```

The following statements then accurately describe the declaration:

1. No structure variables of data type struct account are declared, but the structure tag name is account.

2. The members of struct account are again account_number, *name, balance, and *due_date.

3. The members of struct account can be accessed through variables a1 or a2 only if the following additional declaration is made:

   ```
   struct account a1,a2;
   ```

4. No space is allocated for storage in this situation, only the template for the structure is defined.

To summarize Example 9.1.2 as the statements might appear in a program:

```
struct account{
   int account_number;
   char *name;
   float balance;
   char *due_date;
};
struct account a1, a2;
main()
{
   a1.account_number = 93485;
   a1.name           = "jones";
   a1.balance        = 93.45;
   a1.due_date       = "9/20/88";
}
```

■ **Example 9.1.3**   The tag name may be omitted as in the following declaration:

```
struct {
     int account_number;
     char *name;
     float balance;
     char *due_date;
} a1,a2;
```

The following statements then accurately describe the declaration:

1. The members are again account_number, *name, balance, and *due_date.
2. An additional variable a3 using the same structure can only be declared by repeating the entire structure because no tag name was given above.

To summarize Example 9.1.3 as it might appear in a program:

```
struct {
  int account_number;
  char *name;
  float balance;
  char *due_date;
}a1, a2;

main()
{
  a1.account_number = 93485;
  a1.name           = "jones";
  a1.balance        = 93.45;
  a1.due_date       = "9/20/88";
}
```

Structures that are declared to be external or static may also be initialized by separating the values of the members by commas within brackets as the following example illustrates:

■ **Example 9.1.4**
```
static struct account {
            int account_number;
            char *name;
            float balance;
            char *due_date;
     } a1 ={84762,"Jones",93.45,"9/20/88"};
```

To summarize Example 9.1.4 as it might appear in a program:

```
static struct account{
  int account_number;
  char *name;
  float balance;
  char *due_date;
}a1 = {93485,"Jones",93.45,"9/20/88"};

main()
{
}
```

■ **Example 9.1.5** It is possible to have a member of a structure be itself a structure. This technique is called *nesting structures* and is appropriate to use in situations in which a data item naturally has several components—such as a date. Consider the following declarations and initializations:

```
struct date {
        int month;
        int day;
        int year;
} ;
struct account {
        int account_number;
        char *name;
        float balance;
        struct date due_date;
    } a1;
a1.account_number=84762;
a1.name ="Jones";
a1.balance=93.45;
a1.due_date.month=9;
a1.due_date.day=20;
a1.due_date.year=88;
```

Note that the "." operator again connects the structure name and the member name. In this instance, it connects a1 and its member due_date, and this concatenated pair then is, in turn, a variable of type struct date; hence, "." also connects due_date and members of type struct date. The "." operator associates left to right.

It is also possible to define one or more pointers to a structure and then access the members of that structure through the pointer. The notation is to use the name of the pointer followed by a minus sign and a greater than sign ( → ), followed by the name of the member.

Here is Example 9.1.5 embedded in a program without the comments and with the output:

```
struct date{
  int month;
  int day;
  int year;
};
struct account{
  int account_number;
  char *name;
  float balance;
  struct date due_date;
} a1;
```

```
main()
{
a1.account_number = 93485;
a1.name = "Jones";
a1.balance = 93.45;
a1.due_date.month = 9;
a1.due_date.day = 20;
a1.due_date.year = 88;
printf("a1.account_number = %d\n",a1.account_number);
printf("a1.name = %s\n",a1.name);
printf("a1.balance = %.2f\n",a1.balance);
printf("a1.due_date.month = %d\n",a1.due_date.month);
printf("a1.due_date.day = %d\n",a1.due_date.day);
printf("a1.due_date.year = %d\n",a1.due_date.year);
}


/* OUTPUT */
a1.account_number = 93485
a1.name = Jones
a1.balance = 93.45
a1.due_date.month = 9
a1.due_date.day = 20
a1.due_date.year = 88
```

■ **Example 9.1.6**

```
struct account {
        int account_number;
        char *name;
        float balance;
        char *due_date;
    } a1;
    struct account *a2;
```

In this instance, a1 is of type struct account, but a2 points to a struct account. Initialization could be accomplished as follows:

```
a2=&a1;
(*a2).account_number=84762;
(*a2).name            ="Jones";
(*a2).balance         =93.45;
(*a2).due_date        ="9/20/88";
```

or equivalently

```
a2→account_number=84762;
a2→name            ="Jones";
a2→balance         =93.45;
a2→due_date        ="9/20/88";
```

Here are the various statements captured in a program:

```
struct account{
  int account_number;
  char *name;
  float balance;
  char *due_date;
} a1;
struct account *a2;

main()
{
a2 = &a1;
(*a2).account_number = 93485;
(*a2).name = "Jones";
(*a2).balance = 93.45;
(*a2).due_date = "9/20/88";

a2->account_number = 93485;
a2->name = "Jones";
a2->balance = 93.45;
a2->due_date = "9/20/88";
}
```

∎

The reader should keep in mind that the following four operators associate left to right and have the highest precedence of all operators:

→   used to point to a structure

·   used to connect a structure name and a member

( )   used for argument lists

[ ]   used to access within an array.

The C language permits the programmer to rename data types (but not to create new data types). This can be particularly useful for structure types in that lengthy declarations need only be given once, perhaps in a header file, and then that file may be "included" in the source code of the program to be compiled. This can greatly improve modularity and portability, as well as documentation.

The format for the *typedef* declaration is simply the word typedef followed by the old data type and then a list of the newly associated equivalent names for that data type. Remember, a new data type is not being created, only a new name is being given to an already existing data type. Statements using typedef are similar to using the #define except that the compiler interprets typedefs.

∎ **Example 9.1.7**   The following statement renames the data type int as the data type called whole_numbers. Wherever int would have been used in the program, whole_numbers can now be used:

*typedef int whole_numbers;*

The following statement renames a pointer to a char as simply THE_STRING. THE_STRING then serves as a substitute name for char *, namely THE_STRING is now a pointer to a char:

```
typedef char *THE_STRING;
```
∎

**■ Example 9.1.8**  In the case that follows, a_record is the new name for the structure with members account_number, *name, balance, and *due_date. Then a is declared to be a variable of type a_record and p is declared to be a pointer to a_record.

```
typedef struct {
        int account_number;
        char *name;
        float balance;
        char *due_date;
        } a_record;
a_record a,*p;
```
∎

### Functions and Structures

The only system-independent, absolute guarantee a programmer has with respect to structures is that he or she can access a member of a structure and take the address of a structure. However, on many systems it is now possible to pass a structure to a function as an argument and even to return a structure. It will be assumed that this more liberal environment is available.

The next example assumes that the following declaration is contained in student.h:

```
typedef struct {
        int account_number;
        char *name;
        float balance;
        char *due_date;
        } a_record;
```

One function will be given that assigns values to a record. Note that this function needs a pointer to the record (because everything is passed call by value), as well as the specific values to be assigned. A second function will be written to retrieve the values of a record. In this situation, a pointer to the record must be passed, as well as pointers used to point to each of its members. (Otherwise, the appropriate values could not be passed back.) A third function will be given to print the value of a record.

## ■ Example 9.1.9

```
/*     CHAPTER 9   9.1.9.C    */

#include "/usr/home/eharri/ch9/student.h"

a_record account;

main()
{
  a_record *ptr;
  ptr = &account;
  assignvalues(ptr,2985,"John",93.25,"9/25/89");
  fetchvalues(ptr,2985,"John",93.25,"9/25/89");
  printvalues(ptr);
}

/*****************************************/
assignvalues(p,a,n,b,d)
a_record *p;
int a;
char *n;
float b;
char *d;
{
  p->account_number=a;
  p->name=n;
  p->balance=b;
  p->due_date=d;
}

/*****************************************/
fetchvalues(p,a,n,b,d)
a_record *p;
int a;
char *n;
float b;
char *d;
{
  a = (p ->account_number);
  n = (p ->name);
  b = (p ->balance);
  d = (p ->due_date);
}

/*****************************************/
printvalues(p)
a_record *p;
{
  printf("%d %s %f %s\n",p->account_number,p->name,p->balance,p->due_date);
}


/* INCLUDED FILE */

typedef struct{
  int account_number;
  char *name;
  float balance;
  char *due_date;
} a_record;


/* OUTPUT */

2985 John 93.250000 9/25/89
```

On many systems it is possible to do the following operations on structures. (These operations may not be possible on all systems.)

1. pass a structure (by value) to a function as an argument
2. return a structure from a function via the return statement
3. assign the values of an entire structure to a structure variable with a simple assignment statement
4. pass a structure some of whose members might be arrays to a function by value ∎

The following example is the equivalent of Example 9.1.9 using the return statement to pass back an entire structure.

∎ **Example 9.1.10**

```
/***************************/
/*    CHAPTER 9  9.1.10.C   */
/***************************/


#include "/usr/home/eharri/ch9/student.h"

a_record assignvalues();

/*************************************/
main()
{
  a_record holdrec;
  holdrec = assignvalues(9864,"Jones",98.25,"9/25/88");
  printf("account_number = %d\n",holdrec.account_number);
  printf("name           = %s\n",holdrec.name);
  printf("balance        = %.2f\n",holdrec.balance);
  printf("due_date       = %s\n",holdrec.due_date);
}
/*************************************/
a_record assignvalues(a,n,b,d)
int a;
char *n;
float b;
char *d;
{
  a_record r;
  r.account_number=a;
  r.name=n;
  r.balance=b;
  r.due_date=d;
  return(r);
}


/* INCLUDED FILE */

typedef struct{
  int account_number;
  char *name;
  float balance;
  char *due_date;
} a_record;


/* OUTPUT */

account_number = 9864
name           = Jones
balance        = 98.25
due_date       = 9/25/88
```

∎

## Nested Structures

The last example of this section using structures will show how to use nested structures in an effective manner.

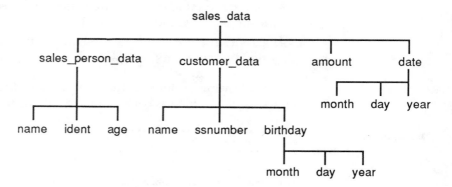

In the construction that follows, the members of the root are specified; and if they are not leaves of the data structure (tree), they are given a label (spd, cd, and d in this case), which is then labeled with the members at the next level down. Whenever the labels are not elementary data types, further labels must be made. The typedefs must appear in the reverse order from that in which they were defined so that all terms are known when the root is finally defined. The constants are, as usual, defined and captured in a file called, perhaps, sales.h.

■ **Example 9.1.11**

```
#include "/usr/home/eharri/ch9/sales.h"
/*******************************************/
main()
{
  d *p;
  d date_data;
  sales_data *ptr;
  sales_data temp;
  ptr = &temp;
  p = &date_data;
  get_date(p);
  enter_data(ptr);
}
/*****************************************/
get_date(pointer)
d *pointer;
{
  printf("Enter the month, day, and year now: ");
  scanf("%s %d %d",pointer->month,&(pointer->day),&(pointer->year));
  printf("\nmonth = %s \n",pointer->month);
  printf("day      = %d\n",pointer->day);
  printf("year     = %d\n",pointer->year);
}
/*****************************************/
```

```
enter_data(p)
sales_data *p;
{
  scanf("%s",p->sales_person_data.name);
  printf("salesperson name: %s\n",p->sales_person_data.name);
  scanf("%d",&(p->sales_person_data.ident));
  printf("salesperson ident: %d\n",p->sales_person_data.ident);
  scanf("%d",&(p->sales_person_data.age));
  printf("salesperson age: %d\n",p->sales_person_data.age);
  scanf("%s",p->customer_data.name);
  printf("customer name: %s\n",p->customer_data.name);
  scanf("%d",&(p->customer_data.ssnumber));
  printf("customer ssnumber: %d\n",p->customer_data.ssnumber);
  scanf("%s",p->customer_data.birthday.month);
  printf("customer bday month: %s\n",p->customer_data.birthday.month);
  scanf("%d",&(p->customer_data.birthday.day));
  printf("customer bday day: %d\n",p->customer_data.birthday.day);
  scanf("%d",&(p->customer_data.birthday.year));
  printf("customer bday year: %d\n",p->customer_data.birthday.year);
  scanf("%f",&(p->amount));
  printf("amount: %.2f\n",p->amount);
  scanf("%s",p->date.month);
  printf("month: %s\n",p->date.month);
  scanf("%d",&(p->date.day));
  printf("day: %d\n",p->date.day);
  scanf("%d",&(p->date.year));
  printf("year: %d\n",p->date.year);
}



/*****************************/
/* included file  "sales.h" */
/*****************************/

#define SALES 10
#define CUSTOMERS 100

typedef struct{
  char month[10];
  int  day;
  int  year;
}d;

typedef struct{
  char name[20];
  int  ssnumber;
  d    birthday;
}cd;

typedef struct{
  char name[20];
  int  ident;
  int  age;
}spd;

typedef struct{
  spd   sales_person_data;
  cd    customer_data;
  float amount;
  d     date;
}sales_data;
```

```
/**********/
/* OUTPUT */
/**********/

Enter the month, day, and year now: Dec 13 1989
month = Dec
day     = 13
year    = 1989
Jones
salesperson name: Jones
9825
salesperson ident: 9825
30
salesperson age: 30
Smith
customer name: Smith
123456789
customer ssnumber: 123456789
Sept
customer bday month: Sept
25
customer bday day: 25
1964
customer bday year: 1964
45.50
amount: 45.50
Sept
month: Sept
30
day: 30
1989
year: 1989
```

∎

## EXERCISES 9.1

1. Suppose the following declaration is made:

   ```
   struct {
           int a;
           int *b;
   } *p;
   ```

   a. Give the equivalent parenthesized version of $++p \rightarrow a$. Does a or p get incremented?

   b. Does $(++p) \rightarrow a$ increment p before or after accessing a?

   c. Does $(p++) \rightarrow a$ increment p before or after accessing a?

   d. Explain what occurs because of $*p \rightarrow b$.

   e. Explain what occurs because of $(*p \rightarrow b)++$.

   f. Explain what occurs because of $*p++ \rightarrow b$.

2. Suppose the following declarations and assignments are made:

   ```
   struct account {
   int account_number;
   char *name;
   ```

```
        float balance;
        char *due_date;
        } a ;
        struct account *p =&a;
        a.account_number=89045;
        a.name="Jones";
        a.balance=89.45;
        a.due_date="9/20/88";
```

Give the equivalent (parenthesized if necessary) expression using the pointer p for each of the following (also give the value of each expression):

a. `a.account_number`

b. `a.name`

c. `a.balance`

d. `a.due_date`

e. `*p → name + 3`

f. `* (p → name + 3)`

3. Put the example of 9.1.9 into a C program that permits the user to interactively enter five records and then print them back to the screen sorted on the name.

## 9.2 | *ARRAYS OF STRUCTURES*

Arrays are designed to hold values of variables, each of which must be of the same data type. This common data type can be elementary, such as int, char, or float, or in fact, it may be a derived data type, such as a structure itself. Consider a program whose purpose is to count the number of sales of each part in a sales count of, say, one hundred maximum different parts. The data might be of the form: widgets 10 gadgets 20 horseshoes 15 widgets 12, and so on, much like on a cash register receipt. Two separate arrays could be used, one to hold pointers to the parts themselves and another to hold the total counts:

```
char *parts[100];
int totals[100];
```

Rather than make two separate arrays of exactly the same size although holding different types of data, it is more convenient to simply define an array of structures as follows:

```
struct info {
      char *parts;
      int totals;
} info_array[100];
```

which defines an array called info_array consisting of one hundred such structures. Alternatively, one could write

```
struct info {
      char *parts;
      int totals;
};
struct info info_array[100];
```

However, one might as well simply initialize the structure when it is defined as follows (set all counts to zero):

```
struct info {
      char *parts;
      int totals;
} info_array[]= {
            "abacus",0, /* or use {"abacus",0}, */
            "brooms",0,
            "catnip",0,
            /*continue with initializers*/
            "widgets",0,
            "zammos",0
};
```

## EXERCISES 9.2

1. Complete the following binary search function that finds the slot in info_array[ ] that holds the part being searched for:

    ```
    binary (searchpart,info_array,slot,n)
    ```

    /*find slot such that info_array[slot]. parts == searchpart*/

    ```
    char *searchpart;
    struct info info_array)[];
    ```

```
int n, slot;
{

/*program code goes here*/
}
```

## 9.3 | *POINTERS TO STRUCTURES*

The primary advantages of using structures are often achieved by having one or more of the members of a structure point to a structure of exactly the same type. First, the simplest case will be examined in which a structure has two members; for example, an integer and a pointer to the same type of structure. It is convenient to capture the definitions in a header file, say, listdec.h:

```
#define NULL 0
```
/*the preprocessor will replace every occurrence of NULL by 0 in the remainder of the file*/

```
typedef into INFO;
```
/*INFO is a new name for the data type int*/

```
struct list {
    INFO i;
    struct list *point;
};
```
/*each struct list has a member of type INFO and a member called "point" that points to a structure of type "struct list" */

```
typedef struct list RECORD;
```
/* the data type struct list will be known as data type RECORD*/

```
typedef RECORD *LINK;
```
/*the data type RECORD will be type *LINK, i.e., LINK points to a record*/

```
RECORD a,b,c;
```
/*a,b, and c are variables of type RECORD*/

■ **Example 9.3.1**   This example will use the definitions above to create the following structures (remember that a RECORD is composed of members of type INFO and \*LINK, a LINK points to a RECORD, and the variables of type RECORD are a, b, and c). Note that in this example the appropriate variables have been declared previously (a, b, and c) and, without a way to allocate space dynamically (available through UNIX and shown in Example 9.3.2), there is no way to access four or more RECORDs.

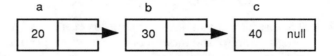

```
#include "/usr/home/eharri/ch9/listdec.h"

main()
{
   a.i      = 20;
   b.i      = 30;
   c.i      = 40;
   a.point  = &b;
   b.point  = &c;
   c.point  = NULL;
   printf("a.i = %d\n",a.i);
   printf("b.i = %d\n",b.i);
   printf("c.i = %d\n",c.i);
}


/*****************/
/* INCLUDED FILE */
/*****************/
#define NULL 0
typedef int INFO;

struct list{
   INFO i;
   struct list *point;
};
typedef struct list RECORD;

typedef RECORD *LINK;

RECORD a,b,c;


/**********/
/* OUTPUT */
/**********/
a.i = 20
b.i = 30
c.i = 40
```

■

■ **Example 9.3.2**  Assume now that variables a, b, and c have not been declared and that the user needs a technique to allocate storage for RECORDs dynamically, that is, during the execution of the program. This is easy to do by using the standard UNIX library function that gives *memory alloc*ation. This function is called *malloc* and it accepts as an argument any ordinary unsigned positive integer, say, x, and returns a pointer to char. Notice that declaring a pointer variable (to a RECORD) called temp and then updating it appropriately permits the programmer to simplify the notation considerably. Here is the program and the output:

```
/**********************/
/* CHAPTER 9  9.3.2.C */
/**********************/
#define NULL 0
typedef int INFO;

struct list{
  INFO i;
  struct list *point;
}*temp;
typedef struct list RECORD;

typedef RECORD *LINK;

LINK head;

main()
{
  head = (LINK)malloc(sizeof(RECORD));
  head->i = 20;
  printf("head->i = %d\n",head->i);
  head->point = (LINK)malloc(sizeof(RECORD));
  head->point->i = 30;
  printf("head->point->i = %d\n",head->point->i);
  head->point->point = (LINK)malloc(sizeof(RECORD));
  head->point->i = 40;
  printf("head->point->i = %d\n",head->point->i);
  head->point->point->point = NULL;
  test_temp();
}
/****************************************************/
/* The following function tests the variable 'temp' */
/****************************************************/
test_temp()
{
  temp = head;
  temp->i = 20;
  printf("temp->i = %d\n",temp->i);
  temp->point = (LINK)malloc(sizeof(RECORD));
  temp = temp->point;
  temp->i = 30;
  printf("temp->i = %d\n",temp->i);
  temp->point = (LINK)malloc(sizeof(RECORD));
  temp = temp->point;
  temp->i = 40;
  printf("temp->i = %d\n",temp->i);
  temp->point = NULL;
}
```

```
/**********/
/* OUTPUT */
/**********/
head->i = 20
head->point->i = 30
head->point->i = 40
temp->i = 20
temp->i = 30
temp->i = 40
```

■

## 9.4 LINKED LISTS

We will see in this section some of the fundamental operations that can be performed on linked lists including the following: creation, counting the number of elements (often records), finding a particular element, concatenation, inserting an element into a desired location, and deleting a desired element. The techniques presented here are very important programming techniques and should be studied carefully to be sure that they are completely understood. Again, it generally will be the case that a header file called listdec.h is included to capture the definitions in a single file.

■ **Example 9.4.1**  First we will write a function to create a linked list from an array of integers. It will be necessary for the function to allocate the storage and assign the necessary values to each record. It will be assumed that the function will copy from the array to the linked list until the integer value zero is encountered. Because a linked list might only be accessible through its first record, the function itself will simply return a pointer to the first record in the linked list.

```
#include "listdec.h"
LINK pointer;
LINK linkarray();
int array[9] = {1,2,3,4,5,6,7,8,0};
/*******************************/
main()
{
   pointer = linkarray(array);
}
/*******************************/
/* FUNCTION: LINKARRAY         */
/*******************************/
LINK linkarray(a)
INFO a[];
{
   LINK head, temp;
   int k;
   head= NULL;
   if (a[0] != 0)
   {
     head = (LINK)malloc(sizeof(RECORD));
     head->i = a[0];
     printf("head->i = %d\n",head->i);
     temp = head;
     for (k=1;a[k] != 0;k++)
     {
```

```
            temp->point = (LINK)malloc(sizeof(RECORD));
            temp = temp->point;
            temp->i = a[k];
            printf("temp->i = %d\n",temp->i);
        }
    }
    return(head);
}

/*****************/
/* INCLUDED FILE */
/*****************/
#define NULL 0
typedef int INFO;

struct list{
    INFO i;
    struct list *point;
};
typedef struct list RECORD;

typedef RECORD *LINK;

RECORD a,b,c;


/***********/
/* OUTPUT */
/***********/
head->i = 1
temp->i = 2
temp->i = 3
temp->i = 4
temp->i = 5
temp->i = 6
temp->i = 7
temp->i = 8
```

■ **Example 9.4.2.**
**Counting records in**
**a linked list:**

```
/*******************************/
/*       CHAPTER 9    9.4.2.C     */
/*******************************/
#include "listdec.h"
int count();
int value;
LINK pointer;
LINK start;
/*******************************/
main()
{
    init_pointer();
    value = count(start);
    printf("value = %d\n",value);
}
/*******************************/
/* FUNCTION: INIT_POINTER     */
/* used to test example.      */
/*******************************/
init_pointer()
{
    start = NULL;
    start = (LINK)malloc(sizeof(RECORD));
    start->i = 61;
    pointer = start;
    pointer->point = (LINK)malloc(sizeof(RECORD));
    pointer = pointer->point;
    pointer->i = 20;
```

```
      pointer->point = (LINK)malloc(sizeof(RECORD));
      pointer = pointer->point;
      pointer->i = 30;
      pointer->point = NULL;
}
/*****************************/
/* FUNCTION: COUNT           */
/*****************************/
int count(head)
LINK head;
{
  LINK temp;
  int k=0;
  if (head == NULL)
    return(k);
  else
  {
    temp = head;
    for (k=1;temp->point != NULL;k++)
      temp = temp->point;
    return(k);
  }
}


/******************/
/* INCLUDED FILE */
/******************/
#define NULL 0
typedef int INFO;

struct list{
  INFO i;
  struct list *point;
};
typedef struct list RECORD;
typedef RECORD *LINK;


/**********/
/* OUTPUT */
/**********/

value = 3
```

■

■ **Example 9.4.3.
Printing INFO fields
in a linked list:**

```
/******************************/
/*    CHAPTER 9    9.4.3.C    */
/******************************/
#include "listdec.h"
int print();
int value;
LINK pointer;
LINK start;
/******************************/
main()
{
  init_pointer();
  print(start);
}
/******************************/
/* FUNCTION: INIT_POINTER     */
/* used to test example.      */
/******************************/
init_pointer()
{
  start = NULL;
  start = (LINK)malloc(sizeof(RECORD));
```

```
    start->i = 61;
    pointer = start;
    pointer->point = (LINK)malloc(sizeof(RECORD));
    pointer = pointer->point;
    pointer->i = 20;
    pointer->point = (LINK)malloc(sizeof(RECORD));
    pointer = pointer->point;
    pointer->i = 30;
    pointer->point = NULL;
}
/*****************************/
/* FUNCTION: PRINT           */
/*****************************/
int print(head)
LINK head;
{
  LINK temp;
  int k=0;
  if (head == NULL)
    printf("There is only an empty list\n");
  else
  {
    for (temp=head;temp->point!=NULL;temp=temp->point)
      printf("%d\n",temp->i);
    printf("%d\n",temp->i);
  }
}

/*****************/
/* INCLUDED FILE */
/*****************/
#define NULL 0
typedef int INFO;

struct list{
  INFO i;
  struct list *point;
};
typedef struct list RECORD;

typedef RECORD *LINK;


/**********/
/* OUTPUT */
/**********/
61
20
30
```

■

■ **Example 9.4.4.
Concatenating two
linked lists:**

```
#include "/usr/home/eharri/ch9/listdec.h"
LINK list1, list2, temp1, temp2;
main()
{
   initialize();
   join(temp1,temp2);
}
/*****************************/
/* FUNCTION: JOIN            */
/*****************************/
join(head1,head2)
LINK head1, head2;
{
  LINK temp = head1;
  LINK head = head1;
  for ( ; temp->point != NULL; temp = temp->point);
```

```
      temp->point = head2;
      while (head->point != NULL)
      {
        printf("%d\n",head->i);
        head = head->point;
      }
      printf("%d\n",head->i);
    }
    /***************************/
    /* FUNCTION: INITIALIZE    */
    /* used for example input  */
    /***************************/
    initialize()
    {
      int j;
      list1 = NULL;
      list2 = NULL;
      list1 = (LINK)malloc(sizeof(RECORD));
      list1->i = 0;
      temp1 = list1;
      for (j=1;j<11;j++)
      {
        list1->point = (LINK)malloc(sizeof(RECORD));
        list1 = list1->point;
        list1->i = j;
      }
      list1->point = NULL;
      list2 = (LINK)malloc(sizeof(RECORD));
      list2->i = 20;
      temp2 = list2;
      for (j=21;j<31;j++)
      {
        list2->point = (LINK)malloc(sizeof(RECORD));
        list2 = list2->point;
        list2->i = j;
      }
      list2->point = NULL;
    }

    /******************/
    /* INCLUDED FILE */
    /******************/
    #define NULL 0
    typedef int INFO;

    struct list{
      INFO i;
      struct list *point;
    };
    typedef struct list RECORD;
    typedef RECORD *LINK;

    /***********/
    /* OUTPUT */
    /***********/
    0
    1
    2
    3
    4
    5
    6
    7
    8
    9
    10
    20
```

```
21
22
23
24
25
26
27
28
29
30
```
■

■ **Example 9.4.5.**
**Inserting a record**
**in its proper place**
**in a linked list:**

This example presupposes that two pointers, say, p1 and p2, have been found (perhaps by marching through a linked list) that point to adjacent records, and that a new record accessed by a pointer called new is to be inserted between those records. Thus, it is assumed that the pointers p1 and p2 are found by another function and that *new is known. It is assumed that neither p1 nor p2 are NULL.

```
/*****************************/
/*    CHAPTER 9    9.4.5.C    */
/*****************************/
#include "/usr/home/eharri/ch9/listdec.h"
LINK temp1, newpt, list1, list2;
main()
{
  initialize();
  insert(list1,newpt,list2);
  print_list();
}
/***************************/
/* FUNCTION: INSERT        */
/* inserts 365 between 0   */
/* and 1.                  */
/***************************/
insert(p1,new,p2)
LINK p1, new, p2;
{
  p1->point = new;
  new->point = p2;
}
/***************************/
/* FUNCTION: INITIALIZE    */
/* used for example input  */
/***************************/
initialize()
{
  int j;
  list1 = NULL;
  list1 = (LINK)malloc(sizeof(RECORD));
  list1->i = 0;
  temp1 = list1;
  for (j=1;j<6;j++)
  {
    list1->point = (LINK)malloc(sizeof(RECORD));
    list1 = list1->point;
    list1->i = j;
  }
  list1->point = NULL;
  list1 = temp1;
  list2 = list1->point;
  newpt = (LINK)malloc(sizeof(RECORD));
  newpt->i = 365;
  newpt->point = NULL;
```

```
}
/*************************/
/* FUNCTION: PRINT_LIST */
/* prints linked list   */
/* after inserting new   */
/* value.               */
/*************************/
print_list()
{
  while (temp1->point != NULL)
  {
    printf("%d\n",temp1->i);
    temp1 = temp1->point;
  }
  printf("%d\n",temp1->i);
}

/******************/
/* INCLUDED FILE */
/******************/
#define NULL 0
typedef int INFO;

struct list{
  INFO i;
  struct list *point;
};
typedef struct list RECORD;

typedef RECORD *LINK;


/**********/
/* OUTPUT */
/**********/
0
365
1
2
3
4
5
```

■

## ■ Example 9.4.6.
## Deleting a record
## from a linked list:

```
#include "/usr/home/eharri/ch9/listdec.h"
LINK list1, temp1;
main()
{
  initialize();
  delete(temp1); /* temp1 points to second element (equals 1) in list */
  printf("The element '1' should be deleted from the list\n");
  while (list1->point != NULL)
  {
    printf("%d\n",list1->i);
    list1 = list1->point;
  }
  printf("%d\n",list1->i);
}
/******************************/
/* FUNCTION: DELETE          */
/******************************/
delete(p)
```

```
LINK p;
{
  LINK q;
  q = p->point;
  p->point = q->point;
  free(q);
}
/***************************/
/* FUNCTION: INITIALIZE   */
/* used for example input */
/***************************/
initialize()
{
  int j;
  list1 = NULL;
  list1 = (LINK)malloc(sizeof(RECORD));
  list1->i = 0;
  temp1 = list1;
  for (j=1;j<11;j++)
  {
    list1->point = (LINK)malloc(sizeof(RECORD));
    list1 = list1->point;
    list1->i = j;
  }
  list1->point = NULL;
  list1 = temp1;
}

/******************/
/* INCLUDED FILE */
/******************/
#define NULL 0
typedef int INFO;

struct list{
  INFO i;
  struct list *point;
};
typedef struct list RECORD;

typedef RECORD *LINK;


/***********/
/* OUTPUT */
/***********/
The element '1' should be deleted from the list
0
2
3
4
5
6
7
8
9
10
```

## Stacks

One of the most important uses of a linked list is to implement the concept of a stack. A stack can also be implemented using an array, but in this section the emphasis will be on using a linked list. A *stack* has the following characteristics:

1. It consists of a set of records with a last or bottom record distinguished by some criterion. In this case, it has a pointer field with value NULL. Every other record has a pointer field whose value is the address of the next record.

2. The only record accessible is the top record distinguished by some criterion. In this case, there is a pointer whose value is the address of the top record.

An easy way to picture a stack is as a set of trays (records) in a cafeteria where only the top tray is accessible. Trays are returned to the top and trays are removed from the top. Trays are divided into two compartments—a data portion and an address portion, which is the address of the tray below it. The last tray is distinguished by the fact that it is at the bottom. That is, it has an address portion whose value is NULL. In addition, there is a pointer whose value is the address of the top tray.

A programmer must be able to implement the following functions when working with stacks:

1. The function empty(p), where p points to the top record (or no record at all) and returns zero if the stack is not empty (when the value of p is a memory address) and one otherwise (when p has value NULL).

2. The function getvalue(p), where p points to the top record, which returns the data value of the top record but does not tamper with the stack itself.

3. The function pop(p,d), where p points to the top record and d is of appropriate data type. This function returns the data value in the top record (through d) and adjusts p so that it now points to the next record, effectively adjusting the pointer to remove the top record from the old stack.

4. The function push(p,d), where the data value d in the record pointed to by p becomes the top record in the new stack, effectively adjusting the pointer to place an additional record on the old stack.

In order to write these four stack operation functions, the following header file called funstack.h will be assumed to be available:

```
#define NULL 0                          /* 0 will be known
                                        as NULL*/

typedef int DATA;                       /* int will be
                                        known as DATA*/

struct stack {
    DATA i;
    struct stack *next;
};                                      /* each record of
                                        type struct stack has
                                        a DATA portion and
                                        a pointer portion,
                                        accessed by next,
                                        which points to a
                                        record of type
                                        struct stack*/

typedef struct stack RECORD;            /* struct stack will
                                        be known as
                                        RECORD*/

typedef RECORD *TOPPOINT;               /* RECORD will be
                                        known as
                                        *TOPPOINT—this
                                        is how records in
                                        the stack will be
                                        accessed*/
```

■ **Example 9.4.7.**
**Checking to see if a**
**stack is empty:**

```
#include "/usr/home/eharri/ch9/funstack.h"
TOPPOINT list, temp;
int isempty();
int value;
main()
{
  init_pointer();
  value = isempty(list);
  while (temp->next != NULL)
  {
    printf("%d\n",temp->i);
    temp = temp->next;
  }
  printf("%d\n",temp->i);
  if (value == 0)
    printf("Stack is not empty\n");
  else
    printf("Stack is empty\n");
}
/**********************/
/* FUNCTION: ISEMPTY */
/**********************/
```

```
isempty(p)
TOPPOINT p;
{
  if (p == NULL)
    return(1);
  else
    return(0);
}
/***************************/
/* FUNCTION: INIT_POINTER */
/* used for sample input   */
/***************************/
init_pointer()
{
  int j;
  list = NULL;
  list = (TOPPOINT)malloc(sizeof(RECORD));
  list->i = 0;
  temp = list;
  for (j=1;j<11;j++)
  {
    list->next = (TOPPOINT)malloc(sizeof(RECORD));
    list = list->next;
    list->i = j;
  }
  list->next = NULL;
  list = temp;
}


/*****************/
/* INCLUDE FILE */
/*****************/
#define NULL 0
typedef int DATA;
struct stack{
  DATA i;
  struct stack *next;
};
typedef struct stack RECORD;
typedef RECORD *TOPPOINT;


/***********/
/* OUTPUT */
/***********/
0
1
2
3
4
5
6
7
8
9
10
Stack is not empty
```

■

■ **Example 9.4.8**
**Finding the top**
**value of a stack:**

```
#include "/usr/home/eharri/ch9/funstack.h"
TOPPOINT list, temp;
DATA getvalue();
int value;
/***********************/
main()
{
  init_pointer();
  value = getvalue(list);
  while (temp->next != NULL)
  {
    printf("%d\n",temp->i);
    temp = temp->next;
  }
  printf("%d\n",temp->i);
  printf("The top value = %d\n",value);
}
/***********************/
/* FUNCTION: GETVALUE */
/***********************/
getvalue(p)
TOPPOINT p;
{
  return(p->i);
}
/***************************/
/* FUNCTION: INIT_POINTER */
/* used for sample input   */
/***************************/
init_pointer()
{
  int j;
  list = NULL;
  list = (TOPPOINT)malloc(sizeof(RECORD));
  list->i = 0;
  temp = list;
  for (j=1;j<11;j++)
  {
    list->next = (TOPPOINT)malloc(sizeof(RECORD));
    list = list->next;
    list->i = j;
  }
  list->next = NULL;
  list = temp;
}



/****************/
/* INCLUDE FILE */
/****************/
#define NULL 0
typedef int DATA;
struct stack{
  DATA i;
  struct stack *next;
};
typedef struct stack RECORD;
typedef RECORD *TOPPOINT;


/**********/
/* OUTPUT */
/**********/

0
1
2
```

```
                              3
                              4
                              5
                              6
                              7
                              8
                              9
                              10
                              The top value = 0
```
                                                                                        ■

**■ Example 9.4.9**
**Popping an element**
**from a stack:**

```c
#include "/usr/home/eharri/ch9/funstack.h"
TOPPOINT list, temp;
int value;
/*********************/
main()
{
  value = 0;
  init_pointer();
  pop(list,value);
  printf("After Pop Function :\n");
  while (temp->next != NULL)
  {
    printf("%d\n",temp->i);
    temp = temp->next;
  }
  printf("%d\n",temp->i);
}
/*********************/
/* FUNCTION: POP       */
/*********************/
pop(p,d)
TOPPOINT p;
DATA d;
{
  TOPPOINT p1;
  p1 = p;
  if (isempty(p1))
    printf("There is an empty stack.\n");
  else
  {
    d = p1->i;
    p = p1->next;
    free(p1);
  }
  temp = p;
}
/*********************/
/* FUNCTION: ISEMPTY */
/*********************/
isempty(p)
TOPPOINT p;
{
  if (p == NULL)
    return(1);
  else
    return(0);
}
/**************************/
/* FUNCTION: INIT_POINTER */
/* used for sample input  */
/**************************/
init_pointer()
{
  int j;
  list = NULL;
  list = (TOPPOINT)malloc(sizeof(RECORD));
  list->i = 0;
```

```
  temp = list;
  for (j=1;j<11;j++)
  {
    list->next = (TOPPOINT)malloc(sizeof(RECORD));
    list = list->next;
    list->i = j;
  }
  list->next = NULL;
  list = temp;
  printf("Before Pop Function :\n");
  while (temp->next != NULL)
  {
    printf("%d\n",temp->i);
    temp = temp->next;
  }
  printf("%d\n",temp->i);
}



/*****************/
/* INCLUDE FILE */
/*****************/
#define NULL 0
typedef int DATA;
struct stack{
  DATA i;
  struct stack *next;
};
typedef struct stack RECORD;
typedef RECORD *TOPPOINT;


/***********/
/* OUTPUT */
/***********/
Before Pop Function :
0
1
2
3
4
5
6
7
8
9
10
After Pop Function :
1
2
3
4
5
6
7
8
9
10
```

■ **Example 9.4.10**
**Pushing an element**
**on a stack:**

```
#include "/usr/home/eharri/ch9/funstack.h"
TOPPOINT list, temp;
int value;
/**********************/
main()
{
  value = 20;
  init_pointer();
  push(list,value);
  printf("After Push Function :\n");
  while (temp->next != NULL)
  {
    printf("%d\n",temp->i);
    temp = temp->next;
  }
  printf("%d\n",temp->i);
}
/**********************/
/* FUNCTION: PUSH     */
/**********************/
push(p,d)
TOPPOINT p;
DATA d;
{
  TOPPOINT p1;
  p1 = (TOPPOINT)malloc(sizeof(RECORD));
  p1->i = d;
  p1->next = p;
  p = p1;
  temp = p;
}
/***************************/
/* FUNCTION: INIT_POINTER */
/* used for sample input  */
/***************************/
init_pointer()
{
  int j;
  list = NULL;
  list = (TOPPOINT)malloc(sizeof(RECORD));
  list->i = 0;
  temp = list;
  for (j=1;j<11;j++)
  {
    list->next = (TOPPOINT)malloc(sizeof(RECORD));
    list = list->next;
    list->i = j;
  }
  list->next = NULL;
  list = temp;
  printf("Before Push Function :\n");
  while (temp->next != NULL)
  {
    printf("%d\n",temp->i);
    temp = temp->next;
  }
  printf("%d\n",temp->i);
}


/****************/
/* INCLUDE FILE */
/****************/
#define NULL 0
```

```
typedef int DATA;
struct stack{
  DATA i;
  struct stack *next;
};
typedef struct stack RECORD;
typedef RECORD *TOPPOINT;


/**********/
/* OUTPUT */
/**********/
Before Push Function :
0
1
2
3
4
5
6
7
8
9
10
After Push Function :
20
0
1
2
3
4
5
6
7
8
9
10
```

■

## Trees

One of the most important concepts in computing is that of a tree, which consists of a finite set of nodes, typically these are records, with the following properties:

1. There is a unique record called the *root* node.

2. The other nodes form a collection of nonoverlapping trees (subtrees) whose own roots are called the children of the root and any root is called a parent of the roots of its subtrees. A node is called a leaf node if it has no children.

A *binary tree* is a tree that has the additional property that any node has at most two children. There are many ways to realize a binary tree, but the easiest is to think of each node as a record with three fields: a left pointer that points to the node's left child or has the value NULL if the node has no left child, a data field, and a right pointer that points to the node's right child or has the value NULL if the node has no right child.

Leaf nodes are then characterized by the fact that both of their pointer fields have the value NULL.

Binary trees are useful in that they permit rapid storage and retrieval of data. For example, if the root is considered level zero, its children level one, and so on, then a data item on level three will be reached by starting at the root and going left or right three times.

Another way to say this is that a data item on level three will be reached by going left or right log 8 (base 2) times ($2 ** 3 = 8$). Thus, if data can be stored in the correct locations in a tree for the application at hand, the programmer can realize significant time savings in searching for a particular data item. Suppose, for example, that 2,047 data items were ordered in an array in ascending order. When a particular data item was then sought, it would take on the average about 1,024 comparisons (lower values take less time, high values take more). On the other hand, if these same 2,047 data items could be arranged in a binary tree in such a way that left children always precede their parent, and right children always follow their parent, then the data items would fit in a binary tree and *any* data item could be located in 11=log 2,048 or fewer comparisons (because $1 + 2 + 2**2 + 2**3 +... + 2**10 = 2**11 - 1 = 2,047$). Taking 11 or fewer comparisons is certainly preferable to taking 1,024 on the average. The time savings become even more significant with the size of the data set—this is often written log n $<<$ n/2 for large n.

Not only is searching time greatly improved with binary trees, but insertion of extra data items is also done much more efficiently. When using a binary tree, the additional data item is simply inserted as a leaf in the tree after log n comparisons; but in a linear list, the additional item would still require an average of n/2 comparisons and then, to add insult to injury, the larger items all have to be moved up one. Significant data transfer is necessary to keep the data items ordered.

Of course, nothing comes totally free. Significant savings in computer time are generally paid for by the necessity to use more computer memory (space). In this case, space is needed to store the pointer fields in each record. Thus, if the data item takes the same amount of space as a pointer, then it would take three times as much space to store the same amount of real data. Usually, however, the data item might itself be an entire record of data, say, 80 characters, while each pointer might take only 8 bytes. In this case, 96 bytes would be needed for each data item instead of only 80 (16/80=20% increase in space), whereas an eight hundred-character data record with 8 bytes for each pointer will necessitate a 16/816=1.96% increase in space. Thus, it is clear that pointers are affordable in typical applications involving large records.

The following header file, bintree.h, will be useful in working with binary trees:

```
#define NULL 0
typedef int DATA;                          /*the data in each
                                           record will be an
                                           integer*/

struct node {                              /*left_child points
    struct node *left_child;               to something of
                                           type struct node */

    DATA i;
    struct node *right_child;
};
typedef struct node RECORD;                /* type struct node
                                           will be known as a
                                           RECORD */

typedef RECORD *BINTREE                     /* type RECORD
                                           will be known as a
                                           *BINTREE, i.e.
                                           BINTREE points to
                                           a RECORD */
```

Assume for a moment that the programmer has constructed a binary tree to fit the particular application at hand. Typically, there are three ways that are often used to record (often called visit) the values of the data items in the tree. These are called *tree traversal* methods. They are *preorder, postorder,* and *inorder* traversals defined as follows. (Each starts the process at the root.)

Preorder: If the node is a parent, visit it; then visit its left subtree followed by its right subtree (recursive definition for visits).

Postorder: Visit the left subtree, followed by the right subtree, followed by the node (starts with the root and is again a recursive definition for visits).

Inorder: Visit the left subtree, followed by the node itself (starts with the root), followed by the right subtree (recursive definition for visits).

Perhaps a more intuitive way to visualize these strategies for visits is in terms of the priority of parents versus children. In a preorder strategy, a parent is visited before either of its children, and the left child before the right child—PARENT FIRST! A postorder strategy dictates that a left child and a right child (in that order) must both be visited before their parents—CHILDREN FIRST! An inorder strategy requires that a left child be visited before its parent, and a parent before its right child.

Because the definitions for these traversals are recursive in nature, the easiest algorithms to implement the visit strategies are also recursive.

■ **Example 9.4.11**
**Inorder traversal:**

```
#include "/usr/home/eharri/ch9/bintree.h"
BINTREE list, temp;
main()
{
  init_tree();
  inorder(list);
}

/***********************/
/* FUNCTION : INORDER */
/***********************/

inorder(pointer)
BINTREE pointer;
{
  if (pointer != NULL)
  {
    inorder(pointer->left_child);
    printf("%d\n",pointer->i);
    inorder(pointer->right_child);
  }
}

/************************/
/* FUNCTION : INIT_TREE */
/************************/
init_tree()
{
  int j;
  list = NULL;
  list = (BINTREE)malloc(sizeof(RECORD));
  list->i = 0;
  temp = list;
  for (j=1;j<11;j++)
  {
    list->left_child = (BINTREE)malloc(sizeof(RECORD));
    list = list->left_child;
    list->i = j;
  }
  list->left_child = NULL;
  list = temp;
  for (j=11;j<21;j++)
  {
    list->right_child = (BINTREE)malloc(sizeof(RECORD));
    list = list->right_child;
    list->i = j;
  }
  list->right_child = NULL;
  list = temp;
}

/*****************/
/* INCLUDED FILE */
/*****************/
#define NULL 0
typedef int DATA;
```

```
struct node{
  struct node *left_child;
  DATA i;
  struct node *right_child;
};
typedef struct node RECORD;
typedef RECORD *BINTREE;


/**********/
/* OUTPUT */
/**********/
10
9
8
7
6
5
4
3
2
1
0
11
12
13
14
15
16
17
18
19
20
```

■

■ **Example 9.4.12 Postorder traversal:**

```
#include "/usr/home/eharri/ch9/bintree.h"
BINTREE list, temp;
main()
{
  init_tree();
  postorder(list);
}

/************************/
/* FUNCTION : POSTORDER */
/************************/

postorder(pointer)
BINTREE pointer;
{
  if (pointer != NULL)
  {
    postorder(pointer->left_child);
    postorder(pointer->right_child);
    printf("%d\n",pointer->i);
  }
}

/************************/
/* FUNCTION : INIT_TREE */
/************************/
init_tree()
{
  int j;
  list = NULL;
  list = (BINTREE)malloc(sizeof(RECORD));
  list->i = 0;
```

```
temp = list;
for (j=1;j<11;j++)
{
  list->left_child = (BINTREE)malloc(sizeof(RECORD));
  list = list->left_child;
  list->i = j;
}
list->left_child = NULL;
list = temp;
for (j=11;j<21;j++)
{
  list->right_child = (BINTREE)malloc(sizeof(RECORD));
  list = list->right_child;
  list->i = j;
}
list->right_child = NULL;
list = temp;
}


/*****************/
/* INCLUDED FILE */
/*****************/
#define NULL 0
typedef int DATA;
struct node{
  struct node *left_child;
  DATA i;
  struct node *right_child;
};
typedef struct node RECORD;
typedef RECORD *BINTREE;

/***********/
/* OUTPUT */
/***********/
10
9
8
7
6
5
4
3
2
1
20
19
18
17
16
15
14
13
12
11
0
```

**■ Example 9.4.13
Preorder traversal**

```
#include "/usr/home/eharri/ch9/bintree.h"
BINTREE list, temp;
main()
{
  init_tree();
  preorder(list);
}

/***********************/
/* FUNCTION : PREORDER */
/***********************/

preorder(pointer)
BINTREE pointer;
{
  if (pointer != NULL)
  {
    printf("%d\n",pointer->i);
    preorder(pointer->left_child);
    preorder(pointer->right_child);
  }
}

/************************/
/* FUNCTION : INIT_TREE */
/************************/
init_tree()
{
  int j;
  list = NULL;
  list = (BINTREE)malloc(sizeof(RECORD));
  list->i = 0;
  temp = list;
  for (j=1;j<11;j++)
  {
    list->left_child = (BINTREE)malloc(sizeof(RECORD));
    list = list->left_child;
    list->i = j;
  }
  list->left_child = NULL;
  list = temp;
  for (j=11;j<21;j++)
  {
    list->right_child = (BINTREE)malloc(sizeof(RECORD));
    list = list->right_child;
    list->i = j;
  }
  list->right_child = NULL;
  list = temp;
}


/******************/
/* INCLUDED FILE */
/******************/
#define NULL 0
typedef int DATA;
struct node{
  struct node *left_child;
  DATA i;
  struct node *right_child;
};
typedef struct node RECORD;
typedef RECORD *BINTREE;
```

```
/**********/
/* OUTPUT */
/**********/
0
1
2
3
4
5
6
7
8
9
10
11
12
13
14
15
16
17
18
19
20
```

■

Of course, to use any of these visit strategies it is necessary to have previously constructed the tree. The next example will do this by starting with an array of integer values, say a[0], a[1], a[2], ..., and mapping them into the data fields of a binary tree. The root will be a[0], and in general the children of a[j] will be a[2*j+1] and a[2*j+2].

■ **Example 9.4.14**

```
#include "/usr/home/eharri/ch9/bintree.h"
BINTREE result;
int array[12], num = 0, s = 10;
BINTREE get_space(), get_record(), make_tree();

/*******************************/

main()
{
  result = make_tree(array,num,s);
}

/*******************************/
/* FUNCTION: GET_SPACE         */
/*******************************/

BINTREE get_space()
{
  return((BINTREE)malloc(sizeof(RECORD)));
}

/*******************************/
/* FUNCTION: GET_RECORD        */
/*******************************/

BINTREE get_record(i1,p1,p2)
DATA i1;
BINTREE p1,p2;
{
  BINTREE p;
  p = get_space();
  p->i = i1;
```

```
  p->left_child = p1;
  p->right_child = p2;
  return(p);
}

/*******************************/
/* FUNCTION MAKE_TREE          */
/*******************************/
BINTREE make_tree(a,i,size)
int i, size, a[];
{
  if (i >= size)
    return(NULL);
  else
    return(get_record(a[i],make_tree(a,2*i+1,size),make_tree(a,2*i+2,size)));
}


/*****************/
/* INCLUDED FILE */
/*****************/
#define NULL 0
typedef int DATA;
struct node{
  struct node *left_child;
  DATA i;
  struct node *right_child;
};
typedef struct node RECORD;
typedef RECORD *BINTREE;
```
■

### Nonbinary Tree

The final topic in this section will involve trees that are not necessarily binary (a parent may have many children). These trees are not efficiently implemented using records with pointer fields simply because the maximum number of pointer fields necessary may not be predictable in advance, and even if it is, it is quite inefficient to set aside storage to accommodate what may be a rare occurrence.

Instead, the technique will be to represent such trees using an array and linked lists; the array p will permit random access, in that p[i] will be a pointer to the i+1th record (one convenient way to count i is simply by preorder) with p[0] pointing to the root. Additionally, each leftmost child will be the beginning of a linked list of siblings (permitting sequential access), terminated with the NULL pointer.

To begin the discussion, let us establish a general header file, called gentree.h, for nonbinary trees:

```
#define NULL 0
typedef int DATA;
struct node    {
```

```
          DATA leftchild;              /* index of node of
                                          left child */
          DATA i;                      /* value of data */
          struct node *sibling;        /* pointer to the
                                          next sibling */
     }
     typedef struct node RECORD;
     typedef RECORD *GENTREE;
     GENTREE get_space()              /* return a pointer
                                         to a sufficient
                                         amount of memory
                                         to hold a
                                         RECORD*/

     {
          return((GENTREE) malloc(sizeof(RECORD)));
     }
     GENTREEget_record(firstborn,i1,brothers)
                                      /*return a pointer to
                                         a RECORD holding
                                         value of i1 */
     DATA firstborn;                  /* pass the number
                                         of the left child! */
     DATA i1;                         /* the actual DATA
                                         in the record*/
     GENTREE brothers;                /* pass the pointer
                                         to the record's first
                                         sibling*/
     {
          GENTREE p;
          p = get_space();            /* get space for new
                                         record*/
          *p.i = i1;                  */ store the data*/
          *p.left_child=firstborn;
          *p.sibling=brothers;
          return(p);
     }
```

■ **Example 9.4.15**   This example shows how to construct a nonbinary tree with array p and p[0] pointing to the node with value one hundred (root). The leftchild field in each node will be set to an array index, even if there is no left child. The value within the array will simply be set to NULL in that case.

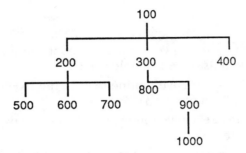

Following the same terminology, p[0] will point to the root (100), p[1] to 100's left child, p[2] to 200's left child, p[3] to 500's left child, and so on, and finally p[10] to 400's left child. Here is the complete program:

```
/***************************/
/*  CHAPTER 9    9.4.15.C  */
/***************************/
#include "/usr/home/eharri/ch9/gentree.h"
GENTREE get_space(), get_record();

main()
{
  GENTREE p[10];
  p[0] = get_record(1,100,NULL);
  p[1] = get_record(2,200,NULL);
  p[1] = get_record(6,300,NULL);
  p[1]->sibling->sibling = get_record(10,400,NULL);
  p[10] = NULL;
  p[2] = get_record(3,500,NULL);
  p[3] = NULL;
  p[2]->sibling = get_record(4,600,NULL);
  p[4] = NULL;
  p[2]->sibling->sibling = get_record(5,700,NULL);
  p[5] = NULL;
  p[6] = get_record(7,800,NULL);
  p[7] = NULL;
  p[6]->sibling = get_record(8,900,NULL);
  p[8] = get_record(9,1000,NULL);
  p[9] = NULL;
}

/*********************************************/
GENTREE get_space()
{
  return((GENTREE)malloc(sizeof(RECORD)));
}

/*********************************************/
GENTREE get_record(firstborn,i1,brothers)
DATA firstborn, i1;
GENTREE brothers;
{
```

```
GENTREE p;
p = get_space();
p->i = i1;
p->leftchild = firstborn;
p->sibling = brothers;
return(p);
}
```

## EXERCISES 9.4

1. Write a recursive routine to count the number of records in a linked list (see Example 9.4.2).

2. Write a recursive routine to print the INFO fields in a linked list (see Example 9.4.3).

3. Write a recursive routine to concatenate two linked lists (see Example 9.4.4).

4. Write a generalized routine to handle the case of Example 9.4.5 in which p1 and/or p2 are NULL.

5. Draw pictures to visualize the before and after results of the four fundamental stack operation functions.

6. Write a C function that takes a string of chars stored in an array, pushes them onto a stack, then pops them from the stack back into the array, but in reverse order.

7. Visit the nodes of *the following tree* using preorder, postorder, and inorder strategies:

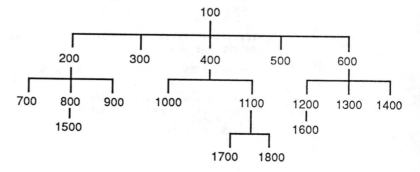

8. Write nonrecursive algorithms that implement the preorder, postorder, and inorder visits for a binary tree.

9. Test Example 9.4.14 with data by combining the functions into a single program.

10. Write code similar to that in Example 9.4.15 to implement the following nonbinary tree:

## 9.5 | *FIELDS AND UNIONS*

A union has essentially the same syntax as a structure except that the keyword *union* replaces *struct.* This single change in syntax forces a single member of the union to be chosen at a given time, and all alternatives for the members will share memory, but not at the same time, that is, different kinds of data can share the same storage area. The amount of memory set aside is the amount necessary to hold the member needing the largest number of bytes. For instance, a double requires more memory than a float, and hence if the declaration is as follows then memory will be set aside to hold a double:

```
union double_or_float {
     double d;
     float f;
} flex;
```

The members of a union are accessed in the same way as those of a structure. So, flex.d accesses the stored value as a double, while flex.f accesses it as a float. Alternatively, if the declaration

```
union double_or_float *pointer;
```

is made, then pointer→d accesses the stored value as a double, while pointer→f accesses it as a float. In any case, the programmer has the responsibility to make the appropriate choice of d or f as the situation dictates. Unions may also appear within structures and arrays as the following example shows.

■ **Example 9.5.1:** Here are two programs with only slightly different statements:

```
/*     CHAPTER 9    9.5.1.C     */


struct{
  int part_number;
  union{
    int    sales_price;
    float  fsales_price;
    char   *description;
  }price;
}info[10];

main()
{
 info[3].price.description = "hammer";
 printf("sales_price = %c\n",*info[3].price.description);
}


/**********/
/* OUTPUT */
/**********/
sales_price = h
```

```
/*      CHAPTER 9    9.5.1.C    */

struct{
  int part_number;
  union{
    int    sales_price;
    float fsales_price;
    char  *description;
  }price;
}info[10];

main()
{
 info[3].price.sales_price = 5;
 printf("sales_price = %d\n",info[3].price.sales_price);
}


/**********/
/* OUTPUT */
/**********/
sales_price = 5
```
■

A *field* is a member of a structure (occupying adjacent bits) that has a bit length specified by following its name with a colon (:) and a non-negative integer constant. This technique permits the programmer to pack information more tightly, compatible with the data, than is normally possible. There are several rules to remember though:

1. The bits assigned to each field are packed in a left-to-right or right-to-left order by the hardware.
2. A single field cannot use more bits than required for a single int.
3. A field might be restricted in a particular implementation to be of type unsigned int, but certain compilers place no restrictions on the data type.
4. An array of fields cannot be defined.
5. Fields cannot have pointers pointing to them.
6. The address operator (&) cannot be applied to a field.
7. Fields can be unnamed and simply used for padding to fill out a word or, alternatively, the special field width of zero forces the next field to begin at the next int.

■ **Example 9.5.2**   Notice the space savings when a 32-bit word is divided into seven fields as follows with two full words making a single structure:

```
struct personal_data {
    unsigned age:4;                    /*age from 0(0000) to 15(1111) */
    unsigned height: 6;                /*height from 0 to 127*/
    unsigned worth: 5;                 /*worth from 0 to 63 dollars*/
    unsigned month: 4;                 /*month from 0 to 15*/
```

```
      unsigned number_of_siblings:3;        /*from 0 to 7*/
      unsigned gender:1:                     /* 1=female, 0=male*/
      unsigned         :9;                   /*align to the next word*/
      float parent_worth;                    /*size of float is 32 bits*/
}
struct personal_data x;                      /*now for the assignments*/
x.age = 12;
x.height=27;
x.worth=63;
x.month=11;
x.number_of_siblings=2;
x.gender=1;                                  /*she is female*/
x.parent_worth=99.45;
```

Here is the complete program with output:

```
/*      CHAPTER 9    9.5.2.C    */
struct personal_data{
  unsigned age: 4;
  unsigned height: 6;
  unsigned worth: 5;
  unsigned month: 4;
  unsigned number_of_siblings: 3;
  unsigned gender: 1;
  unsigned         : 9;
  float parent_worth;
};
struct personal_data x;

main()
{
  x.age                = 12;
  x.height             = 27;
  x.worth              = 63;
  x.month              = 11;
  x.number_of_siblings = 2;
  x.gender             = 1;
  x.parent_worth       = 99.45;
  printf("age                  = %d\n",x.age);
  printf("height               = %d\n",x.height);
  printf("worth                = %d\n",x.worth);
  printf("month                = %d\n",x.month);
  printf("number of siblings = %d\n",x.number_of_siblings);
  printf("gender               = %d\n",x.gender);
  printf("parent worth         = %.2f\n",x.parent_worth);
}

/**********/
/* OUTPUT */
/**********/
age                 = 12
height              = 27
worth               = 31
month               = 11
number of siblings = 2
gender              = 1
parent worth        = 99.45
```

■

## EXERCISES 9.5

1. Define appropriate structures to handle the following data: (for faculty) year_started, rank, salary; (for students) age, credits_ earned, present_classes Now define a union that permits the user to select one of these structures. Finally, define a personnel_ record that has as its members: name, address, and the union specified above.

2. Binary coded decimal notation uses four bits to represent a single digit ranging from 0 to 9: 0000=0, 0001=1, 0010=2,...,1001=9 Write functions using fields that convert back and forth from BCD to binary. For example 0000 0101 1001 0110 0111 0100 0001 0011 is converted back to 05967413, while 23945868 would be converted back to 0010 0011 1001 0100 0101 1000 0110 1000.

3. Write a function which can be passed any float and which will in turn print out its bit representation.

4. Write a program which prints the bit representation of all characters.

## 9.6 | CHAPTER SUMMARY

## EXERCISES 9.5

1. Structures permit the user to group nonhomogeneous data together and to access individual members with the "." operator.

2. A structure can be stored as a component of an array or structures can be linked together by defining one or more of the members of a structure as pointers to the structure itself.

3. If a bit length is specified for an individual member of a structure, then that member is called a field.

4. The purpose of a union is to permit members of a structure to share common storage.

5. Structures may be declared with an optional structure tag name.

6. Structures may be declared with an optional structure tag name without any declaration of variables of that data type until later in the program.

7. External and static structures may be initialized.

8. Nested structures are permitted, that is, a member of a structure may itself be a structure.

9. A member of a structure may be accessed by declaring a pointer to the structure and then using pointer→member, with an appropriate choice of pointer and member.

10. The operators having the highest precedence are →, ., (), and [ ].

11. C permits the programmer to rename data types with user-defined names (particularly useful for structures) with the typedef statement.

12. A programmer is only guaranteed to be able to access a member of a structure and to be able to take the address of a structure. All other structure operations are system dependent.

# CHAPTER  10

## UNIX System Calls and the UNIX C Library

**10.1** | ***INTRODUCTION***

It is now time to expand upon the various tools that can be used in the construction of a C program. These fall into three categories, as stated in Chapter 1:

1.  Built-in functions, called UNIX C functions, that cannot stand alone, but rather must be part of a C program

    a.  Type I UNIX C functions. These are *system calls* and are part of UNIX itself. There are about 60 and they should be standard on every UNIX, or UNIX look-alike, system. System calls provide the interface between application programs plus shell and UNIX utilities and the "kernel" of UNIX, which performs low-level operating system services. The kernel communicates with the hardware and peripherals. System calls are available to C programs automatically and without the necessity of declaring them in the C program.

    b.  Type II UNIX C functions. These are *library functions,* are add-ons to the operating system, and typically use system calls to perform their tasks. They may not be standard across UNIX systems, although they in fact often are. Some but not all of the library functions must be declared in the C program to make them available, and/or compiler options must be stated for the cc compiler on the command line itself.

2.  UNIX commands or sequences of UNIX commands stored in a file called a shell script can stand alone in UNIX and can also be called from a C program. In fact, they are called via one of the library functions, the special one that is named system.

3.  User-written functions

In addition to the powerful "hooks" from C into UNIX described above, it is quite easy to run a C program mixed within a sequence of UNIX commands stored in a file. This is often done, for example, to make a C program interactive.

The intention in this chapter is not to give a complete synopsis of all the system calls or the library functions that are available, but rather to provide insights into how they are used, considerations to take into account, and other related matters. To this end, only certain of the UNIX C functions will be explored. The reader can find out about the others by referring to the appropriate UNIX manual.

All of the Type I UNIX C functions (system calls) are automatically made available to any C program by UNIX itself. The user does have to know the type of value returned (if any), the number and type of arguments needed (if any), and whether external variables and header files are needed. Type I Unix C functions are documented in Section 2 of the System V UNIX Programmer's Manual. Thus, for example, the system call named access() will appear in the manual under the heading access(2).

Some of the Type II UNIX functions (library functions), on the other hand, are not *automatically* made available to a C program by UNIX. That is to say, some require the user to invoke a particular preprocessor #include directive inside the C program and/or give special options to the cc compiler on the command line. The various possibilities will be discussed in this chapter.

It should be noted that the library functions may actually use, or call (without the programmer's knowledge), the system calls to do their work. Also note that Type II UNIX C functions are documented in Sections 3 through 6 of the UNIX Programmer's Manual. Section 3 is further divided into subsections labeled 3C, 3F, 3M, 3S, and 3X. Incidentally, Section 1 of the UNIX Programmer's Manual documents the UNIX utilities that can be entered at the command line.

There are generally five major groupings of functions. These groupings do not coincide with Sections 1 through 6 of the manual. In fact, some functions in groups 1 and 2 are the same ones. (The basic I/O package is part of the standard C library.) Here are the five groupings, and they are not mutually exclusive:

Group 1. These functions found in Sections 3C, 2, and 3S of the UNIX manual constitute the *standard C library (libc)* and are automatically loaded by the cc compiler without any #include directive. The necessary declarations and headers for some of these functions must be obtained by putting the appropriate #include directive within the C program.

Group 2. Section 3S is part of the standard C library and constitutes the *basic I/O package*. The declarations for these functions may be obtained by putting

*#include <stdio.h>*

in the C program.

Group 3. Section 3M is the *mathematics library (libm)*. These functions are only loaded if the -lm option is given to the cc compiler, as in

*$ cc prog.c -lm*

The declarations for these functions may be obtained by putting

*#include <math.h>*

in the C program.

Group 4. Section 3X is the *specialized library*, which includes such functions as curses for CRT screen handling and plot for graphics interface routines. Various #include directives need to be given, and sometimes even compiler directives as, for example, with curses.

Group 5. Section 3F is the *Fortran library (libF77)* and these functions are automatically available to the Fortran compiler.

## 10.2 CHMOD(2), ACCESS(2), KILL(2), ERRNO, AND PERROR(3C)

This section will introduce the reader to two system calls, chmod(2) and kill(2), one library function perror(3C), and an external variable named errno. The system call access(2) will be explored and then studied in exercises.

### errno

Each time a system call is executed and for some reason is not able to faithfully perform its avowed purpose, the variable named errno of type int will be set to an otherwise impossible value (usually -1). (See intro(2) in the introduction to system calls and error numbers in the manual.) The value of this variable can be manually reset within a C program, but barring that kind of programmer intervention, errno simply retains its most recent value set after an unsuccessfully executed system call. If the programmer wishes to actually use errno in a program, the following declaration must be used:

*extern int errno;*

If that declaration is made, printf() references to errno in the program will simply print its int value (as expected). For example, if a system call has failed (say, errno==30 is true), the user will be forced to go to intro(2) to determine the symbolic representation and meaning of that value of errno. In this particular instance, intro(2) will indicate that error number 30 is associated with the symbolic representation EROFS (*error read only file system*), meaning that the user attempted to modify a file or directory for which he or she only had read permission. The intro(2) section of the manual lists values of errno that range from 1 to 45, and it is possible to use the symbolic representations in the program, rather than just the numbers, by including the header file <errno.h>:

```
#include <errno.h>
```

So, system calls may (and do!) fail to successfully execute, and then the programmer has four choices:

1. Omit the declaration of errno and the header file <errno.h> and have no idea exactly *why* a system call may have failed within a program. (Clearly this is *never* the preferred method!)

2. Include the declaration of errno *only* and set the option to printf() errno's int value in case a system call fails; then look in the manual for its associated symbolic representation and explanation. (For example, errno==27 is explained in intro(2) as "file too large.")

3. Include the declaration of errno and the header file <errno.h>; then, if a system call fails, use the value of errno *or* the symbolism in the program to decipher the meaning. (For example, if errno==27 *or* if errno==EFBIG could be used in the program.)

4. Use the library function perror(3C), which is the best way of all. It puts the last error message encountered by a system call at the disposal of the programmer (on the standard error output) by permitting the use of errno as the value of a subscript in the external array sys_errlist[] (which is an array of pointers to char) of all error messages. Perror(3C) also keeps track of the largest integer associated with an error in the external variable sys_nerr.

### chmod

Each of the four previous techniques will be illustrated here with the system call chmod(2). Note that there is also a UNIX command called chmod whose programming actually includes a call to chmod(2).

First, there will be a brief discussion of how the manual describes UNIX C functions. Each of the UNIX C functions is described in Sections 2 and 3 of the UNIX manual with the following headings:

1. name of the function with the section of the manual in parentheses, as in chmod(2)

2. NAME section giving the name of the function and its description, as in

    *NAME*

    *chmod--change mode of a file.*

3. SYNOPSIS section summarizing the data types of the function's parameters, the data type returned, and related functions and variables (none in this case), as in

    ```
    SYNOPSIS
        int chmod(path,mode)
        char *path;
        int mode;
    ```

4. DESCRIPTION section explaining what the function does and the associated error messages. For example, chmod(2) can fail with any of the following symbolic error messages: ENOTDIR==20 (illegal file name because a component of the path is not a searchable directory), ENOENT==2 (the file does not exist), EACCES==13 (no access granted on a component of the path), EPERM==1 (effective user ID does not match the owner of the file), EROFS==30 (the specified file is read only), or EFAULT==14 (the path is outside the allocated address space of the process).

    Access permission bits for chmod are: 04000—set user ID on execution; 02000—set group ID on execution; 00400—read by owner; 00200—write by owner; 00100—execute (search if a directory) by owner; 00070—read, write, and execute (search) by group; 00007—read, write, and execute (search) by others; and various combinations based on octal arithmetic.

5. other sections, such as SEE ALSO (related topics), BUGS, and DIAGNOSTICS (gives both the normal and the unsuccessful return values of the function in question)

The first example has code that might have chmod(2) failing, but the *reason* for failure would be unknown because no error checking is performed by the programmer. In the output shown, chmod(2) is successful because the given file is readable.

■ **Example 10.2.1**
```
#define READ 00400
main()
{
  char file[40];
  printf("This program permits the user to determine whether\n");
  printf("the access mode of a file is 'read' --\n");
  printf("enter the full pathname of the file now ");
  scanf("%80s",file);
  if (chmod(file,READ) == 0)
    printf("%s is readable.\n",file);
  else
    printf("%s might not be readable.\n",file);
}



/**********/
/* OUTPUT */
/**********/
This program permits the user to determine whether
the access mode of a file is 'read' --
enter the full pathname of the file now /usr/home/eharri/ch9/bintree.h
/usr/home/eharri/ch9/bintree.h is readable.                          ■
```

The second example uses errno to pinpoint the reason for failure of chmod(2), but the user would still have to go to the manual to find the symbolic representation associated with the integer error message "2" ENOENT (the file does not exist). Note that zero would be returned in the case that the file is readable—chmod is successful.

■ **Example 10.2.2**
```
#define READ 00400
main()
{
  char file[40];
  extern int errno;
  printf("This program permits the user to determine whether\n");
  printf("the access mode of a file is 'read' --\n");
  printf("enter the full pathname of the file now ");
  scanf("%80s",file);
  if (chmod(file,READ) == 0)
    printf("%s is readable.\n",file);
  else
  {
    printf("%s might not be readable.\n",file);
    printf("The value of errno is %d\n",errno);
  }
}



/**********/
/* OUTPUT */
/**********/
This program permits the user to determine whether
the access mode of a file is 'read' --
enter the full pathname of the file now /usr/home/eharri/ch10/nofile
/usr/home/eharri/ch10/nofile might not be readable.
The value of errno is 2
                                                                     ■
```

The third example shows how to use the symbolic representation to catch an error (say, ENOTDIR).

■ **Example 10.2.3**

```
#include <errno.h>
#define READ 00400
main()
{
  char file[40];
  extern int errno;
  printf("This program permits the user to determine whether\n");
  printf("the access mode of a file is 'read' --\n");
  printf("enter the full pathname of the file now ");
  scanf("%80s",file);
  if (chmod(file,READ) == 0)
    printf("%s is readable.\n",file);
  else
  {
    printf("%s might not be readable.\n",file);
    printf("The value of errno is %d\n",errno);
    if (errno = ENOTDIR)
      printf("one of the components of the path was not a directory\n");
  }
}


/**********/
/* OUTPUT */
/**********/
This program permits the user to determine whether
the access mode of a file is 'read' --
enter the full pathname of the file now /usr/hoem/eharri/ch10/testfile
/usr/hoem/eharri/ch10/testfile might not be readable.
The value of errno is 2
one of the components of the path was not a directory                    ■
```

### perror

The fourth example shows how to use perror(3C) to capture the description of any error associated with trying to determine whether a file is readable. The library function perror(3C) is in the standard C library. It has no return value (type void) and has as its argument a pointer to a char, typically the name of the system call:

*void perror(s)*

*char *s;*

The function perror() prints the string s, followed by a colon and a blank, then an error message and newline. All of this is printed on the standard error output, which by default is the terminal.

■ **Example 10.2.4**

```
#define READ 00400
main()
{
  char file[40];
  printf("This program permits the user to determine whether\n");
  printf("the access mode of a file is 'read' --\n");
  printf("enter the full pathname of the file now ");
  scanf("%80s",file);
  if (chmod(file,READ) == 0)
    printf("%s is readable.\n",file);
  else
  {
    printf("%s might not be readable.\n",file);
    perror("chmod");
  }
}


/**********/
/* OUTPUT */
/**********/
This program permits the user to determine whether
the access mode of a file is 'read' --
enter the full pathname of the file now /usr/home/eharri/ch10/testfile
/usr/home/eharri/ch10/testfile is readable.                            ■
```

Note that perror() is able to use the external variable errno because it is declared as an external variable in that function; it was not necessary to declare it again in the full program. Also note that perror() sends its output to the standard error not to the standard output. If the programmer wants the output to be redirected, he or she must redirect the standard output (file descriptor 2).

In the description of perror(3C), the synopsis includes references to external variables:

*extern int errno;*

*extern char *sys_errlist[];*

*extern int sys_nerr;*

It is not necessary to use or declare these external variables, but they are in the synopsis because they all relate to error processing. They can be used independently of perror(3C) itself. The external variable errno has already been discussed. The value of errno is often used as a subscript in the array sys_errlist, each of whose elements point to a char. For example, sys_errlist[1] points to the error message associated with an errno==1 (EPERM—not owner of file). The external variable sys_nerr is the largest value of errno provided for in the array. Be careful in that sys_nerr may have been updated on the system itself with new error codes, but not in the documentation.

## access

The system call access(2) is used to determine whether a file can be accessed for reading, writing, executing, existence, or any combination thereof. Its synopsis is as follows:

```
int access(path,amode)
char *path;
int amode;
```

Thus access requires two parameters, path and amode, where path is a pointer to a char and amode is an int with 00=existence, 01=execute (search), 02=write, and 04=read. So, for instance, access(myfile,04) tries to determine if myfile is readable. A value of errno will be automatically set if access(2) is unsuccessful. The function access(2) also returns 0 if it is successful, and −1 otherwise. Remember—access(2) is designed to be used to work with existing files, not to create new ones. This function gives the C programmer a way to determine whether a particular file can be accessed for a particular task.

The reader will recall that in UNIX each file has an associated owner, group, and others. If a C programmer uses access() on a particular file for which he or she belongs to the group or other categories, then the bit pattern is interpreted as the group or other mode bits, respectively. Exercises 10.2 ask the reader to write elementary programs using access(2).

## kill

The last system call studied in this section is kill(2) whose purpose is to send a signal to a process or group of processes. Its synopsis is:

```
int kill(pid,sig)
int pid, sig;
```

Thus, kill() returns an integer (which as usual for system calls is 0 if successful and −1 otherwise) with the accompanying setting of errno. Reasons for an unsuccessful call include, among others, such cases as sig not being a valid signal number and/or no existing process corresponding to pid. The function kill() requires two integer parameters: pid is the process identification number of the process or group of processes and sig is either zero or the signal to be sent (the list is specified in signal(2) with possibilities ranging from 0 to 19). Because signal(2) is related to kill(2), signal(2) appears in the "SEE ALSO" section of kill(2).

There are protections built into the system so that kill cannot be executed willy nilly. Every user is identified by a positive integer called a real user ID. Every user is also a member of a group, which is identified by a positive integer called a real group ID. Every process then has a real user ID and a real group ID that are simply the real user ID and the real group ID of whoever created the process. In addition, every process has an effective user ID and an effective group ID. The effective user ID and the effective group ID of a process are typically identical to the real user ID and the real group ID of that process. However, it is possible that the effective user ID and the effective group ID of a process are not the same as the real user ID and the real group ID of that process. This happens if that process or an ancestor of it evolved from a file that had the set-user ID or set-group ID bit set.

For example, chmod(myfile,04000) sets the user ID of myfile while chmod(myfile,02000) sets the group ID of myfile. In the first case, a subsequent call to execl(2) with myfile as the first parameter would then set the effective user ID of the new process created to the owner ID of myfile. In the latter case, a subsequent call to execl(2) with myfile as the first parameter would set the effective group ID of the new process created to the group ID of myfile.

To use kill(2), the real or effective user ID of the sending process in which kill() is embedded must match the real or effective user ID of the receiving process unless the effective user ID of the sending process is the superuser. Lack of these conditions causes failure—a return of the value $-1$. In other words, processes can only receive signals if the sending process has the same effective user as the receiving process, or is a superuser. This provides protection from signals being sent willy nilly to any process. Without this protection chaos would reign!

The system called getpid(2) that appears in the "SEE ALSO" section of kill(2) has as its purpose to return the process ID of the calling process, which has no arguments: int getpid().

Suppose a user has a program running with unknown pid that he or she wishes to generate the interrupt signal—SIGINT==02—see signal(2)—when x==20000. The following will do the job:

■ **Example 10.2.5**

```
main()
{
    int x=10;
    for (; x > 0; )
    {
                                      /*do something with
                                      x here*/
```

```
if (x ==20000)
     kill(getpid(),02);
```
/*get the process id of the calling process and send signal 02——the interrupt signal*/

/* exit(1); would do just as well—the system call exit(2)—Section 2 of the manual—terminates the program and returns the value of the argument—arbitrarily chosen to be 1 here*/

```
     }
}
```
/*end for */

■

## EXERCISES 10.2

1. Write a C program that uses the external variable sys_nerr and external array sys_errlist[] to print out the error messages associated with the various possible values of errno.

2. Look up the system call access(2), which is used to determine accessibility to a file. Now write a program that lets the user input a name of a file and:
   a. determine whether the file is writable with no error checking
   b. determine whether the file is writable with errno only used for error checking
   c. determine whether the file is writable using perror(3C)
   d. determine whether the file is writable using *sy_errlist[]

3. List all the header files (those that end with .h) in /usr/include/ yours, where yours==your login identification number.

4. Look up the system call mknod(2) in the UNIX manual and specify the number of arguments, the type of each argument, the type of value returned, and the number of possible values that errno can be set to.

5. Look in intro(2) for the definitions of proc0 and proc1. Then look at kill(2) to determine how proc0 and proc1 may be excluded from the kill(2) function.

## 10.3 MORE SYSTEM CALLS FOR INPUT AND OUTPUT: CREAT(2), OPEN(2), CLOSE(2), READ(2), WRITE(2), AND LSEEK(2)

This section will primarily deal with the system calls that allow programmers to do low-level file input and output. These system calls should not be expected to be in non-UNIX operating systems. Without a program, there may be a need to be able to:

1. create files or prepare them to be rewritten

   [creat(2)]

2. open files for reading or writing or both [open(2)]
3. close files [close(2)]
4. read from files that have been opened for reading [read(2)]
5. write to files that have been opened for writing [write(2)]
6. move through an opened file without reading or writing [lseek(2)]

Within a given C program, there may be as many as 20 files open at once, numbered consecutively from 0 to 19 with an integer called a *file descriptor*. Three of these files are always open in any C program: the standard input with file descriptor 0, the standard output with file descriptor 1, and the standard error with file descriptor 2. The first file that is explicitly opened or created in a program is assigned file descriptor 3, the second 4, and so on. Once a file descriptor (*filedes*) has been assigned to a file in a program, that file descriptor is always used to refer to that file in read, write, close, and lseek system calls. In addition, the parameter "mode" uses 0 for read, 1 for write, and 2 for read and write. The name of the file is pointed to by the pointer variable named path.

Here are the various synopses, return values, and comments:

```
int creat (path, mode)
char *path;
int mode;                    /* path is a character string
                             specifying the file; mode is a 3-digit
                             octal code specifying the protection
                             assigned to the owner, group, and
                             others; returns a file descriptor
                             when successful and −1 otherwise;
                             if the file already existed, it is
                             truncated to length 0 */
```

```
int open (path, mode)
char *path;
int mode                    /* mode of 0 is for read, 1 for write,
                               and 2 for both; returns a file
                               descriptor when successful and −1
                               otherwise */

int close (filedes)
int filedes;                /* returns 0 if successful and −1
                               otherwise */

int read (filedes, buf, nbytes)
int fildes;
char *buf;
unsigned nbytes;            /* returns the number of bytes read
                               if successful, 0 if end of file has
                               been reached, or −1 otherwise
                               (plus it sets errno). The read is into
                               a buffer pointed to by buf which
                               must be defined by the programmer.
                               The read also causes the pointer to
                               advance in preparation for another
                               read. At most one line can be read if
                               fildes is 0 (standard input)*/

int write (filedes, buf, nbytes)
int fildes;
char *buf;
unsigned nbytes;            /* returns the number of bytes
                               written if successful or −1
                               otherwise (plus it sets errno). The
                               write is from a buffer pointed to by
                               buf which must be defined by the
                               programmer. The write also causes
                               the pointer to advance in
                               preparation for another write */

long lseek (filedes,offset,whence)
int filedes;
long offset;
int whence;                  /* moves the read/write file pointer
                               of the file with file descriptor filedes
                               offset bytes measured from: the
                               beginning if whence is 0; the
```

current location if whence is 1; the end if whence is 2. Returns the number of bytes from the beginning that file pointer is positioned on (if successful) and −1 otherwise (plus sets errno). */

■ **Example 10.3.1**   The following program creates a file named myfile with read, write, and execute permission for the owner; execute only for the group; and execute only for the others. In the program itself, this file is known by the integer value (file descriptor) of fd.

```
main()
{
  int fd;
  fd = creat("myfile",0711);
  system("ls -al myfile");
}

/**********/
/* OUTPUT */
/**********/
-rwx--x--x   1 eharri   student        0 Dec 14 18:51 myfile        ■
```

■ **Example 10.3.2**   The following program opens myfile for reading and writing:

```
int fd;
main()
{
  fd = open("myfile",2);
  system("ls -al myfile");
}

/**********/
/* OUTPUT */
/**********/
-rwx--x--x   1 eharri   student        0 Dec 14 18:51 myfile        ■
```

■ **Example 10.3.3**   The following program opens myfile for reading and then immediately closes it:

```
int fd;
main()
{
  fd = open("myfile",0);
  close(fd);
}
```
                                                                    ■

■ **Example 10.3.4**   The following program opens myfile for reading and then reads 50 characters into the buffer named buff:

```
/*    CHAPTER 10  10.3.4.C   */

int fd;
char buff[50];
main()
{
  fd = open("myfile",0);
  read(fd,buff,50);
  printf("%s\n",buff);
}


/**********/
/* OUTPUT */
/**********/
The following 50 characters will be read into the
```
■

■ **Example 10.3.5**   The following program opens myfile for reading, reads 50 characters of myfile into buff, opens myfile2 for writing, and then writes those 50 characters into myfile2:

```
/*   CHAPTER 10  10.3.5.C  */

int fd1, fd2;
char buff[50];

main()
{
  fd1 = open("myfile",0);
  read(fd1,buff,50);
  fd2 = open("myfile2",1);
  write(fd2,buff,50);
  close(fd1);
  close(fd2);
}


/***********/
/* MYFILE2 */
/***********/
The following 50 characters will be read into the
```
■

■ **Example 10.3.6**   The following program opens myfile for reading, and moves the pointer to 10 characters from the end of myfile:

```
/*    CHAPTER 10   10.3.6.C    */

main()
{
  int fd;
  long where;
  fd = open("myfile",0);
  where = lseek(fd,10,2);
  printf("where = %d\n",where);
}
```
■

Before looking at any more examples of the use of these system calls, the reader should review how to use command line arguments, argc and argv. The number of arguments on a command line is declared as

```
int argc; /*always at least one*/
```

and the first characters of the arguments themselves are pointed to by an array of pointers declared as

```
char *argv[];
```

Thus,

**$ cc prog1.c file1**

has argc==3, argv[0] points to the first c in cc, argv[1] points to the p in prog1.c, and argv[2] points to the f in file1. Because argv[1] is a pointer to p, argv[1][0] has value p itself, and so on.

The first example will open an existing file, change every character to uppercase, and print the contents back to a new file.

■ **Example 10.3.7**

```
/*      CHAPTER 10    10.3.7.C    */

#include <ctype.h>
#define SIZE 5

main(argc,argv)
int argc;
char *argv[];
{
  int fd1, fd2;
  char buff[SIZE], hold[SIZE];
  int i;
  int j;
  if (argc != 3)
  {
    printf("wrong number of arguments for prog %s\n",argv[0]);
    exit(2);
  }
  if ((fd1= open(argv[1],0)) == -1)
  {
    perror(argv[0]);
    exit(3);
  }
  fd2 = creat(argv[2],1);
  while ((i = read(fd1,buff,SIZE)) > 0)
  {
    for (j=0;j<=SIZE;j++)
      hold[j] = toupper(buff[j]);
    write(fd2,hold,i);
  }
  close(fd1);
  close(fd2);
}


/***************/
/* INPUT FILE */
/***************/
The following 50 characters will be read into the
buffer named buff.
```

```
/***************/
/* OUTPUT FILE */
/***************/
THE FOLLOWING 50 CHARACTERS WILL BE READ INTO THE
BUFFER NAMED BUFF.
```
∎

## EXERCISES 10.3

1. Write a program that will open any file, find the first character of the file, the last character, and the middle character, and print them in that order.

2. Write a program that will open any file and prints the contents of that file to another file where each successive set of 25 characters is printed in reverse order on separate lines. Any leftover characters should be printed in the order read, not reverse order, on the last line.

3. Write a program that will take any two files and concatenate them together into one big file. Make your program so the user can decide which file is the first part of the big file.

4. Write a program that will take all the files in a specified directory, sort them by name, and then zap every other file to length zero.

## 10.4 THE STANDARD I/O LIBRARY: FOPEN(3S), FCLOSE(3S), GETC(3S), PUTC(3S), FPRINTF(3S), PRINTF(3S), AND OTHERS

This section will describe a set of *standard* I/O functions (Section 3S of the UNIX manual) that is basically standard across full implementations of C. These functions can be used in lieu of the low-level system calls described in Section 10.3 that *demand* a UNIX implementation. It is often the case that the standard I/O functions (approximately 25–30 in number) have been programmed to do their work by making calls to the system calls that were described in Section 10.3. Their real advantage is that they use a buffered approach so that reading or writing is done from (or to) a buffer rather than performing a disk access for each input/ output operation. There are many important points to be covered in this section, and they will be handled systematically and methodically.

The first question to be answered is, *how is a programmer able to access the standard I/O library from within a C program?* Answer: At the very minimum, the programmer must include in the program the file named stdio.h, which contains a set of definitions that all such standard I/O functions will use:

```
#include <stdio.h>
```

The second question is then, *what exactly is in the file stdio.h?* The UNIX utility cat will reveal this.

**$ `cat /usr/include/stdio.h`**

Answer: Several pieces of information are in stdio.h, including a structure that describes a FILE; the definitions of standard input, standard output, and standard error; the definitions of NULL and EOF; declarations of various functions; various preprocessor #define statements; the buffer size; and other information (dependent on the system).

For example, on the author's system the size of the buffer used for input and output is defined as follows to be 1,024 bytes:

*#define BUFSIZ 1024*

A file, on the other hand, is defined to be a structure consisting of two fields, _cnt and *ptr:

```
typedef struct {
    int _cnt;
    unsigned char *_ptr:
} FILE;
```

The field _cnt counts the number of bytes remaining in the buffer as measured by _ptr, which points to the current position in the buffer. Thus, the first getc() in a C program (the standard I/O equivalent of the read system call) will fill the buffer with the first 1,024 characters in the file, set _cnt to 1,024, set _ptr to point to the first char in the buffer, read that first char, and then decrement _cnt to 1,023 while advancing _ptr to point to the second char in the buffer.

The identifiers NULL and EOF are often defined to be 0 and 1 respectively as follows:

*#define NULL 0*
*#define EOF (-1)*

The maximum number of files that can be opened is defined as 20 as specified by _NFILE (if not previously defined):

*#ifndef    _NFILE*
*#define    _NFILE    20*

An array named _iob is defined as an array of FILEs as follows:

*extern FILE    _iob[_NFILE];*

At the same time, standard input, standard output, and standard error are indexed to be the addresses of the initial three files in this array:

```
#define stdin  (&_iob[0])
#define stdout (&_iob[1])
#define stderr (&_iob[2])
```

Additional definitions in stdio.h are such things as the return values of functions in the package including:

```
extern FILE *fopen();      /* the function fopen() returns a
                              pointer to FILE */

extern int fclose();       /* the function fclose() returns
                              an int */
```

Finally, the standard I/O functions getchard() and putchar() are implemented as macros if stdio.h is included; this is because of the following preprocessor directives in stdio.h:

```
#define getchar()  getc(stdin)
#define putchar(x) putc((x),stdout)
```

There are thus many different statements in stdio.h and the interested reader is encouraged to study them in detail. The examples given here are certainly not exhaustive.

The third question to be answered is, *what exactly are the standard I/O functions in the standard I/O library that can be accessed from within a C program?* Answer: There are approximately 25–30 such functions made available by the inclusion of stdio.h depending on the system, and they might have the following synopses:

### Function 1

```
char *ctermid(s)
char *s;
```

> /* ctermid() generates the filename for the terminal that is controlling the current process by returning a pointer to the appropriate char array*/

■ **Example 10.4.1**    This program returns a pointer to /dev/tty5 and any subsequent file references to terminal then automatically refer to the terminal.

Here is a program using ctermid:

```
/*   CHAPTER 10   10.4.1.C   */

char terminal[10];
main()
{
  strcpy(terminal,ctermid("/dev/tty5"));
  printf("terminal = %s\n",terminal);
}



/**********/
/* OUTPUT */
/**********/
terminal = /dev/tty
```

## Function 2

```
char *cuserid(s)

char *s;
```

/* cuserid() gets the character login name that the owner of the current process is logged in under*/

■ **Example 10.4.2**   Here is a program using cuserid:

```
/*   CHAPTER 10   10.4.2.C   */

char name[70];
main()
{
  strcpy(name,cuserid("/usr/home/eharri"));
  printf("%s\n",name);
}



/**********/
/* OUTPUT */
/**********/
eharri
```

## Function 3

```
int fclose(fptr)        /* and also fflush(fptr) */
FILE *fptr;
```

/* fclose() empties any buffers *and* breaks any connections to the file that fptr points to; it returns 0 if successful and −1 if unsuccessful, such as trying to write to a file that has not been opened for writing; fflush() has exactly the same synopsis and result except that *it does not break the connections to the file that fptr points to* */

## Function 4

```
int ferror(fptr)
```
/* and also feof(fptr), clearerr(fptr), and fileno(fptr) */

```
FILE *fptr;
```

/* all of these functions are implemented as macros in stdio.h— hence they cannot be declared or redeclared. The function ferror() returns nonzero when a previous read or write attempt generated an I/O error, and 0 otherwise; the function feof() returns nonzero when a previous read found EOF, and 0 otherwise; the function clearerr() resets the error indicator returned by ferror() and the EOF indicator both to 0; the function fileno() returns the file descriptor associated with fptr (the one returned by the system call open(2)) */

## Function 5

```
FILE *fopen(filename,filemode)
char *filename, *filemode;

FILE *freopen(filename,filemode,fptr)
char *filename, *filemode;
FILE *fptr;

FILE *fdopen(filedes,filemode)
int filedes;
char *filemode;
```

/* Each of these three functions opens a file and returns a pointer to FILE. The possible file modes are r (for read), w (for write), and a (for append). The file pointer returned points to the first char in the file if the mode is r or w (be careful about destroying the contents of the file in this case), and at the end of the file in the case of a (a NULL pointer is returned if unsuccessful). A mode of w or a will create the file if it does not presently exist. The function freopen permits the programmer to override the old value of fptr with the actual value of "filename" (and simultaneously closing the original file that fptr pointed to) thus eliminating the need to declare separate fptrs for each distinct file. This function can in fact be used to attach previously defined fptrs associated with stdin, stdout, or stderr to other files. The function fdopen permits the programmer to associate a fptr with a file descriptor (obtained from a system call such as open(2)).*/

## Function 6

```
int fread(ptr,size, nitems,fptr)          /*same
                                           synopsis for
                                           fwrite*/

char *ptr;
int size,nitems;
FILE *fptr;
```

/*These functions perform buffered binary input and output respectively. They return the number of items read or written respectively, and 0 if no read or write took place. The read is into an array pointed to by ptr; of nitems of data (each of length size); from the current position of fptr in the file.*/

■ **Example 10.4.3**

```
char a[80];
FILE *fptr, *fopen();
fptr=fopen("myfile","r");
```

/* i=fread(a,4,10,fptr); would be interpreted as reading ten 4 byte chunks from the current position of fptr into the array pointed to by a; normally then setting i to 40; and advancing fptr 40 bytes. If EOF or an error condition arises during the read then less than 40 bytes might be transferred. The fwrite() function writes from an array pointed to by ptr; of at most n items of data (each of length size again); to the current position of fptr in the file. Thus i=fwrite(a,4,10,fptr) would be interpreted as writing ten 4 byte chunks from the array pointed to by a into the file pointed to by fptr; normally then setting i to 40; and advancing fptr 40 bytes. If an error condition on fptr arises during the write then less than 40 bytes might be transferred.*/

Here is a complete program using fread:

```
/**************************/
/* CHAPTER 10   10.4.3.C  */
/**************************/
#include "stdio.h"

char a[80];
int i;
FILE *fptr;
main()
{
  fptr = fopen("myfile","r");
  i = fread(a,4,10,fptr);
  printf("%s\n",a);
}


/**********/
/* OUTPUT */
/**********/
THE FOLLOWING 50 CHARACTERS WILL BE READ
```

### Function 7

```
int fseek(fptr,offset,place)
FILE *fptr;
long offset;
int place;


void rewind(fptr)
FILE *fptr;


long ftell(fptr)
FILE *fptr;
```

/* fseek() moves the file pointer fptr to a specified position determined by the values of offset and place in the file where the next I/O operation will take place (if place is 0 then position fptr offset bytes from the beginning of the file; if place is 1 then position fptr offset bytes from the current position of fptr; if place is 2 then position fptr offset bytes from the end of the file); rewind() moves the file fptr to the beginning of the file; and ftell() returns the number of bytes that fptr is from the beginning of the file. These functions do no input or output—they simply permit the user to reposition fptr or find out where fptr is. The function fseek() will return 0 if it is successful and non-zero otherwise.*/

■ **Example 10.4.4**

*fseek(fptr,10L,2);*

positions fptr 10 bytes from the end of the file pointed to by fptr while

*fseek(fptr,0L,0);*

positions fptr 0 bytes from the beginning of the file pointed to by fptr which is the equivalent of

*rewind(fptr);*                                                         ■

## Function 8

```
int getc(fptr)
FILE *fptr;
```
/* getc() is a macro that returns the next byte from the file pointed to by fptr, stores it as an integer, and moves the file pointer fptr ahead one byte—it returns EOF if there is an error or end-of-file is reached. */

```
int getchar()

int fgetc(fptr)
FILE *fptr;
```
/* getchar() is also a macro and returns the next byte from the file pointed to by stdin—i.e., getchar() is defined as getc(stdin). On the other hand, fgetc() performs the same job as getc(), but does it as a function rather than as a macro—because fgetc() is a function it has the advantages of taking less memory per invocation than getc() and its name can be passed as an argument to a function, but a negative aspect is that it runs more slowly. */

```
int getw(fptr)
FILE *fptr;
```
/* getw() fetches the next word from the file pointed to by fptr, and then increments fptr to point to the next word (no alignment assumed). Because the size of a word varies from machine to machine (and is the size of an integer) special care should be taken when using getw(). */

**■ Example 10.4.5**  Programmers should be especially careful about storing the return values of any of the functions getc(), getchar(), fgetc(), and getw() in a variable of type char and then comparing it to the int value EOF because the comparison may not succeed due to machine dependency of sign-extension of a char to an integer—so, do *not* use the following:

```
char c;
while(EOF != (c=getc(fptr)))        /* use the following
                                       instead*/

while(EOF != (getc(fptr))                                    ■
```

## Function 9

```
char *gets(s)
char *s;
```
/* The purpose of gets() is to transfer standard input into an array pointed to by s. The transfer takes place until the newline character \n is encountered (end of stdin file). The newline char is *not* transferred to s, but rather the null character is substituted for it—thus providing normal termination for the resultant string */

```
char *fgets(s,n,fptr)
char *s;
int n;
FILE *fptr;
```
/*The purpose of fgets() is to transfer input *from the file pointed to by fptr* into an array pointed to by s. The transfer takes place until n-1 chars have been read or a newline character is encountered or end-of-file is found, whichever occurs first. The null character terminates the resultant string in all cases. The function fgets() returns the value of its first parameter—the pointer to the resultant string, unless a read error occurs or no characters get read (end-of-file encountered immediately) in which case a NULL pointer is returned. */

Function 10

```
FILE *popen(command,type)
char *command, *type;

int pclose(fptr)
FILE *fptr;
```

/* When a program is running (i.e., a *process is executing*) it is sometimes desirable to create a pipe from that program to a particular UNIX shell command (pointed to by command) to be executed (from within that program). The value of type points to either r for read or w for write. With either type (r or w) a file pointer is returned permitting writing to the associated file by capturing the standard input of the command (in the case of w) or permitting reading from the associated file by capturing the standard output of the command (in the case of r). The essential difference of the functions popen() and fopen() is that the former uses a command as the first argument, while the latter uses a filename. */

■ **Example 10.4.6**  Consider the following code:

```
FILE *fptr;
char *buf;
fptr =popen("ls","r");
```

/* the standard output of the ls utility is temporarily associated with the value of fptr, permitting subsequent reads of that "standard output" to take place */

| | |
|---|---|
| `fgets(buf,n,fptr);` | /* a read takes place into the string pointed to by buf from the file fptr points to */ |
| `FILE *fptr;` `char *buf;` `fptr=popen("cat","w");` | /*the standard input to the cat utility is temporarily associated with the value of fptr, permitting subsequent writes to that "standard input" to take place */ |
| `fputs(buf,fptr);` | /* a write takes place from the string pointed to by buf to the file fptr points to */ |

Any file opened with popen() should be closed with pclose(). The function popen() returns a NULL pointer if files or processes cannot be created.

Here is a complete program without all the comments:

```
/**************************/
/*  CHAPTER 10  10.4.6.C  */
/**************************/
#include "stdio.h"

FILE *fptr;
char *buf;
int n;
main()
{
  fptr = popen("ls","r");
  fgets(buf,n,fptr);
  printf("%s\n",buf);
  fptr = popen("cat","w");
  fputs(buf,fptr);
  printf("%s\n",buf);
}
```

## Function 11

```
int printf(format,arg...)
char *format;

int fprintf(fptr,format,arg...)
FILE *fptr;
char *format;

int sprintf(s,format [ , arg]...)
char *s, *format;
```

Each of these functions produces formatted output. In the case of printf, the output goes to stdout; fprintf, on the other hand, sends its output to the file pointed to by fptr; and sprintf sends its output to the string pointed to by s (naturally terminated by the null character (\0) to make it a valid string). The statements printf() and fprintf (stdout,format,arg...) are equivalent if their formats and args are identical. Each of the functions returns the number of chars outputted, excluding the null char for sprintf().

An argument list is simply a list of expressions separated by commas, such as:

```
4.06,x, y, z
4.06,x+y, z
4.06,4, x-7/2
```

Each of the output functions accepts an argument list that is converted to the format specified and subsequently output. The format itself consists of a string of two types of objects:

1. plain characters
2. format specifications, one per arg, which consist of the percent symbol(%), followed optionally by minus sign, field width, period, specified precision, character l or L, or possibly the * char, and then one of the conversion characters d,o,x,u,e,f,g,c,s. (Extra args are ignored while extra format specifications cause an error.) Not all combinations are valid, but all *must begin with a % and end with a conversion character.*

The plain characters are output exactly as is, while the format specifications are paired in sequential fashion with the arguments enabling them to be outputted according to those specifications.

Conversion characters are defined as follows:

| | |
|---|---|
| d | convert to a decimal integer |
| o | convert to a octal integer |
| x | convert to a hexadecimal integer |
| u | convert to an unsigned decimal integer |
| e | convert to a floating point number with an exponent |
| f | convert to a floating point number without an exponent |
| g | convert to the shorter of e or f |
| c | convert to a single char |
| s | convert to a string |

■ **Example 10.4.7**    `printf("%d %o %x %u %e %f %g %c %s", 46,`
`46,46,46, 79.8,79.8, 79.8, 'a', "how are you");`

In this case, there are nine format specifications and nine arguments. The following will be printed with varying amounts of space (defaults) between them:

```
46   56    2e     46     7.980000e+01     79.80000079.8
a    how are you
```

Note that decimal 46 is octal 56 ( $5 * 8 + 6$ ) and hexadecimal 2e ( $2 * 16 + 14$ ). Note also that the conversion characters e and f default to six digits after the decimal point. The character a is printed in %c format (character) while the string "how are you" is printed in %s format (string). It is a good idea (unless the reader expects the unexpected) to match integers with %d format, reals with %e, %f, or %g format, and so on.

Here is a complete program with output:

```
main()
{
  printf("%d %o %x %u %e %f ",46,46,46,46,79.8,79.8");
  printf("%g %c %s\n",79.8,'a',"how are you");
}


/**********/
/* OUTPUT */
/**********/
46 56 2e 46 7.980000e+01 79.800000 79.8 a how are you
```

Each of the arguments is output in its *field*. Normally, the argument is right aligned in its field; however, the minus sign forces left alignment. The field has a *field width*, whose default value is whatever is required to output the value of the arg. For example, the decimal integer 255 when output with %d format will require three spaces; however, when output with %x format, it will require two spaces because 255 base 10 is equal to ff base 16.

Fortunately, the defaults can be overridden. Between the % sign and the conversion character, the following characters may be used, as mentioned before: minus sign, field width, period, specified precision, character l or L, or possibly * char.

The default value of the field width can be overridden by simply specifying the width as in %10d (convert the arg to decimal and output it in a field of width 10, using blanks for any necessary padding on the *left*). If a minus sign is also present as in %-10d, the arg is converted to decimal and it is output in a field of width 10, but now using blanks for any necessary padding on the *right*. If the field width is specified too narrow, as in %2d for the output of 201, then the field width is simply expanded to the default to accommodate the value (201 is *not* truncated). The user also has the option of padding with zeros instead of blanks by simply beginning the field width with the digit 0, as in %010d .

The period (.) is used to separate the field width from the *precision,* which in the case of %e and %f formats is simply the number of digits to be output to the right of the decimal point, and in the case of %s format is the maximum number of characters to be output. Thus, %10.2f will output 123.456 into a field of width 10 (right justified) with 2 digits after the decimal:

```
123.45
```

while %-10.2e will output 123.456 into a field of width 10 (left justified because of the minus sign) with 2 digits after the decimal:

```
1.23e+02
```

Note also that the precision specification %.10s will output "how are you" as a string truncated to 10 chars:

```
how are yo
```

The char l (ell) or L is used to specify that the conversion character d, o, x, or u corresponds to an argument of type long, as in %10Ld being used to output any long integer.

The field width or precision (or indeed both) may be specified by the char *, which means that an integer arg is used to provide the field width or precision. The args that specify field width or precision must appear before the arg to be converted. Thus, the specification *.*e can be used with args 10,2,123.456 to output 123.456 into a field of width 10 and precision 2 as:1.23e+02

The reader should be aware that precision as used in formatting output is considerably different than when used to refer to storage in a machine. Recall that the former indicates how many digits are to be output to the right of the decimal point, or in the case of strings, how many characters are to be output. In the case of storage, while it is true that variables of type float and double can be assigned a number with many digits to the right of the decimal, it is a fact that only about 6 significant digits are stored for type float, and about 16 significant digits in the case of type double. Thus, when formatting precision exceeds machine precision one should expect unpredictable output.

### Function 12

```
int putc(c,fptr)      /* putc is a macro that writes the char
int c;                c onto the file pointed to by fptr and
```

`FILE *fptr;`

moves the file pointer fptr ahead one byte—it returns the value written if successful and EOF if there is an error such as the file pointed to by fptr is not open for writing. */

`int putchar(c)`
`int c;`

/* putchar() is a macro and writes the char c onto the file pointed to by stdin—i.e. putchar(c) is defined as putc(c,stdin). On the other hand, fputc() performs the same job as putc(), but does it as a function rather than as a macro—because fgetc() is a function it has the advantages of taking less memory per invocation than getc() and its name can be passed as an argument to a function, but a negative aspect is that it runs more slowly. */

`int putw(w,fptr)`
`int w;`
`FILE *fptr;`

/* putw() writes the word w (defined as an integer which implies its size is machine dependent) to the file pointed to by fptr (no alignment is considered). Because the size of a word varies from machine to machine, special care should be taken when using putw(). */

/* The function setbuf(3S)—function 15 may be used to change a file's output buffering which normally defaults to the following:

1. stderr is unbuffered—i.e., written to stderr as each char is output.

2. output to the terminal is line buffered—i.e., written to the terminal as a block of chars when \n is output or when terminal input is requested.

3. output to a plan file is buffered—i.e., written to the file as a block of chars of predetermined size.*/

Function 13

```
int puts(s)
char *s;
```

/* The purpose of puts() is to transfer from a string pointed to by s (terminating with \0) to stdout. The transfer takes place until the null character \0 is encountered (end of string). The null char is *not* transferred to stdout, but rather the newline character is substituted for it. */

```
int fputs(s,fptr)
char *s;
FILE *fptr;
```

/* The purpose of fputs() is to transfer from a string pointed to by s (terminated again with \0) *to the file pointed to by fptr.* The transfer takes place until a null character is encountered. The null character is not transferred to the file, and a newline character is not written either. The function fputs() returns the number of chars written if successful and EOF if the file has not been opened for writing. */

Function 14

```
int scanf(format,arg,...)
char *format;

int fscanf(fptr,format,arg...)
FILE *fptr;
char *format;

int sscanf(s,format [ , arg]...)
char *s, *format;
```

Each of these functions reads input according to a specified format, often called a control string, and stores the results in the addresses specified by the args. In the case of scanf, the input comes from stdin; fscanf, on the other hand, gets its input from the file pointed to by fptr; and sscanf gets its input from the string pointed to by s (naturally terminated by the null character \0 to make it a valid string). The statements scanf() and fscanf (stdout,...) are equivalent if their formats and args are identical. Each of the functions returns the number of successfully matching input items, which could be zero (if the first arg conflicts with the first format specification) or even EOF if input ends before any conflicts.

An argument list is simply a list of pointer arguments separated by commas, such as:

```
    &i,string, &string[10]
  where int i; char string[20];
```

Each of these input functions accepts an argument list of pointer arguments that specifies where the converted input should subsequently be stored. The format itself consists of a string of the following three types of chars:

1. white space (blanks, form feeds, new lines, or tabs), which *usually* causes input to be read *up to* the next non-white-space char in the input.

2. non-white-space characters (excluding the char %), which must match the next character in the input file.

3. conversion specifications, one per arg, which consist of the percent symbol (%), followed optionally by a * char, which indicates assignment suppression, an integer defining a maximum field width, or the character l or h, and then one of the conversion characters d,o,x,u,e,f,c,s, or [string]. (Any extra args are ignored while extra format specifications cause an error.) Not all combinations are valid, but all *must begin with a % and end with a conversion character,* just as for formatted output.

The format specifications are paired in sequential fashion with the arguments enabling them to be input according to those specifications.

Conversion characters are defined as follows:

| | |
|---|---|
| d | interpret as a decimal integer |
| o | interpret as a octal integer |
| x | interpret as a hexadecimal integer |
| u | interpret as an unsigned decimal integer |
| e | interpret as a floating point number |
| f | interpret as a floating point number (same as e) |
| c | interpret as a single char |
| s | interpret as a string |
| [string] | special string |

■ **Example 10.4.8**

```
int i,n;
char c;
char string[12];
n=scanf("%d   , %*s      %c      %3s      %s",
              &i,              &c, string, &string[4])
```

input---> 4 , per_hour @ his_sal

/* Summary: Find a decimal number and place its value in address i—thus 4 is placed in i; match a comma and essentially ignore it; find a string and ignore it (because of the * char)—thus the string "per _hour" is ignored; find a char and place it in c—thus @ is placed in c; find a 3 character string, terminate it, and place it in address string pointed to by s—thus h goes in string[0], i in string[1], s in string[2], *and \0 in string[3];* find a string and place it in &string[4]—thus '_' in string[4], 's' in string[5], 'a' in string[6], '1' in string[7], '\0' in string[8]. The variable n will have the value 5 because 5 successful conversions were made.*/ ■

Some of the finer points about the input functions:

1. The %ld, %lo, and %lx can be used to convert to a long int, while %le and %lf are used to convert to a long float (double); similarly, %hx, %ho, and %hx convert to a short int.

2. An input field is simply a single char in the case of %c, and the next set of contiguous nonwhite characters that make sense for the conversion—this set will end if the field width has been used. For example, if

    *char string[12]*

    then the specification %5s with the argument named string will simply look for the next nonwhite char plus four more contiguous chars, and then pad with the terminator \0. On the other hand, %s with the argument named string will cause scanning for the next nonwhite char continuing until white space occurs. This may mean that \0 might not terminate string.

3. Floating point numbers will appear in the input as an optional sign (+ or −), followed by a digit string with or without a decimal point, followed by an optional exponent part (e or E), followed by an optional sign, followed by a digit string. The following all will be interpreted as valid floating point numbers: +12.34e–99, 12.34, −12.34, 1234, and 1234E+2.

4. The user can specify the characters that may be read into a string by the specification %[string] where string is the set of chars or the complement of the set of chars. The latter occurs if the first char of string is the char ^ . For example, the specification %[aeiou] will input a string consisting only of vowels and will stop at the first nonvowel (even a blank). On the other hand, %[ ^ aeiou] will input string consisting only of nonvowels and will stop at the first vowel.

5. Chars in the control string other than the special char % are searched for in the input.

6. White space in the control string is ignored.

7. Scanf() returns the number, possibly zero, of successful conversions and EOF if end-of-file is reached.

**Function 15**

```
void setbuf(fptr,buffer)
FILE *fptr;
char *buffer

int setvbuf(fptr,buf,type, size)
FILE *fptr;
char *buf;
int type, size;
```

/* It is possible for a programmer to specify the buffer to be used after a file has been opened, provided it has not been read or written. The size of the buffer should agree with the constant BUFSIZ (usually 512 or 1024) defined in <stdio.h>.*/

■ **Example 10.4.9**   To use the array buf for reading the file filename, the programmer could do the following:

```
/***************************/
/* CHAPTER 10  10.4.9.C */
/***************************/
#include "stdio.h"
char buf[BUFSIZ];
FILE *fptr;
main()
{
  fptr = fopen("myfile","r");
  setbuf(fptr,buf);
}
```

■

The programmer can also explicitly specify the buffer to be used. The following are types of buffering, as defined in <stdio.h>:

| | |
|---|---|
| _IOFBF | input and output are fully buffered. |
| _IOLBF | output is line buffered—that is, the buffer will be written when a newline is encountered, the buffer is full, or input is requested. |
| _IONBF | input and output are not buffered. The defaults are that output to a terminal is line buffered, and all other I/O is fully buffered. |

■ **Example 10.4.10** The following program will cause myfile to be opened for reading, and the input buffer used will be buf of size BUFSIZ, and output is line buffered. Note also that if a buffer space is declared as an automatic variable in a block, then the file should be closed in that same block.

```
/**************************/
/* CHAPTER 10  10.4.10.C  */
/**************************/
#include "stdio.h"

char buf[BUFSIZ];
FILE *fptr;
main()
{
  fptr = fopen("myfile","r");
  setvbuf(fptr,buf,_IOLBF,BUFSIZ);
}
```
■

## Function 16

```
#include <setjmp.h>              /*section 3C */
int setjmp(env)
jmp_buf env;


void longjmp(env,val)
jmp_buf env;
int val;
```
/* The purpose of setjmp() (which returns the integer 0) is to save the stack environment (values of registers, values of *local* variables, etc.) so that errors and interrupts encountered in a function can be diagnosed. The environment is saved in a variable of type jmp_buf that is defined in the file <setjmp.h>. The function longjmp() is used to restore the environment saved by setjmp() and causes program execution to begin gain as if setjmp had returned val. If longjmp() is

invoked with val==0, setjmp will return 1. When setjmp() is returned to, the local variable values are as they were when setjmp() returned the first time—but global variables are not considered part of the stack environment.*/

■ **Example 10.4.11**   Consider the following program:

```
/*************************/
/* CHAPTER 10 10.4.11.C */
/*************************/

#include <setjmp.h>

jmp_buf env;
int i = 0;

main()
{
  void exit();
  if (setjmp(env) != 0)
  {
    printf("value of i on 2nd return is: %d\n",i);
    exit(0);
  }
  printf("value of i right now is: %d\n",i);
  i=1;
  g();
}
g()
{
  longjmp(env,1);
}



/***********/
/* OUTPUT */
/***********/
value of i right now is: 0
value of i on 2nd return is: 1
```

Contrast that program with the following:

```
#include <setjmp.h>

jmp_buf env;

main()
{

        int i =0;            /*local variable for main() */
        void exit();         /*must be declared because
                             this system call returns a
                             noninteger */

                             /* the if statement that follows
                             is not executed immediately
                             because setjmp() does return
                             0 */
```

```
    if (setjmp(env) !=0) {
          printf("value of i on 2nd return is:
          %d\n",i);
          exit(0);
    }
    printf({value of i right now is: %d\n", i);
    i=1;
    g();
}
g()
{
    longjmp(env,1);
}
```

PRINTOUT: value of i right now is: 0

value of i on 2nd return is: 0                                              ∎

## Function 17

```
#include <stdio.h>
FILE *stdin, *stdout, *stderr;
```

/* A file with buffering is called a stream and a pointer is used to refer to that stream. There are normally three open files: stdin (the standard input file), stdout (the standard output file), and stderr (the standard error file). */

## Function 18

```
int system(string)
char *string;
```

/* The purpose of the function system() is to pass the string as a command, just as if it had been typed at the terminal, to the command interpreter sh(1). The current process waits until the shell has completed executing string, and then returns the exit status of the shell. The function system() actually creates a child process of the current process—that child process executes sh, which in turn executes string. If the fork fails or sh cannot be executed, then system returns a negative value and errno is set.*/

## Function 19

```
FILE *tmpfile()
```
/* Sometimes during a process it is desirable to generate a temporary file, opened for update ("w+") by using tmpfile(), which will be given a name by the function tmpnam(). (See Function 20.) The function tmpfile() returns a pointer to that file, if successful, and a NULL pointer otherwise. */

## Function 20

```
char *tmpnam(s)
char *s;

char *tmpnam(dir,pfx)
char *dir, *pfx;
```
/*The purpose of these functions is to generate file-names for files that are temporary only in the sense that they are in a directory intended for temporary use. The path of the file is predefined in <stdio.h> as P_tmpdir . If the pointer s is not NULL, then it should be the name of an array of at least L_tmpnam (length of the temporary name) bytes, where L_tmpnam is defined in <stdio.h>. The function tmpnam() places its result in that array and returns s.*/

**■ Example 10.4.12**

```
char *s;
char t[L_tmpnam];
s = tmpnam(t);
```

The second version of tempnam permits the user to specify the directory for the file, as well as the first five or fewer characters of that file's name. Thus, if the user wanted the temporary files to begin with KEM and to be located in the directory /user/kem/tmp, then the following would be coded:

```
char *s
char t[L_tmpnam];
s = tmpnam(/usr/kem/tmp,KEM);
```

■

Function 21

```
int ungetc(c,fptr)      /* ungetc() can be used to push
int c;                     the char c back into the buffer that
FILE *fptr;                is associated with fptr during
                           input. */
```

**■ Example 10.4.13**  Suppose that reading is being done into the buffer from the file associated with fptr and the current read position is as follows:

```
now is the time for all
       ^
```

Suppose the user wants to change the h to an i in the buffer. The following will do just that:

```
ungetc('i',fptr);
```

The very next time a getc() call is made, i will be returned. If the stream is stdin, then one char may be pushed onto the buffer without a previous read; otherwise, one char of pushback is guaranteed assuming at least one char has been read and buffering has been used. An attempt to push EOF onto the buffer has no effect on the buffer and in that case ungetc() simply returns EOF, as it does if a character cannot be pushed back. ■

## EXERCISES 10.4

1. On your machine make the following declarations and assignments

```
char c;
int i,j,k;
c='d';
```

```
i=10;
j=100;
k=999999999;
```

a. What format would be used to print the value of c in a field of width 5, left aligned?

b. What format would be used to print the value of j in a field of width 3, right aligned? Do the same but with the added conditions of converting j to octal and hexadecimal.

c. What format would be used to print the value of -j in a field of width 4, left aligned?

d. Specify the format to do parts a–c with the added condition that padding will be done with zeros.

2. On your machine make the following declarations and assignments

```
double x;
double y,z;
x=123.456789123456789;
y=z=123.456789123456789e-10;
```

In each case specify the appropriate format to print the following:

| EXPRESSION | PRINT VALUE | FORMAT |
|---|---|---|
| COLUMNS ⟶ | 12345678901234 | |
| x | 123.456789 | |
| x | 123.4 | |
| x | 123.456 | |
| x | 123.456 | |
| x | 123.456789123 | |
| y | 123.456e+02 | |
| y | 123.456e+02 | |
| z | .000000 | |
| z | 1.23456e−08 | |
| z | 1.2e−08 | |
| z | 1.23e−08 | |
| z | 1.23456789e−08 | |

3. On your machine make the following declarations and assignments

```
static char s[]="C is the language"
static char t[]="Unix is powerful"
```

COLUMNS————————→ 12345678901234567

In each case specify the appropriate format to print the following:

| Expression | Print Value | Format |
|---|---|---|

COLUMNS————————→ 12345678901234567890

| | | |
|---|---|---|
| s | C is the language | |
| t | Unix is powerful | |
| t | Unix is powerful | |
| t | Unix is | |
| t | Unix is power | |
| t | Unix is | |

4. Consider the input: 40 5.68 123 Elm with:

```
int conversions, hours; float salary; char
address[20]
conversions=scanf("%d %f %s", &hours,
&salary, address);
```

Give the value of hours, salary, address, and conversions.

5. Consider the input: 050 55.68 89 123Elm with:

```
int hours, days; float salary; char
address[20];
scanf("%o %ld %f %*d %*[123]
%s",&hours,&days,&salary,address);
```

Show that the value of hours is 40, the value of day is 5, the value of salary is 5.68, and the value of address is Elm\0.

## 10.5 | C PROGRAMS CALLED IN UNIX SHELL SCRIPTS

The design of a C program varies with the type of data that it manipulates. For example, if it needs information from a file (or files) for input, then those file(s) may be listed on the command line as arguments when running a.out. As has been seen, argv[0] points to the a in a.out, argv[1] points to the first character in the second string, and so forth, while argc counts the strings on the command line (always at least one because a.out is present). This technique of using the command line to hold the arguments is an effective technique in many situations. It is certainly more useful than specifying the names of the files to be read within the program.

It is of course possible to simply use an interactive program that prompts the user at the appropriate times. This method is generally less desirable than the method of using command line arguments if the input is extensive.

Other possibilities include (1) combining interactive input and command line arguments, (2) writing a function whose purpose is to generate interactive input and using it in those programs where it is appropriate, (3) writing a shell script that combines interactive input and command line arguments, and (4) writing a function in C that can be called from other C programs. The last two techniques will be illustrated in the following examples.

■ **Example 10.5.1**   Suppose the user has written a program called count whose purpose is simply to count and then send to standard output the number of uppercase letters in an existing file, say, the first command line argument. Suppose also that the executable code is stored in a.out. A good interactive version follows (stored in intercount):

```
$ cat intercount
echo This shell script uses the C program called count
echo to count the number of uppercase letters in a
echo specified file. Please indicate the file at this
echo time

read filename
answer= `count $filename `      #capture the output in the
                               #shell variable answer
echo The number of uppercase letters in $filename is
echo $answer
$
```

A second example will show how to write a version of the C program count so that it can be called from other programs (building your own library function).

■ **Example 10.5.2**

```
/* CHAPTER 10   10.5.2.C */

#include <stdio.h>
main()
{
  count("myfile");
}
count(filename)
char *filename;
{
  int ch;
  int number=0;
  FILE *fptr;
  if ((fptr = fopen(filename,"r")) == NULL)
  {
    fprintf(stderr,"count: cannot open %s\n",filename);
    return(-1);
  }
  while ((ch = getc(fptr)) != EOF)
  {
    if ((ch > 1) && (ch < 30))
      number++;
  }
}
```

■

## 10.6 | *CHAPTER SUMMARY*

1. System calls and library functions are typically used in C programs.

2. The library function "system" permits a C program to call a shell script or a UNIX command.

3. The standard C library consists of those functions described in Sections 3C, 2, and 3S of the UNIX Programmer's Manual.

4. The variable errno and the library function perror(3C) are useful in determining why a system call might have failed to execute successfully.

5. System calls may be used to create, open, close, read, and write files (available only in UNIX environments).

6. Input and output that is done with system calls associates a file descriptor with each file in question.

7. Random access to a file can be done with the system call lseek().

8. Input and output that is done with library functions associates a file pointer with each file in question.

9. The file stdio.h contains a set of definitions that all standard I/O functions use.

10. The inclusion of stdio.h gives the programmer access to approximately 25–30 library functions.

11. Random access to a file can be done with the library function fseek().

12. Formatted output can be done with the library function printf().

13. It is often desirable to have a shell script that combines interactive input with command line arguments.

14. It is often desirable to write a function in C that can be called from other C programs.

# *The UNIX-C Interface*

A good deal of time was spent in Chapter 10 studying how to use UNIX C functions (system calls and library functions) within C programs. Knowledge of these techniques lets you use the C language effectively without having to write a C function for each individual task that needs to be done. In fact, that's the point: use *C functions* (system calls, library functions, and user-written C functions) as modular programming tools that can be inserted into C programs. By doing so you can have at your disposal a wide variety of functions that will increase your productivity, and at the same time decrease your programming errors. You may have noticed that the compactness of the C language is greatly enhanced by the richness and diversity of the UNIX C functions; they effectively extend and enrich the language itself.

This chapter will provide additional techniques that may be used for a rich and productive interface between C programs and the UNIX operating system. The interface involves individual techniques, such as the following, which may be combined in natural ways:

1. linking (two or more) C programs (binary code), say, prog_i and prog_i+1, in serial fashion using the piping techniques, so that the output of prog_i is the input to prog_i+1

   $ `prog_i | prog_i+1`

2. using a C program (binary code again), say, prog, with redirection so that its standard input can be redirected to come from a file (say, newinput) and so its standard output can be redirected to go to another file (say, newoutput).

   $ `prog <newinput >newoutput`

3. using a C program, say, prog, so that its input can come from the standard input or from command line arguments (files such as file1, file2, and file3).

   $ `prog file1 file2 file3`

4. using a C program to fetch certain information (often via system calls) from the UNIX operating system, such as the time, access permissions, and such.

5. using a C program to accept command line options to influence the output of the program. For example, prog might be a C program that gives the age of a file (say, filename) in days (-d option) or in hours (-h option).

```
$ prog -d filename
```

## 11.1 | *Access of Standard Input and Opened Files in a C Program*

The first program will show how to write a single program with the options to accept standard input, or redirected input from another file, or actually open an input file within the program. The purpose of this program is simply to count the number of times each of the single digits zero through nine appears in the input file.

■ **Example 11.1.1**

```
$ countdigits                      /* count the single digits in an input file*/
or (for a file named "filename")
                                   /* the usage is either as simply (for
$ countdigits filename                standard input)
     */
#include <stdio.h>
main(argc,argv)
int argc;                          /*always at least one*/
char *argv[ ];                     /*pointers to the command line arguments*/
{
FILE *fptr;
                                   /* watch for standard input or a file that cannot be
                                   opened */
if (argc ==1)                      /* there is no file specified, so use terminal input* /
    adddigits(stdin);
                                   /* now for the case where a file is specified */
else {
```

```
    if ((fptr=fopen(argv[1],"r")) == NULL) {
        perror(argv[0]);
        exit(1);              /* if the file cannot be opened for reading, then print an
                                 appropriate error message and leave the program */

    }
    else {
        adddigits(fptr);
        fclose(fptr);         /* do the counting of the digits and then close the file */
    }
}
}
#include <ctype.h>            /*includes the macro isdigit */
                             /* see Section 11.2 for a discussion of <ctype.h> */

adddigits(fptr)
FILE *fptr;
{
int subscript;               /*the index into an array that holds the counts for each
                               digit */
int howmany[10];             /* the array that holds individual counts*/
int inchar;                  /*the character presently read */
for (subscript=0; subscript < 10; ++subscript)
    howmany[subscript] =0; /*initialize each slot to zero */
                             /* at this point we are ready to begin reading the characters
                               in the standard input or the opened file—loop as long as
                               end of file is not encountered */
while( (inchar = getc(fptr)) != EOF )
{    if (isdigit(inchar))
        howmany[inchar — '0']++

}
                             /* now print the results */
for ( subscript=0; subscript <=9; ++subscript)
    printf("%3d %10d\n", subscript, howmany[subscript]);
}
```

Here is the program with output and no comments:

```
/*    CHAPTER 11    11.1.1.C   */


#include <stdio.h>
#include <ctype.h>

main(argc,argv)
int argc;
char *argv[];
{
  FILE *fptr;
  if (argc == 1)
    adddigits(stdin);
  else
  {
    if ((fptr=fopen(argv[1],"r")) == NULL)
    {
      perror(argv[0]);
      exit(1);
    }
    else
    {
      adddigits(fptr);
      fclose(fptr);
    }
  }
}

adddigits(fptr)
FILE *fptr;
{
  int subscript;
  int howmany[10];
  int inchar;
  for (subscript=0; subscript < 10; ++subscript)
    howmany[subscript] = 0;
  while ((inchar = getc(fptr))!= EOF)
  {
    if (isdigit(inchar))
      howmany[inchar - '0']++;
  }
  for (subscript=0; subscript <=9; ++subscript)
    printf("%3d %10d\n",subscript,howmany[subscript]);
}



/*********/
/* INPUT */
/*********/
a.out myfile


/**********/
/* OUTPUT */
/**********/
  0          0
  1          0
  2          0
  3          0
  4          0
  5          0
  6          0
  7          0
  8          0
  9          0
```

## EXERCISES 11.1

1. Write a C program that counts the number of times each of the letters of the alphabet appears in the input file. As in the example, write the program so that standard input may be used if desired, or an input file may be opened within the program.

2. Write a C program that opens a file and then counts the number of characters in that file, as well as the number of times each of the letters of the alphabet appears in that file. Furthermore, print the relative frequency of each letter count to the total count of characters, and then print the table of those frequencies in descending order.

## 11.2 | <CTYPE.H> MACROS

Recall that macros are preprocessor directives that are defined with the #define directives. Their judicious use permits the programmer to avoid the use of functions, and to be more succinct. For example, instead of writing

*y\*y\*y*

each time a variable needs to be cubed, it would be easier to define the macro cubed as follows:

*#define cubed(x) ((x)\*(x)\*(x))*

which permits the use of cubed(x) instead of ((x)\*(x)\*(x)) in source code, and can indeed be used for any appropriate data type (int or real). In effect, *every* reference to cubed(x) in source code gets replaced by ((x)\*(x)\*(x)). The parentheses are necessary as the reader will verify in the exercises.

One of the more important set of macros can be made available, as it was in the last program, by the directive:

*#include <ctype.h>*      /\*section 3C of the UNIX manual \*/

The set of macros made available via <ctype.h> is handy to classify characters according to whether they are letters, such as isalpha(), or other criteria:

*int isalpha(c)*
*int c;*

They all have the same synopsis as isalpha. That is, they each need an int c between (-1), which is the value of EOF), and 127, except for is-ascii, which is defined for *all* integers. They each return an int—nonzero for true and zero for false.

| | |
|---|---|
| `isalpha(c)` | alphabetic character |
| `isupper(c)` | uppercase letter |
| `islower` | lowercase letter |
| `isdigit(c)` | zero through nine |
| `isxdigit(c)` | hexadecimal digit, zero through nine, A–F, a–f |
| `isalnum(c)` | letter or digit |
| `isspace(c)` | space, tab, carriage return, newline, vertical tab, or formfeed |
| `ispunct(c)` | punctuation character |
| `isprint(c)` | printing character, 32 (space) through 126 (tilde) |
| `isgraph(c)` | printing, *excluding* space (33–126) |
| `iscntrl(c)` | control character (0–31) or delete character (127) |
| `isascii(c)` | ASCII character (0–127) |

## EXERCISES 11.2

1. Modify the program in Section 11.1 to count uppercase and lowercase alphabetic characters. It will be helpful to use the macro isalpha() in <ctype.h>. Indexing can be achieved by using inchar - 'a' instead of inchar -'0' as in the example.

2. Specify the difference between howmany[(inchar-'0')++] and howmany[inchar-'0']++ . Pay close attention to the priority of the various operators.

3. Run the program given in this section with standard input and also with data file input. Then run it again by combining the run with a pipe to lp to produce four columns of output per line.

4. Show why the macro definition given by

    #define cubed(x) x*x*x

    will produce erroneous results for cubed(x+2) and x/cubed(x).

## 11.3 OPTIONS FOR C PROGRAMS

Before giving an example of how to process options for C programs, a short review will be given of argc and argv. Recall that argc counts the number of arguments on the command line and is always, therefore, at least one, while argv[ ] is an array of pointers to the arguments themselves. The appropriate declarations are:

```
int argc;
char *argv[];        /* or alternatively char **argv; */
```

An effective method to examine a series of command line arguments is to use:

```
argc--;
argv++;
```

■ **Example 11.3.1**    Suppose the following command line is given:

```
$ a.out -p f1 f2
```

In this case, argc--4; argv is the address of the array whose elements are argv[0], argv[1], argv[2], and argv[3]. The array argv[0] is the address of argv[0][0], argv[1] is the address of argv[1][0], argv[2] is the address of argv[2][0], and argv[3] is the address of argv[3][0]. Schematically, the whole situation might be like this:

| Address | Value | Name |
|---------|-------|------|
| 100 | 4 | argc |
|  | 1000 | argv |
| 1000 | 2000 | argv[0] |
| 1001 | 3000 | argv[1] |
| 1002 | 4000 | argv[2] |
| 1003 | 5000 | argv[3] |
| 2000 | 'a' | argv[0][0] |
| 2001 | '.' | argv[0][1] |
| etc. | | |
| 3000 | '-' | argv[1][0] |
| 3001 | 'p' | argv[1][1] |
| 4000 | 'f' | argv[2][0] |
| 4001 | 'l' | argv[2][1] |
| 5000 | 'f' | argv[3][0] |
| 5001 | '2' | argv[3][1] |

Now suppose the following C statement is executed:

```
printf("%u %u %c \n", argv, argv[0], argv[0][0]);
                                  /* prints 1000 2000 a */
```

Now suppose the following C statements are executed:

```
argc--
argv++
```

Then the memory above is modified to the following:

| Address | Value | Name |
|---------|-------|------|
| 100 | 3 | argc |
| | 1001 | argv |
| 1001 | 3000 | argv[0] |
| 1002 | 4000 | argv[1] |
| 1003 | 5000 | argv[2] |
| 3000 | '-' | argv[0][0] |
| 3001 | 'p' | argv[0][1] |
| 4000 | 'f' | argv[1][0] |
| 4001 | 'l' | argv[1][1] |
| 5000 | 'f' | argv[2][0] |
| 5001 | '2' | argv[2][1] |

Notice that as soon as argv has the value 1001, argv[0] has the value 3000, which means that argv[0][0] has the value '-'. Effectively, a shift left has occurred in the arguments. ■

In Section 11.1, a program countdigits was written simply to count the number of times each of the digits from zero through nine appeared in standard input or in an ordinary data file. In this section, the reader will learn how to provide options for C programs.

Recall that an option is simply a command line argument that customizes, or alters, the default running of a program. Many UNIX utilities, normally written in C, are equipped with options. The approach here is to begin options with hyphens and sandwich them between the name of the program and its arguments. For example, it might be desirable to run countdigits on inputfile, but to print out the relative frequencies of each digit as a percentage. This will be called the -p option, and would be run as follows (where countdigits is the renamed a.out associated with countdigits.c):

$ <u>countdigits -p inputfile</u>

There are two main ideas that the new and improved countdigits must contend with: first, it must be reprogrammed so that the main() function can determine whether an option is present. Second, it must have the auxiliary adddigits() function reprogrammed not only to add digits, as it did before, but also to compute percentages for each *when that option is present*. Thus, in effect, adddigits() must perform two tasks: the incrementing of each slot in the array and the computing of the percentages, if the -p option is present.

The option will be set by a flag, that is to say, by a variable whose value will be set to one if the option is present and zero otherwise. This flag may be defined as an external variable so that it can be shared by any and all functions (main and adddigits in this case), or, alternatively, it may have its value passed as a parameter to the function adddigits. The latter is the desirable avenue to follow because the adddigits function is the only one that needs the value of the flag. In general, the use of global variables (external) should be minimized as much as possible.

■ **Example 11.3.2**    This program counts the single digits in an input file with a -p option for the percentages of each digit present. The usage is:

$ <u>countdigits [-p] [filename]</u>

If the filename is absent, standard input is used. Here is the program run with its output shown:

```
/*    CHAPTER 11    11.3.2.C   */


#include <stdio.h>
#include <ctype.h>

main(argc,argv)
int argc;
char *argv[];
{
  FILE *fptr;
  int flag = 0;
  while ((argc > 1) && (argv[1][0] == '-'))
  {
    if (argv[1][1] == 'p')
      flag = 1;
    else
    {
      fprintf(stderr,"The program %s used and unknown option %d\n",argv[0],argv[1
      exit(1);
    }
    argc--;
    argv++;
  }
  if (argc == 1)
    adddigits(stdin,flag);
  else
  {
    if ((fptr=fopen(argv[1],"r")) == NULL)
    {
      perror(argv[0]);
      exit(1);
    }
    else
    {
      adddigits(fptr,flag);
      fclose(fptr);
```

```
        }
      }
    }

    adddigits(fptr,option)
    FILE *fptr;
    int option;
    {
      int subscript;
      int howmany[10];
      int inchar;
      int total=0;
      for (subscript=0; subscript < 10; ++subscript)
        howmany[subscript] = 0;
      while ((inchar = getc(fptr))!= EOF)
      {
        if (isdigit(inchar))
        {
          howmany[inchar - '0']++;
          total++;
        }
      }
      if (total == 0)
      {
        printf("no digits found\n");
        exit(2);
      }
      if (option == 0)
      {
        for (subscript=0; subscript <=9; ++subscript)
          printf("%3d %10d\n",subscript,howmany[subscript]);
      }
      else
      {
        for (subscript=0; subscript <=9; ++subscript)
          printf("%d %10d %6d\n",subscript,howmany[subscript],(100*howmany[subscript]
      }
    }


    /**********/
    /* INPUT */
    /**********/
    a.out -p myfile


    /**********/
    /* OUTPUT */
    /**********/
    no digits found
```

■

## EXERCISES 11.3

1. Modify the program in Section 11.3 to count uppercase and lowercase alphabetic characters with the -p option availability. It will be helpful to use the macro isalpha() in <ctype.h>. Indexing can be achieved by using inchar - a instead of inchar -0 as in the example.

2. Suppose the command line is as follows:

$ <u>at the sound of the bell</u>

a. What is the value of argv[2]?

b. What is the value of argv[2][3]?

c. After argv++, what is the value of argv[2][3]?

d. What does argv[2]++ cause to occur?

## 11.4 | *MULTIPLE FILES FOR C PROGRAMS*

The next step is to modify the countdigits program so that it can process more than one file. That is to say

$ <u>countdigits file1 file2 file3</u>

should open file1, process it, close it, and then repeat the sequence for file2 and file3. The -p option should still be available.

■ **Example 11.4.1**

/* count the single digits in one or more files with a -p option for the percentages of each digit present */

/* the usage is: $ countdigits [-p] [filename . . .] if the filename is absent, standard input is used */

```
#include <stdio.h>
main(argc,argv)
int argc;
char *argv[];
```

/*always at least one*/

/*pointers to the command line arguments*/

```
{
FILE *fptr;
int flag=0;
```

/* 1 for presence of -p option, 0 otherwise—assume initially there is no -p option present */

```
int cnt=1;
int filesflag=0
```

/* 1 if there is more than one file to process, 0 otherwise*/

/* Loop through to search for an argument beginning with a hyphen. The arguments will be successively shifted left with the count of the number of arguments decreased by 1 each time. The body of the following loop only executes when there is still at least one argument following the name of the program (argc > 1) *and* when that argument begins with a hyphen (argv[1][0]==`-` ). When an argument begins with a `-` the flag is set to 1; otherwise if there is a second argument and it begins with a hyphen an unconditional exit is made from the program. */

```
while ((argc > 1) && (argv[1][0] =='-'))        {
```

/* if true and p follows, then set flag */

```
if (argv[1][1] == 'p')
    flag =1;
```

/* if true and p does not follow, then print error message and leave */

```
else      {
    fprintf(stderr, "the program %s used an unknown
    option %s \n", argv[0],argv[1]);
    exit(1);
    }
argc--;
argv++;
}
```

/* watch for standard input or a file that cannot be opened */

```
if (argc >=3) filesflag = 1;
if (argc == 1)
```

/* there is no file specified, so use terminal input* /

```
    adddigits(stdin,flag);
```

/* now for the case where *one or more files are* specified */

```
else {
    while (argc > 1)         {
```

/* if a file cannot be opened, print error and leave the program */

```
            if ((fptr=fopen(argv[cnt],"r")) == NULL){
            perror(argv[0]);
            exit(2);                          /* if the file cannot be opened for
                                              reading, then print an appropriate
                                              error message and leave the
                                              program */

                }
            else if (argc ==2)
            {
                if (filesflag == 1)
                printf("The name of the current file is
                %s\n,argv[cnt]);
                adddigits(fptr,flag);
                fclose(fptr);
                exit(3);
            }
            else {
                if (filesflag==1)
                    printf("\nthe name of the current file
                    is %s",argv[cnt]);
                adddigits(fptr,flag);
                fclose(fptr);                 /* do the counting of the digits and
                                              then close the file */

                cnt++;
                argc--;
            }
        }
    }
}

    #include <ctype.h>                        /*includes the macro isdigit */
                                              /*see Section 11.2 for a discussion of
                                              <ctype.h> */

adddigits(fptr,option)
FILE *fptr;
int option;
{
```

```
    int subscript;                          /* the index into an array that holds
                                             the counts for each digit */

    int howmany[10];                         /* the array that holds individual
                                             counts*/

    int inchar;                              /*the character presently read */

    int total=0;                             /*total number of digits found */

    for (subscript=0; subscript < 10; ++subscript)
        howmany[subscript] =0;               /*initialize each slot to zero */
```

/* at this point we are ready to begin reading the characters in the standard input or the opened file—loop as long as end of file is *not* encountered */

```
while( (inchar = getc(fptr)) != EOF )
    if (isdigit(inchar))    {
        howmany[inchar — '0']++ ;
        total++;
        }
```

/* now print the results *based on the option* */

```
if (total == 0)      {
        printf("no digits found");
    }
else if (option == 0)     {
    for ( subscript = 0; subscript <=9; ++subscript)
    printf("%3d %10d\n", subscript, howmany[subscript]);
    }
else {
    for (subscript =0; subscript <=9;++subscript)
        printf("%d %10d %6d
        \n",subscript,howmany[subscript] , (100*
        howmany[subscript])/total);
    }
}
```

Here is the complete program shown with input and output:

```
/*    CHAPTER 11    11.4.1.C    */


#include <stdio.h>
#include <ctype.h>

main(argc,argv)
int argc;
char *argv[];
{
  FILE *fptr;
  int flag = 0;
  int cnt = 1;
  int filesflag=0;
  while ((argc > 1) && (argv[1][0] == '-'))
  {
    if (argv[1][1] == 'p')
      flag = 1;
    else
    {
      fprintf(stderr,"The program %s used and unknown option %d\n",argv[0],argv[1
      exit(1);
    }
    argc--;
    argv++;
  }
  if (argc >= 3)
    filesflag = 1;
  if (argc == 1)
    adddigits(stdin,flag);
  else
  {
    while (argc > 1)
    {

      if ((fptr=fopen(argv[cnt],"r")) == NULL)
      {
        perror(argv[0]);
        exit(2);
      }
      else if (argc == 2)
      {
        if (filesflag == 1)
          printf("The name of the current file is %s\n",argv[cnt]);
        adddigits(fptr,flag);
        fclose(fptr);
        exit(3);
      }
      else
      {
        if (filesflag == 1)
          printf("The name of the current file is %s\n",argv[cnt]);
        adddigits(fptr,flag);
        fclose(fptr);
        cnt++;
        argc--;
      }
    }
  }
}
adddigits(fptr,option)
FILE *fptr;
int option;
{
  int subscript;
```

```
int howmany[10];
int inchar;
int total=0;
for (subscript=0; subscript < 10; ++subscript)
  howmany[subscript] = 0;
while ((inchar = getc(fptr))!= EOF)
{
  if (isdigit(inchar))
  {
    howmany[inchar - '0']++;
    total++;
  }
}
if (total == 0)
  printf("no digits found\n");
else if (option == 0)
{
  for (subscript=0; subscript <=9; ++subscript)
    printf("%3d %10d\n",subscript,howmany[subscript]);
}
else
{
  for (subscript=0; subscript <=9; ++subscript)
    printf("%d %10d %6d\n",subscript,howmany[subscript],(100*howmany[subscript]
}
}


/*********/
/* INPUT */
/*********/
1 2 3 4 5 6 7 8 9 0
a b c d e f g h i j
99999 4444


/**********/
/* OUTPUT */
/**********/
0          1      5
1          1      5
2          1      5
3          1      5
4          5     26
5          1      5
6          1      5
7          1      5
8          1      5
9          6     31
```

■

## *EXERCISES* **11.4**

1. Write a C program whose purpose is to count the number of sentences in one or more files. If filenames are not given, standard input should be used.

2. Write a C program whose purpose is to add the ASCII values associated with the last ten bytes in one or more files. If filenames are not given, standard input should be used.

3. Write a C program whose purpose is to find all the nonprinting characters in one or more files, and then write those nonprinting characters to a single file.

## 11.5 | *ACCESS OF SYSTEM INFORMATION IN A C PROGRAM: GETENV(3C), GETLOGIN(3C), TIME(2), CTIME(3C)*

Recall that a C program typically consists of user-written functions, systems calls, and other C library functions. The most important of the library functions are in Section 3C or 3S of the UNIX programmer's manual—remember the 3C functions and the 3S functions are automatically loaded by the C compiler, but some of these functions do require the inclusion of a header file (the synopsis for a function will indicate whether the header file is necessary). Of course the 3S functions do require the inclusion of the header file <stdio.h>. In this section we will illustrate how system calls and library functions can be used to obtain information for a C program from UNIX.

The discussion begins by providing a summary of the four functions to be used in our program: getenv(3C), getlogin(3C), time(2), and ctime(3C).

The function *getenv(3C)* has the following synopsis:

```
char *getenv(name)
char *name;
```

The possible values of name are found in environ(5). They include PATH (the sequence of directory prefixes to be used in searching for a file with an incomplete filename), HOME (the name of the user's login directory), TERM (the type of terminal for any output), TZ (time zone information), and any shell variable names whose values have been set and exported, for example,

```
AGE=10
export AGE
```

The value returned by getenv() is NULL if the variable named name is not present in the environment, and is its value otherwise.

The function *getlogin(3C)* has the following synopsis:

```
char *getlogin()
```

The function getlogin() returns a pointer to the login name found in /etc/utmp.

The function *time(2)* has the following synopsis:

```
long time((long *) 0)
long time (tloc)
long *tloc;
```

The function time(2) returns the number of seconds since 00:00:00 GMT, January 1, 1970. If a pointer to a long is the argument to time(), then that pointer (i.e., that address) is where the time is stored. Thus, if the declaration

```
long thetime;
```

is made, then the following statement will place the time in seconds since January 1, 1970, in the address specified by thetime:

```
time(&thetime);
```
/* the time() function can actually place the time in another variable, say, alsothetime, by using its return value as in:

*long thetime;*

*long alsothetime;*

*alsothetime= time(&thetime); */*

The function time(2) can also return the time in seconds since January 1, 1970, by passing it a null address pointing to a long as in:

```
thetime = time(0);
```

In either case, unsuccessful completion returns a value of -1 and the variable errno is set.

The function *ctime(3C)* has the following synopsis:

```
#include <time.h>
char *ctime(clock)
long *clock;
```

It accepts an address of a long integer pointed to by clock (the number of seconds since January 1, 1970) and returns a pointer to a 26-character string of the following form:

```
Mon Dec 26 17:33:52 1988 \n\0
```

The following example will show how a systems administrator can use a function to determine who used a particular program, what the users' HOME variables are, and when the program was used. Imagine that the program to be monitored in compiled code is called payroll, with source code saved in payroll.c, and that the monitoring C function named checkit is saved in checkit.c:

```
$ cc -o payroll payroll.c checkit.c
```

Usage of the payroll program will be reported in the file called /usr/you/keeptrack, which can be cat with typical output as follows:

```
$ cat keeptrack
```
jim with home directory /usr/jim used payroll on
Fri May 20 at 12:30:55 EST

jane with home directory /usr/jane used payroll
on Mon May 23 at 08:30:42 EST
```
$
```

Note also that anyone who uses payroll must have write permission to /usr/you/keeptrack:

```
$ chmod a+w /usr/you/keeptrack
```

■ **Example 11.5.1**                              /* payroll.c program */

```
main()
{
    /* code for payroll goes here
    ...
    ...
                                    */
    checkit();
}
```

/* the next function, checkit() is saved in checkit.c */

/* the checkit() function will be called when payroll is executed */

```
#include <stdio.h>
checkit()
{
    FILE *fptr;
    char *getenv(), *ctime(), *getlogin();
    long time();
    long thetime;
```

/* these functions must be declared because they do not return an int */

```
    time(&thetime);
```

/* thetime is in seconds */

/*if the file keeptrack cannot be opened for appending print an error message and leave */

```
    if ((fptr =fopen(/usr/you/keeptrack,"a")) == NULL) {
        perror("checkit");              exit(1);
        }
```

/* otherwise report the required usage
data */

```
else {
    fprintf(fptr, "%s with home directory %s used payroll
    on %s \n",getlogin(),getenv("HOME"),
    ctime(&thetime));
    }
}
```

■

### EXERCISES 11.5

1. Redesign checkit so that it can be effectively used to monitor any program that /usr/you wants to monitor, rather than just payroll. Use the C library string functions for this purpose.

## 11.6 | *INODE INFORMATION: STAT() AND FSTAT()*

Each data file has an inode entry that provides essential information about the file (see number 3 below).

Recall that the information concerning a data file is essentially located in three places:

1. The data itself is stored one character per byte on disk.
2. The data file has a (single!) parent called a directory file, and in that file is a set of entries, one for each of its children. Each individual entry consists of a user-selected name for the particular file and its inode number (integer).
3. The data file has an inode entry stored on disk that has the following information: disk location of the first byte of the data itself, number of bytes in the data file, date and time when the file was last used, date and time when the file was last modified, owner of the file, inode number assigned to the file, and other information that is all captured in a structure defined in the header file named /usr/include/sys. This header file actually uses other definitions and information defined in the file named /usr/include/types.h.

In System V, the equivalent of the following declaration, combined here for brevity from the two header files mentioned above, appears for the capture of inode information:

```
struct stat
{
```

```
short            st_dev;
```
/* ID number of the device that has a directory entry for this file */

```
unsigned short st_ino;
```
/* inode number of the file */

```
unsigned short st_mode;
```
/* the file mode captured in 16 different bits, labeled 0 through 15—other information available in mknod(2) */

```
short st_nlink;
```
/* the number of links to the file */

```
unsigned short st_uid;
```
/* the user ID of the file's owner */

```
unsigned short st_gid;
```
/* the group ID of the file's owner */

```
short st_rdev;
```
/* ID of device and only used for character special and block special files */

```
long st_size;
```
/*the size of the file in bytes */

```
long st_atime;
```
/*the time that the file was last accessed */

```
long st_mtime;
```
/* the time that the file was last modified */

```
long st_ctime;
```
/* the time that the file had its file status changed */

```
};
```

In actuality, the data types given in the structure defined above often have other names. For example, instead of seeing

```
short            st_dev;
```

in /usr/include/sys/stat.h , the fact is that

```
dev_t            st_dev;
```

appears in /usr/include/sys/stat.h, and

```
typedef short dev_t
```

appears in /usr/include/sys/types.h.

This is why both of the following include statements must appear in a C program that attempts to obtain inode information:

```
#include <sys/types.h>
#include <sys/stat.h>
```

These statements give the program access to the data type struct stat, and, hence, the user can then declare a variable of that type to hold the information, as in:

```
struct stat inode_info;
stat("myfile",&inode_info);        /* inode_info now has
                                      all the inode information
                                      available in it */
```

Additional information about <sys/type.h> can be located in the UNIX manual under TYPES(5).

### stat(2) and fstat(2)

The system calls that are used to fetch inode information are stat(2) and fstat(2). The former should be used if the actual name of the file is referenced, while the latter is used if its file descriptor is used. Their synopses are as follows:

```
#include <sys/types.h>
#include <sys/stat.h>

int stat(path,buf)
char *path;
struct stat *buf;

int fstat(fd,buf)
int fd;
struct stat *buf;
```

The parameter "path" is a pointer to a string that is the name of a file. The user must be able to search all directories in the pathname, but need not have any permission to the file in question. The value of fd, on the other hand, will have been obtained from a successful open, creat, or other appropriate system call. The functions will fail if a component of the path is not a directory, the file does not exist, search permission is denied for one or more of the path components, and so on. The value 0 is returned if successful, -1 otherwise with errno set to indicate the error.

The following program accesses some important information about a specified file.

■ **Example 11.6.1**

```
/*    CHAPTER 11    11.6.1.C   */

#include <sys/types.h>
#include <sys/stat.h>

main(argc,argv)
int argc;
char *argv[];
{
  struct stat inode_info;
  int catcherror;
  catcherror = stat(argv[1],&inode_info);
  if (catcherror == -1)
    printf("problem with %s\n",argv[1]);
  else
  {
    printf("The file %s has %d links\n",argv[1],inode_info.st_nlink);
    printf("and the user ID is %d\n",inode_info.st_uid);
    printf("it has %d bytes\n",inode_info.st_size);
  }
}


/*********/
/* INPUT */
/*********/

1 2 3  4 5 6 7 8 9 0
a b c d e f g h i j
99999 4444


/***********/
/* OUTPUT */
/***********/
The file inputfile has 1 links
and the user ID is 10026
it has 54 bytes                                                    ■
```

The reader has seen that one of the members of the struct stat structure defined in /usr/include/sys/stat.h is named st_mode of data type unsigned short (two-byte integer). It contains a wealth of information in its 16 bits labeled bit 15 down through bit 0, including:

- file permissions for others (read, write, execute: set with bits 2 down through 0, respectively)
- file permissions for the group (read, write, execute: set with bits 5 down through 3, respectively)
- file permissions for the user (read, write, execute: set with bits 8 down through 6, respectively)
- the sticky bit (set with bit 9)
- set gid (set with bit 10)
- set uid (set with bit 11)

- file type information: regular file (set with bit 15)
- block special file (set with bits 13 and 14)
- character special file (set with bit 13)
- directory file (set with bit 14)

The most convenient way to specify the bit patterns that are appropriate for a given file is by using base 8 (octal) notation. Each possible set of three binary digits (bits), beginning with bits 2 down through 0, can be represented by a single octal digit (0 through 7) as follows. Octal numbers will be indicated by a leading 0. Bit 15, the leading bit, will be represented by the binary digit 0 or 1. Here is the complete pattern:

| octal | binary |
|-------|--------|
| 0 | 000 |
| 1 | 001 |
| 2 | 010 |
| 3 | 011 |
| 4 | 100 |
| 5 | 101 |
| 6 | 110 |
| 7 | 111 |

■ **Example 11.6.2**   If the octal representation of bits 15 down through 0 is 0040731, with the leading 0 indicating octal, the next 0 interpreted as a binary digit, and the remaining digits as octal digits of three binary digits each, then the file it refers to has the following characteristics:

1. It is *not* a regular file because 0 indicates bit 15 is off.
2. It is a directory file because 4 indicates bit 14 is on.
3. The set uid, set gid, and sticky bits are off because of the octal 0.
4. The user has read, write, and execute permission because of the octal 7 (binary 111).
5. The group has write and execute permission because of the octal 3 (binary 011).
6. The others have execute permission only because of the octal 1 (binary 001). ■

Within the header file /usr/include/sys/stat.h, the reader can find the definition of the data type struct stat and symbolic definitions of various bit patterns that facilitate the checking of whether a file has certain characteristics.

These definitions are as follows:

```
#define S_IFMT      0170000        /* file type mask */
#define S_IFDIR     0040000        /* directory bit is on */
#define S_IFCHR     0020000        /* character special file
                                      bit is on */
#define S_IFBLK     0060000        /* block special file bit
                                      is on */
#define S_IFREG     0100000        /* regular file bit is on */
#define S_IFIFO     0010000        /* first in first out bit is
                                      on */
#define S_ISUID       04000        /* set user ID on exe-
                                      cution */
#define S_ISGID       02000        /* set group ID on exe-
                                      cution */
#define S_ISVTX       01000        /* set sticky bit */
#define S_IREAD     0000400        /* owner has read per-
                                      mission */
#define S_IWRITE    0000200        /* owner has write per-
                                      mission */
#define S_IEXEC     0000100        /* owner has execute/
                                      search permission */
```

It is not necessary to use any of the symbolic notations, but they do make code more readable than simply using the octal digits. Other symbolic notations could be added, but the ones given are the most important ones.

It is important to realize that if the following declaration is made in a C program with the inclusion of the two header files:

```
#include <sys/types.h>
#include <sys/stat.h>
struct stat inode_info
```

then one *cannot* check to see if myfile is a directory file with the following code:

```
stat("myfile",&inode_info);
if (inode_info.st_mode ==S_IFDIR) {

        . . .

    }
```

The problem is that a file will be a directory file solely on the basis of whether bit 14 is set (and, hence, bits 15, 13 and 12 should be off); but checking against S_IFDIR checks to see if bit 14 is set *and all other bits are off.* Thus, it is necessary to isolate only bit 14 (and implicitly bits 15, 13, and 12) if one wants to determine whether a file is a directory file. This can be done by using the bitwise and & operator, which has the following properties:

$$0 \& 0 == 0$$
$$0 \& 1 == 0$$
$$1 \& 0 == 0$$
$$1 \& 1 == 1$$

More succinctly, 1 & bit == bit, while 0 & bit == 0 . The and operator can also be used to "and" corresponding bits in bit strings of the same length—simply "and" corresponding bits and concatenate all such bits. This operator should not be confused with the address operator using the same & symbol. Watch the context to determine meaning.

**■ Example 11.6.3** Hence, the proper way to check to see if myfile is a directory file is with the following code. The & operator will individually "and" the corresponding bits. Furthermore, in the comment, alphabetic letters represent a binary digit, 0 or 1:

```
stat("myfile",&inode_info);
if (inode_info.st_mode & S_IFMT ==S_IFDIR) {
        ...
   }
```

/* a bcd efg hij klm npq
& 1 111 000 000 000 000
== 0 100 000 000 000 000 will be true exactly when a==0; b==1, c==0; d==0, and the rest ==anything; i.e., when inode_info.st_mode begins with 0100; i.e., when "myfile" is a directory */                          ■

The moral of the above story is, if you want to determine if certain bits are set or off (in our case if inode_info.st_mode begins with 0100) and other bits can have any value (in our case bits 11 down through 0 of inode_info.st_mode can have any value), simply use the and (&) operator combining the unknown values with a mask having the bits on that must have a certain value against another constant having only 1s where desired.

**■ Example 11.6.4** Suppose the user wants to check to determine if a sequence is as follows (where x = don't care):

```
x10x01
```

The appropriate mask in this case is

011011     /* ones where you care */

The check would be: **x10x01**

&011011
==010001     /*which is always true—independent of the value
of x, *and never true if any of the determined 0s or
1s in the x10x01 sequence are changed* */     ■

In addition to the & operator, there are two other binary operators. The or (|) operator and the not (~) operator can be used to *set* bits on or turn them off. So, use & to check, and | or ~ to set on or off.

Specifically, the or | operator has the following properties:

0 | 0 == 0
0 | 1 == 1
1 | 0 == 1
1 | 1 == 1

More succinctly, 1 | bit == 1, while 0 | bit == bit. The or (|) operator can also be used to "or" corresponding bits in two-bit strings of the same length. Simply "or" corresponding bits and concatenate all such bits.

The not (~) operator is a unary operator operates on single bits by changing 0 to 1, and 1 to 0:

~0 == 1
~1 == 0

Again, the not operator can also be used on a string of bits by defining the not of a bit string to mean "not" each individual bit and concatenate all such answers.

Suppose the user wants to set a certain bit or bits in mystring on and leave all the others alone. The correct way to do this is to assign mystring the or of mystring and a string with ones where the set should take place and zeros elsewhere.

■ **Example 11.6.5**  Let mystring= 100 010. Suppose the user wants to set mystring==101 110 (turn bits 3 and 2 on). The solution is: mystring = mystring | 001 100 or in shorthand, mystring |= 001 100 because

        100 010
    | 001 100
    == 101 110

Thus, if a bit is already on it stays on; if off, it stays off. ■

Suppose the user wants to turn off a certain bit or bits in mystring and leave all the others alone. The correct way to do this is to assign mystring the or of mystring and a string, *which is the negation of one,* with ones where the set should take place and zeros elsewhere.

■ **Example 11.6.6**  Let mystring= 100 011. Suppose the user wants to set mystring= =000 010 (turn bits 5 and 0 off). The solution is: mystring = mystring ~ 100 001 or in shorthand, mystring = ~100 001 because

```
        100  011
¦      ~100  001
==      000  010
```
■

## EXERCISES 11.6

1. Modify Example 11.6.1 to obtain the same information for any number of files given on the command line after the program name.
2. Repeat Example 11.6.2 for the case in which st_mode has the following value: 0061345.
3. Show the corresponding code to Example 11.6.3 to check to see if a file is a regular file.
4. Explain how one would check to see if a sequence of binary digits is x 001 100 111 11x x10 where x indicates don't care (see Example 11.6.4).
5. Show an efficient way to give others read and write permission for a specific file without changing any of the other bits in its st_mode member.
6. Write a C program that shows the user the names of all of his or her C programs ( .c as the suffix) and then prompts interactively as to whether others should be granted execute permission; if affirmative, such permission should be granted.
7. Write a C program that copies one file to another with appropriate error checking for the following cases:
   a. The first file cannot be opened.
   b. The number of arguments is not correct.
   c. The first cannot be located.
   d. The first file is not a data file.
   e. The second file exists already but is not a data file.
   f. The second file name is the same as the first.
   g. The second file exists already, but the user is given a chance to overwrite it.

h. The first file cannot be read.

i. The second file cannot be written to.

## 11.7 FILE PERMISSIONS: CREAT(), CHMOD(), AND UMASK()

Recall that the system call *creat*(2) creates a new file or rewrites an existing one. This was explained in Chapter 10, including its synopsis:

```
int creat(path,mode)
char *path;
int mode;
```

where path points to the name of the file and mode is most easily given ask an octal number as was discussed in st_mode (from /usr/include/ sys/stat.h ). However, any mode that is passed to the function creat(2) is actually altered by a default file creation mask, generally 0022 octal, which is 000 010 010 binary. This file creation mask is used to turn the group write and the "other" write permissions off by the following calculation (as discussed in the previous section):

```
mode = mode & ~0022
```

So, if the user programs

```
creat("myfile",0664)
```

then the actual mode that myfile receives is:

```
110 110 100      == 110 110 100
&~000 010 010      &111 101 101
                 == 110 100 100 (0644).
```

However, the user may change the default file creation mask by issuing a call to the system call *umask*(2). The synopsis of umask(2) is:

```
int umask(csmask)
int cmask;
```

The function umask(2) sets the file creation mode mask to cmask and returns the previous value of the mask, generally 0022. Only the low-order bits of cmask (bits 8 down through 0) are used.

Recall that the chmod command can be used to set file permissions from within a UNIX shell script. It can be used with symbolic notation or with octal notation. Thus, for example, the following command lines each give (1) the owner read, write, and execute permission; (2) the group write only; and (3) others read only:

```
$ chmod 0724 myfile
```

or

```
$ chmod u=rwx myfile
$ chmod g=w myfile
$ chmod o=r myfile
```

There is a way to get to the UNIX utility chmod from within a C program, from the library function system(3S) as discussed in the next section. Another way to change permissions on a file from within a C program is the system call *chmod(2)* whose synopsis is as follows:

```
int chmod(path,mode)
char *path;
int mode;
```

This was discussed in Section 10.2.

■ **Example 11.7.1**   Suppose the user has a file called myfile, which generally only has read permission for the owner. But the owner wishes to run a program that fetches the file and actually updates it by writing to it. In that case, the following lines of code would sandwich the actual processing from within the C program:

```
chmod("myfile",0600)
chmod("myfile",0400)
```

Here is the complete program with its output:

```
/*      CHAPTER 11    11.7.1.C    */

main()
{
  chmod("myfile",0600);
  system("ls -al myfile");
  chmod("myfile",0400);
  system("ls -al myfile");
}


/**********/
/* OUTPUT */
/**********/
-rw-------   1 eharri    student      0 Aug 22 09:09 myfile
-r--------   1 eharri    student      0 Aug 22 09:09 myfile
```

■

**1.** Write the code so that in the creation of a file, no matter what mode is passed to it, the file will not have execute permission for the owner, and will not have read permission for others, and will not have write permission for the group.

**2.** Write the code with umask(2) so that in the creation of a file no masking is done.

## 11.8 *COMMAND FILES IN A C PROGRAM: SYSTEM(3S), EXECL(2), FORK(2), GETPID(2), WAIT(2)*

The purpose of the UNIX C function *system(3S)* is to issue a command to the shell from within a C program. Its synopsis is as follows:

```
#include <stdio.h>
int system(string)
char *string;
```

This causes the string to be passed to sh(1) just as if the string had been typed on the command line itself. The value of string may be one of the UNIX utilities in Section 1, or indeed, it may be the name of an executable shell script. The process that had been executing simply waits until the shell has finished executing the UNIX command given by string, and then the system(3S) function returns the exit status of the shell. The child process that is forked by system(3S) executes /bin/sh, which, in turn, forks another process to execute string. While string is executing, /bin/sh is sleeping. When string finishes execution, /bin/sh awakens. Finally, /bin/sh dies and the original process is awakened.

The function system(3S) returns a negative value and sets errno if it is unsuccessful; otherwise it returns the exit status of the shell itself. The string that is executed via system(3S) inherits the same file connections that the C program had (the calling function). This means that if redirection was used with the calling program, it will also be used with string.

It is interesting to note that system(3S) was actually constructed using execl(2), fork(2), and wait(2).

■ **Example 11.8.1.** The following program prints the list of files in the working directory of the user:

```
/*     CHAPTER 11    11.8.1.C    */

main()
{
  printf("Here are the files in your working directory\n");
  system("ls -l");
  printf(" good day !\n");
}

/**********/
/* OUTPUT */
/**********/
total 83
-rw-r--r--    1 eharri    student         955 Dec 20 13:07 11.1.1
-rwx------    1 eharri    student         712 Dec 14 13:08 11.1.1.c
-rw-r--r--    1 eharri    student        1409 Dec 20 13:08 11.3.2
-rwx------    1 eharri    student        1298 Aug 21 15:02 11.3.2.c
-rw-r--r--    1 eharri    student        2071 Dec 20 13:08 11.4.1
-rwx------    1 eharri    student        1741 Aug 21 15:44 11.4.1.c
-rw-r--r--    1 eharri    student         671 Dec 20 13:08 11.6.1
-rwx------    1 eharri    student         468 Aug 21 16:29 11.6.1.c
-rw-r--r--    1 eharri    student         312 Dec 20 13:10 11.7.1
-rwx------    1 eharri    student         149 Aug 22 09:11 11.7.1.c
-rwx------    1 eharri    student         153 Aug 22 09:13 11.8.1.c
-rw-r--r--    1 eharri    student         361 Aug 22 09:25 11.8.2.c
-rw-r--r--    1 eharri    student         179 Aug 22 09:30 11.8.2b.c
-rw-r--r--    1 eharri    student         186 Aug 22 09:33 11.8.3.c
-rw-r--r--    1 eharri    student         231 Aug 22 09:55 11.8.4.c
-rw-r--r--    1 eharri    student         277 Aug 22 10:24 11.8.5.c
-rw-r--r--    1 eharri    student         306 Aug 22 10:31 11.8.6.c
-rw-r--r--    1 eharri    student         461 Aug 22 10:37 11.8.7.c
-rw-r--r--    1 eharri    student         473 Aug 22 11:06 11.9.2.c
-rw-r--r--    1 eharri    student         602 Aug 22 11:10 11.9.3.c
-rw-r--r--    1 eharri    student          99 Aug 22 09:56 Cfiles
-rwxr-xr-x    1 eharri    student       22509 Dec 20 13:10 a.out
-rw-r--r--    1 eharri    student           9 Aug 21 15:01 input
-rwxrwxrwx    1 eharri    student          54 Aug 21 15:04 inputfile
-r--------    1 eharri    student           0 Aug 22 09:09 myfile
-rw-r--r--    1 eharri    student           0 Dec 20 13:11 out
Here are the files in your working directory
 good day !
```

■ **Example 11.8.2** Here is an example of a program that actually builds the command line within the C program:

```
/*     CHAPTER 11    11.8.2.C    */

main()
{
  char command_buf[80];
  char options_buf[40];
  printf("What shell script do you want to run ? \n");
  scanf("%s",command_buf);
  printf("add options now, if any \n");
  scanf("%s",options_buf);
  strcat(command_buf," ");
  strcat(command_buf,options_buf);
  system(command_buf);
  printf("all finished now\n");
}
```

```
/*********/
/* INPUT */
/*********/
What shell script do you want to run ?
cat
add options now, if any
inputfile


/**********/
/* OUTPUT */
/**********/
1 2 3 4 5 6 7 8 9 0
a b c d e f g h i j
99999 4444
all finished now                                        ■
```

In the exec(2) entry of the manual the user will find six functions named: execl(2), execv(2), execle(2), execve(2), execlp(2), and execvp(2).

These are related functions, but for purposes of clarity, we will concentrate simply on *execl(2)*—execute and leave. It is very much like system(3S) in that it permits the user to run a command file from a C program.

The synopsis of execl(2) is:

```
int execl(path,arg0,arg1,...,argn,0)
char *path,*arg0, *arg1,...,*argn;
```

where path points to the name of the file holding a command that is to be executed, arg0 points to a string that is the same as path (or at least its last component), arg1 through argn are pointers to the arguments for the command, and 0 simply marks the end of the list of arguments.

There are key differences between system(3S) and execl(2):

1. Execl(2) does not create a new process: it simply overlays the original program with the called command.

2. Because execl(2) does not create a new process, the command that is executed has the same process ID as the calling program.

3. Because an overlay has taken place, code that follows the call to execl(2) is not executed.

4. Note that execl(2) requires the full pathname and will not expand partial pathnames. Execle(2) will, however.

The next example is a version of Example 11.8.1, but is different in that the message of the last line is not printed.

■ **Example 11.8.3**

```
main()
{
    printf("Here are the files in your working directory\n");
    execl("/bin/ls","ls","-l",0);
    printf("This line is not printed\n");
}


/**********/
/* OUTPUT */
/**********/
total 84
-rw-r--r--   1 eharri    student        955 Dec 20 13:07 11.1.1
-rwx------   1 eharri    student        712 Dec 14 13:08 11.1.1.c
-rw-r--r--   1 eharri    student       1409 Dec 20 13:08 11.3.2
-rwx------   1 eharri    student       1298 Aug 21 15:02 11.3.2.c
-rw-r--r--   1 eharri    student       2071 Dec 20 13:08 11.4.1
-rwx------   1 eharri    student       1741 Aug 21 15:44 11.4.1.c
-rw-r--r--   1 eharri    student        671 Dec 20 13:08 11.6.1
-rwx------   1 eharri    student        468 Aug 21 16:29 11.6.1.c
-rw-r--r--   1 eharri    student        312 Dec 20 13:10 11.7.1
-rwx------   1 eharri    student        149 Aug 22 09:11 11.7.1.c
-rw-r--r--   1 eharri    student       1875 Dec 20 13:11 11.8.1
-rwx------   1 eharri    student        153 Aug 22 09:13 11.8.1.c
-rw-r--r--   1 eharri    student        587 Dec 20 13:14 11.8.2
-rw-r--r--   1 eharri    student        361 Aug 22 09:25 11.8.2.c
-rw-r--r--   1 eharri    student        179 Aug 22 09:30 11.8.2b.c
-rw-r--r--   1 eharri    student        186 Aug 22 09:33 11.8.3.c
-rw-r--r--   1 eharri    student        231 Aug 22 09:55 11.8.4.c
-rw-r--r--   1 eharri    student        277 Aug 22 10:24 11.8.5.c
-rw-r--r--   1 eharri    student        306 Aug 22 10:31 11.8.6.c
-rw-r--r--   1 eharri    student        461 Aug 22 10:37 11.8.7.c
-rw-r--r--   1 eharri    student        473 Aug 22 11:06 11.9.2.c
-rw-r--r--   1 eharri    student        602 Aug 22 11:10 11.9.3.c
-rw-r--r--   1 eharri    student         99 Aug 22 09:56 Cfiles
-rwxr-xr-x   1 eharri    student      19751 Dec 20 13:15 a.out
-rw-r--r--   1 eharri    student          9 Aug 21 15:01 input
-rwxrwxrwx   1 eharri    student         54 Aug 21 15:04 inputfile
-r--------   1 eharri    student          0 Aug 22 09:09 myfile
-rw-r--r--   1 eharri    student          0 Dec 20 13:15 out
```
■

The system call execl(2) cannot be used directly to execute shell scripts that contain metacharacters *, ?, [, and others. However, there is a way around it. The idea is to make sure that a new shell is spawned, because it *does* recognize metacharacters. The command interpreter, sh, can then be given a -c option that tells it to interpret the string following it as a list of arguments, rather than as a single argument. For example,

**$ sh -c ls -l**

will spawn two processes, one running another shell, sh, which in turns spawns a process running ls with the -l option.

Here is a revised Example 11.8.3, which shows an alternative way to print a directory.

■ **Example 11.8.4**

```
main()
{
  printf("Here are the files in your working directory\n");
  execl("/bin/sh","sh","-c","ls -l",0);
  printf("This line is not printed\n");
}
```

```
/**********/
/* OUTPUT */
/**********/
total 88
-rw-r--r--    1 eharri    student         955 Dec 20 13:07 11.1.1
-rwx------    1 eharri    student         712 Dec 14 13:08 11.1.1.c
-rw-r--r--    1 eharri    student        1409 Dec 20 13:08 11.3.2
-rwx------    1 eharri    student        1298 Aug 21 15:02 11.3.2.c
-rw-r--r--    1 eharri    student        2071 Dec 20 13:08 11.4.1
-rwx------    1 eharri    student        1741 Aug 21 15:44 11.4.1.c
-rw-r--r--    1 eharri    student         671 Dec 20 13:08 11.6.1
-rwx------    1 eharri    student         468 Aug 21 16:29 11.6.1.c
-rw-r--r--    1 eharri    student         312 Dec 20 13:10 11.7.1
-rwx------    1 eharri    student         149 Aug 22 09:11 11.7.1.c
-rw-r--r--    1 eharri    student        1875 Dec 20 13:11 11.8.1
-rwx------    1 eharri    student         153 Aug 22 09:13 11.8.1.c
-rw-r--r--    1 eharri    student         587 Dec 20 13:14 11.8.2
-rw-r--r--    1 eharri    student         361 Aug 22 09:25 11.8.2.c
-rw-r--r--    1 eharri    student        1966 Dec 20 13:16 11.8.2b
-rw-r--r--    1 eharri    student         179 Aug 22 09:30 11.8.2b.c
-rw-r--r--    1 eharri    student         186 Aug 22 09:33 11.8.3.c
-rw-r--r--    1 eharri    student         231 Aug 22 09:55 11.8.4.c
-rw-r--r--    1 eharri    student         277 Aug 22 10:24 11.8.5.c
-rw-r--r--    1 eharri    student         306 Aug 22 10:31 11.8.6.c
-rw-r--r--    1 eharri    student         461 Aug 22 10:37 11.8.7.c
-rw-r--r--    1 eharri    student         473 Aug 22 11:06 11.9.2.c
-rw-r--r--    1 eharri    student         602 Aug 22 11:10 11.9.3.c
-rw-r--r--    1 eharri    student          99 Aug 22 09:56 Cfiles
-rwxr-xr-x    1 eharri    student       19763 Dec 20 13:16 a.out
-rw-r--r--    1 eharri    student           9 Aug 21 15:01 input
-rwxrwxrwx    1 eharri    student          54 Aug 21 15:04 inputfile
-r--------    1 eharri    student           0 Aug 22 09:09 myfile
-rw-r--r--    1 eharri    student           0 Dec 20 13:16 out
```

■ **Example 11.8.5**  This example prints the names of all the programs in the working directory that end with .c.

```
main()
{
  printf("Here are the files in your working directory\n");
  printf("that end with '.c'\n");
  execl("/bin/sh","sh","-c","ls *.c ",0);
  printf("This line is not printed\n");
}
```

```
/**********/
/* OUTPUT */
/**********/
11.1.1.c
11.3.2.c
11.4.1.c
11.6.1.c
11.7.1.c
11.8.1.c
11.8.2.c
```

```
11.8.2b.c
11.8.3.c
11.8.4.c
11.8.5.c
11.8.6.c
11.8.7.c
11.9.2.c
11.9.3.c
```

■

The *fork*(*2*) and the *getpid*(*2*) system calls have very simple synopses:

```
int fork()

int getpid()
```

The system call getpid(2) simply returns the process ID of the process that called it.

The appearance of fork(2) in a C program, on the other hand, is a bit more interesting. It literally causes the remainder of the code to be considered as two identical but separate processes (running in a time-sharing mode). The nomenclature is that the parent process—the original process before the fork() call—has spawned a child process, which is the newly hatched process with a different PID. Both processes have the same environment, including file descriptors.

The child process that is spawned by fork() does return a different int than the parent. The child returns 0, while the parent returns the process ID of the child itself.

## ■ Example 11.8.6

```
main()
{
  int return_value;
  printf("This program forks another process\n");
  fork();
  printf("The process id is %d and the return_value is %d\n",getpid(),return_value);
  execl("/bin/ls","ls",0);
  printf("say no -- do not print\n");
}


/**********/
/* OUTPUT */
/**********/
This program forks another process
The process id is 3351 and the return_value is 0
The process id is 3350 and the return_value is 0
11.1.1
11.1.1.c
11.3.2
11.3.2.c
11.4.1
11.4.1.c
11.6.1
11.6.1.c
11.7.1
11.7.1.c
11.8.1
11.8.1.c
11.8.2
```

```
11.8.2.c
11.8.2b
11.8.2b.c
11.8.3
11.8.3.c
11.8.4
11.8.4.c
11.8.5.c
11.8.6.c
11.8.7.c
11.9.2.c
11.9.3.c
Cfiles
a.out
input
inputfile
myfile
out
11.1.1
11.1.1.c
11.3.2
11.3.2.c
11.4.1
11.4.1.c
11.6.1
11.6.1.c
11.7.1
11.7.1.c
11.8.1
11.8.1.c
11.8.2
11.8.2.c
11.8.2b
11.8.2b.c
11.8.3
11.8.3.c
11.8.4
11.8.4.c
11.8.5.c
11.8.6.c
11.8.7.c
11.9.2.c
11.9.3.c
Cfiles
a.out
input
inputfile
myfile
out
```

Note that once a process forks, it is impossible to tell in advance which process will get the CPU's time. It is running in time-share mode, so one run may differ from the next. In this run, the assumption will be that the parent has a process ID of 283 and the child of 291, and that the child runs first.

A typical run would then be as follows:

```
$ cc -o for_ex fork.c

$ for_ex
```

this program forks another process

the process id is 291 and the return_value is 0

/* now comes the list of files from the child process */

**the process id is 283 and the return_value is 291**

/* now comes the list of files from the parent process */ ■

■ **Example 11.8.7** In this example, only the child process will execute the second printf, because it is the process that returns 0. Assume here that the parent has process ID 283, the child has 291, and that the parent runs first:

**$ cc -0 for_ex2 newfork.c**

**$ for_ex2**

**this program forks another process**

/* now comes the list of files from the parent process */
the process id is 283 and the return_value is 0

Here is the program and its actual output:

```
main()
{
  int return_value;
  printf("This program forks another process\n");
  if ((return_value = fork()) == 0)
    printf("the process id is %d and the return_value is %d\n",getpid(),return_value
  execl("/bin/ls","ls",0);
  printf("say no -- do not print !\n");
}


/**********/
/* OUTPUT */
/**********/
This program forks another process
the process id is 3369 and the return_value is 0
11.1.1
11.1.1.c
11.3.2
11.3.2.c
11.4.1
11.4.1.c
11.6.1
11.6.1.c
11.7.1
11.7.1.c
11.8.1
11.8.1.c
11.8.2
11.8.2.c
11.8.2b
11.8.2b.c
11.8.3
11.8.3.c
11.8.4
11.8.4.c
11.8.5
11.8.5.c
```

```
11.8.6.c
11.8.7.c
11.9.2.c
11.9.3.c
Cfiles
a.out
input
inputfile
myfile
out
11.1.1
11.1.1.c
11.3.2
11.3.2.c
11.4.1
11.4.1.c
11.6.1
11.6.1.c
11.7.1
11.7.1.c
11.8.1
11.8.1.c
11.8.2
11.8.2.c
11.8.2b
11.8.2b.c
11.8.3
11.8.3.c
11.8.4
11.8.4.c
11.8.5
11.8.5.c
11.8.6.c
11.8.7.c
11.9.2.c
11.9.3.c
Cfiles
a.out
input
inputfile
myfile
out
```

■

Finally, we look at the *wait*(*2*) system call, whose purpose is to force the parent process to wait for a child process to stop or terminate. Its synopsis is:

```
int wait(stat_loc)
int *stat_loc;
int wait ((int *) 0)
```

The purpose of stat_loc is to point to a status location of information that can be used to distinguish between suspended processes and terminated child processes, as well as the cause of the termination of a child process. This information is passed to the parent process. The reader should consult the UNIX manual (2) for further details. Normally, the wait(2) function returns the PID of the child process in the case of a stopped or terminated child process and -1 otherwise.

■ **Example 11.8.8**  In this example, there is no question that the wait(2) function forces the parent to wait for the child. This is essentially how the system(3S) function would be constructed from scratch. Assume again that the parent has process ID 283 and the child, 291:

```
main()                                              /*forkwait.c */
{
    int return_value;
    int status_info;
    int wait_id;
    printf("this program forks and waits for another process");
    if ( (return_value = fork()) == 0).
    printf("the process id is %d and the return_value is
    %d\n",   getpid(),return_value);        /*only the child
                                             process will print
                                             this */

    wait_id = wait(&status_info);           /*the parent now must
                                             wait for the child
                                             process to finish */
    printf("the wait id is %d and the status is %d\n",wait_id,
    status_info);
    execl("/bin/ls","ls",0);
    printf("say no--do not print !\n");
}

    $ cc -0 forkwait forkwait.c
    this program forks and waits for another process
    the process id is 291 and the return_value is 0
    the wait id is 291 and the status is 0
                                             /* the files from the
                                             child process are listed
                                             here */

    the wait id is 291 and the status is 0
                                             /* the files from the
                                             parent process are
                                             listed here */           ■
```

The following rules apply when using the fork(2) and wait(2) system calls:

1. A parent process can spawn several child processes with calls to the fork(2) function several times.

**2.** A parent process can be made to wait for each of its child processes to terminate by placing the wait(2) function in the process several times.

**3.** The return value of wait(2) can be used to loop through a sequence of statements until the desired child is located or until there are no children left. In this case, -1 is returned.

```
int return_value;
int status_info;
int wait_id;
return_value=fork();
while ( (wait_id=wait(&status_info)) !=
return_value
        && wait_id ! = -1);
```

/* this says to loop as long as there are more child processes and the child processes have a different wait_id than the value returned by the fork(2) function */

Here is the program and its actual output:

```
main()
{
  int return_value;
  int status_info;
  int wait_id;
  printf("This program forks and waits for another process\n");
  if ((return_value = fork()) == 0)
    printf("the process id is %d and the return_value is %d\n",getpid(),return_value
  wait_id = wait(&status_info);
  printf("the wait id is %d and the status is %d\n",wait_id,status_info);
  execl("/bin/ls","ls",0);
  printf("say no -- do not print !\n");
}


/**********/
/* OUTPUT */
/**********/
This program forks and waits for another process
the process id is 3386 and the return_value is 0
the wait id is -1 and the status is 0
11.1.1
11.1.1.c
11.3.2
11.3.2.c
11.4.1
11.4.1.c
11.6.1
11.6.1.c
11.7.1
11.7.1.c
```

```
11.8.1
11.8.1.c
11.8.2
11.8.2.c
11.8.2b
11.8.2b.c
11.8.3
11.8.3.c
11.8.4
11.8.4.c
11.8.5
11.8.5.c
11.8.6
11.8.6.c
11.8.7.c
11.9.2.c
11.9.3.c
Cfiles
a.out
input
inputfile
myfile
out
the wait id is 3386 and the status is 0
11.1.1
11.1.1.c
11.3.2
11.3.2.c
11.4.1
11.4.1.c
11.6.1
11.6.1.c
11.7.1
11.7.1.c
11.8.1
11.8.1.c
11.8.2
11.8.2.c
11.8.2b
11.8.2b.c
11.8.3
11.8.3.c
11.8.4
11.8.4.c
11.8.5
11.8.5.c
11.8.6
11.8.6.c
11.8.7.c
11.9.2.c
11.9.3.c
Cfiles
a.out
input
inputfile
myfile
out
```

## EXERCISES  11.8

**1.** Write a C program that gives the user the opportunity to remove any or all of the files in the working directory. The name of a file should appear followed by a prompt as to whether it should be removed.

**2.** Write a C program that interactively asks whether a new process should be started. In either case, have the program list the process status of all processes.

## 11.9 | *TRAP SIGNALS: SIGNAL()*

It is often important to know why a particular process might have executed abnormally. The system call *signal*(2) can be used to determine what the problem was, and even override the system defaults to deal with the aberration, if that is the desired action.

The system call signal(2) has the following synopsis:

```
#include <signal.h>
int (*signal(sig,func))()
int sig;
void (*func)();
```

Note that sig is the value of the signal itself and func, which is a pointer to the function func(), specifies one of three ways to deal with the signal.

First, a discussion of the possible values of sig. They have been given symbolic names in <signal.h>, but they can also be designated by number. Some values have been omitted from the following list:

| | | |
|---|---|---|
| SIGHUP | 01 | sent when the phone is hung up |
| SIGINT | 02 | typically sent by depressing the ctrl-c key |
| SIQUIT | 03 | typically sent by depressing the ctrl-\ key |
| SIGILL | 04 | typically sent by an illegal instruction |
| SIGTRAP | 05 | trace trap |
| SIGFPE | 08 | typically sent by a floating point exception |
| SIGKILL | 09 | kill (cannot be caught or ignored) |
| SIGSYS | 12 | typically sent when a bad argument to a system call is detected |
| SIGPIPE | 13 | typically sent when a write occurs on a pipe with no process to read it |
| SIGUSR1 | 16 | user-defined signal 1 |
| SIGUSR2 | 17 | user-defined signal 2 |

|  |  |  |
|---|---|---|
| **SIGCLD** | 18 | death of a child |
| **SIGPWR** | 19 | power fail |

Here are the three possible ways to deal with a value of sig. Func will be assigned one of these three values.

1. **SIG_DFL** a pointer to the system default function SIG_DFL(); the action is to terminate the process upon receipt of the signal.

2. **SIG_IGN** a pointer to the system ignore function SIG_IGN(); the action is to ignore the sig that is sent. Note that SIGKILL cannot be ignored. Do not use signal(SIG_IGN,SIGKILL);

3. **function address** When the signal sig is received, the process is to execute the function pointed to by func, with sig as its only argument. After the function pointed to by func is executed, the process that received the signal will resume execution at the point that it was interrupted. Before func is executed, the value of func for the caught signal will be set to SIG_DFL unless the signal is SIGILL, SIGTRAP, or SIGPWR.

The value returned by a successful execution of signal is the previous value of the second argument of signal for the specified sig—namely, a pointer to a function—either SIG_DFL, SIG_IGN, or the user-defined func. Unsuccessful calls to signal return a -1 with errno also set to isolate the error. Note then that often this return value will initially be SIG_DFL (in the case of foreground processes) and SIG_IGN (in the case of background processes that ignore for example SIGINT and SIGQUIT).

■ **Example 11.9.1**   Suppose the user wishes for a program to ignore the interrupt key (ctrl-c). In that case, the following statement should appear as the *first* statement in the C program, or should be placed at the point in the program where trapping should first begin:

```
signal(SIGINT,SIG_IGN);     /* or alternatively, but this is
                               more likely to be system
                               dependent */

signal(2,SIG_IGN);          /* or alternatively system("trap"
                               2 ") */
```

The program can be reset to system defaults for signals at any place in the program by the following statement:

```
signal(SIGINT,SIG_DFL);
```                                                                     ■

Note that when the signal() function catches a signal and takes an action other than SIG_IGN, it resets the action to the default. *Thus, it is important to reset the action to whatever is desired after a signal is caught.*

■ **Example 11.9.2**  This program will trap the signal 2 and take alternative action defined by a function called new_action, which does not return a value—hence is defined as type void:

```
#include <signal.h>
   int iteration;
   void new_action();
main()                              /* any function that does not return an
                                       int must be declared */

{
   printf("this program is going to have a trap
set to take new action based on the signal '2' " );
   signal(SIGINT,new_action);       /* set the trap to take new_action, a
                                       pointer to the function new_action(), in
                                       case the signal SIGINT is received by the
                                       program */
   for ( iteration=0; iteration < 20; ++iteration) {
       printf(" i am now doing iteration %d", iteration);
       sleep(1);                    /*suspend the program for 1
                                       second */
       }
   }
void new_action()
{
   signal(SIGINT,new_action);       /* the signal SIGINT has been caught if
                                       this line is executed; hence the trap is
                                       reset here so that the next ctrl-c will also
                                       generate a new action—otherwise the
                                       default action for the signal SIGINT will
                                       be taken which will simply be to
                                       terminate the program */
   printf("you must have pressed the ctrl-c");
}
```

Here is the complete program and its output:

```
/*      CHAPTER 11    11.9.2.C    */

#include <signal.h>

int iteration;
void new_action();

main()
{
  printf("This program is going to have a trap set to take new \n");
  printf("action based on the signal '2'\n");
  signal(SIGINT,new_action);
  for (iteration=0; iteration < 20; ++iteration)
    {
      printf("I am now doing iteration %d\n",iteration);
      sleep(1);
    }
}
void new_action()
{
  signal(SIGINT,new_action);
  printf("you must have pressed the ctrl-c\n");
}


/**********/
/* OUTPUT */
/**********/
This program is going to have a trap set to take new
action based on the signal '2'
I am now doing iteration 0
I am now doing iteration 1
you must have pressed the ctrl-c
I am now doing iteration 2
I am now doing iteration 3
you must have pressed the ctrl-c
I am now doing iteration 4
I am now doing iteration 5
I am now doing iteration 6
you must have pressed the ctrl-c
I am now doing iteration 7
I am now doing iteration 8
I am now doing iteration 9
you must have pressed the ctrl-c
I am now doing iteration 10
I am now doing iteration 11
I am now doing iteration 12
I am now doing iteration 13
I am now doing iteration 14
I am now doing iteration 15
I am now doing iteration 16
I am now doing iteration 17
I am now doing iteration 18
I am now doing iteration 19
you must have pressed the ctrl-c
```

The preceding program cannot be terminated by the SIGINT signal, but could still be terminated by the SIGQUIT signal (usually control backslash—ctrl \). The default actions, to be taken when SIGINT or SIGQUIT is received, are almost identical—they both will terminate the process. SIGQUIT goes one step further and actually causes a copy of the running program to be placed in a file named core in the user's working directory, which can then be used to assist in the debugging.

Other signals, namely, SIGILL, SIGTRAP, SIGIOT, ASIGEMT, SIGFPE, SIGBUS, SIGSEGV, and SIGSYS, also will attempt to create the file named core. If the interrupted program had an effective user ID that is different from the real user ID, then the core file is not produced. Information concerning core can be found in core(4), signal(2), exit(2), usr/include/sys/param.h, /usr/include/sys/user.h, and /usr/include/sys/reg.h.

Finally, a few words about signals and how they relate to background processes—those invoked by

$ **a.out &**

or any executable file that is run in the background. Generally speaking, background processes will not be interrupted by SIGINT and SIGQUIT. However, if the programmer has a program in which an action is explicitly stated for SIGINIT or SIGQUIT, those actions will *override* the system defaults to ignore such signals received by background processes.

The following program will show how the programmer can run a process that will do exactly what often is needed: ignore SIGINT entirely if the program is run in the background but take new_action if the program is run in the foreground.

■ **Example 11.9.3**

```
#include <signal.h>
    int iteration;
    void new_action();                    /* any function that
                                             does not return an int
                                             must be declared */

main()
{
    printf("this program is going to have a trap set to take
    new action based on the signal '2', but the trap will be
    disabled if the program runs in the background");
```

```
    if ( signal(SIGINT,SIG_IGN) != SIG_IGN)
        signal(SIGINT,new_action);
```
/* set the trap to take new_action, a pointer to the function new_action(), in case the signal SIGINT is received by the program. This new_action will not however be activated if the program is run in the background. */

```
    for ( iteration=0; iteration < 20; ++iteration) {
        printf(" i am now doing iteration %d", iteration);
        sleep(1);
```
/*suspend the program for 1 second */

```
        }
    }
void new_action()
{
    signal(SIGINT,new_action);
```
/* the signal SIGINT has been caught if this line is executed; hence the trap is reset here so that the next ctrl-c will also generate a new action—otherwise the default action for the signal SIGINT will be taken, which will simply be to terminate the program */

```
        printf("you must have pressed the ctrl-c");
        }
```

The analysis of the program is as follows:

CASE 1: Suppose the program has just begun running *in the background*. Thus, precisely because it is a background process, SIG_IGN is set for SIGINT since background processes ignore SIGINT. The if condition is checked—signal() returns SIG_IGN. Hence, the condition is false and the signal SIGINT will be ignored the first time it is set. Now suppose SIGINT is sent again. This time the same thing happens: the if condition is still false because the return value of signal() is SIG_IGN, previous second argument for signal(); moreover, SIG_IGN is still set for SIGINT.

CASE 2: Suppose the program has just begun running *in the foreground.* Thus, precisely because it is a foreground process, SIG_DFL is set for SIGINT since foreground processes do not ignore SIGINT. The if condition is checked—signal() returns SIG_DFL. Hence, the condition is true and the signal SIGINT will cause new_action to be taken. Now suppose SIGINT is sent again. This time the same thing happens: the if condition is still true because the return value of signal() is new_action, previous second argument for signal(); moreover, new_action is still set for SIGINT.

Here is the program and its actual output:

```
/*     CHAPTER 11    11.9.3.C     */


#include <signal.h>

int iteration;
void new_action();

main()
{
  printf("This program is going to have a trap set to take new \n");
  printf("action based on the signal '2', but the trap will be\n");
  printf("disabled if the program runs in the background\n");
  if (signal(SIGINT,SIG_IGN) != SIG_IGN)
    signal(SIGINT,new_action);
  for (iteration=0; iteration < 20; ++iteration)
  {
    printf("I am now doing iteration %d\n",iteration);
    sleep(1);
  }
}
void new_action()
{
  signal(SIGINT,new_action);
  printf("you must have pressed the ctrl-c\n");
}


/**********/
/* OUTPUT */
/**********/
This program is going to have a trap set to take new
action based on the signal '2', but the trap will be
disabled if the program runs in the background
I am now doing iteration 0
you must have pressed the ctrl-c
I am now doing iteration 1
I am now doing iteration 2
I am now doing iteration 3
you must have pressed the ctrl-c
I am now doing iteration 4
I am now doing iteration 5
you must have pressed the ctrl-c
```

```
I am now doing iteration 6
I am now doing iteration 7
I am now doing iteration 8
you must have pressed the ctrl-c
I am now doing iteration 9
I am now doing iteration 10
I am now doing iteration 11
you must have pressed the ctrl-c
I am now doing iteration 12
I am now doing iteration 13
I am now doing iteration 14
you must have pressed the ctrl-c
I am now doing iteration 15
I am now doing iteration 16
I am now doing iteration 17
I am now doing iteration 18
you must have pressed the ctrl-c
I am now doing iteration 19
```

## EXERCISES 11.9

1. Write a program segment that provides a nice exit for when the phone is hung up.

2. Write a program that traps the signal 3 and takes some interesting action based on that signal.

## 11.10 CHAPTER SUMMARY

1. Two or more C programs (binary code) may be piped together in serial fashion so that the output of one becomes the input to the next.

2. Redirection of standard input and standard output can be used on the command line with a.out.

3. C programs can be written to access command line arguments, which will often simply be the names of files.

4. System calls can be called from C programs to obtain information from the UNIX operating system.

5. C programs can be written to accept command line options to influence the output of the program.

6. The file ctype.h contains a number of useful macros for dealing with data types.

7. The proper way to march through arguments on the command line is with argc − − and argv + +.

# CHAPTER 12

# UNIX C Files

## 12.1 DYNAMIC MEMORY ALLOCATION: MALLOC(), REALLOC(), CALLOC(), AND FREE()

The dynamic allocation of memory permits the programmer to use only as much memory as needed and only for the part of the program that actually needs it. This allows unused memory to be returned to the operating system for another program or user. The alternative, namely, assigning as much memory as could *possibly* be used by any run, is very ineffective indeed. The programmer often has no way of knowing whether a program will be run with a few or many data items and the size of the data items is unpredictable. So, reserving memory for the worst, or most demanding, case is simply not acceptable because only limited memory is available.

Section 12.1 will present the tools to gain access to additional main memory during the execution of a program, and thus to use space wisely.

The first tool to be examined is *malloc(3C)*, which is related to realloc(3C), calloc(3C), and free(3C). Each has its own uses and the following are their synopses from the UNIX manual:

```
char *malloc(size)
unsigned size;

char *realloc(ptr,size)
char *ptr;
unsigned size;

char *calloc(nelem,elsize)
unsigned nelem, elsize;

void free(ptr)
char *ptr;
```

The function *malloc(3C)* is passed a "size" indicating the number of bytes to make available, up to a maximum of the largest unsigned integer available, and it returns a pointer to the very first byte of the *contiguous* space that is returned. The memory that has now been made available must then be accessed through that pointer. Malloc(3C) might need to

.

call sbrk (see brk(2)) if it is necessary to go to the operating system to get adequate space. A NULL pointer is returned if unsuccessful. Note that because malloc returns a pointer to a char, not an integer, it must be declared.

The function *realloc(3C)* is also passed a size indicating the number of bytes to be made available and *a pointer* to an existing block of memory. It returns a pointer to the first byte of size bytes (returning NULL only if unsuccessful). In addition, realloc(3C) keeps the same values stored as were in the old block of memory. It is possible that ptr will need to be moved to find size bytes, but the programmer can use realloc to guarantee that ptr points to a sufficient amount of contiguous memory.

The function *calloc(3C)* is passed two values, the number of elements for which space must be allocated, nelem, and also the size of an individual element, elsize. It also returns a pointer to the very first allocated byte (NULL if unsuccessful) and furthermore it *initializes each byte in the allocated space to zero*.

The function *free(3C)* is passed a pointer to a block of memory that has previously been allocated by malloc(3C). It frees that space for future allocation, but the contents of the various memory locations are not changed.

With each of the allocation functions, the programmer has the option of using pointer arithmetic to traverse from one instance of a data structure to another instance, or may choose to embed a pointer as one of the *fields* of a data structure so that it can point to the next instance of a data structure. Each approach has its merits.

■ **Example 12.1.1** This first example will show how to use malloc(3C) to allocate just enough storage space to hold each field of a single data structure. The program will prompt the user for *only one instance* of a name, address, hometown, and state, and then simply print them back.

```
#include <stdio.h>

main()
{
    char a[25];
    char *name, *address, *hometown, *state;
    char *malloc();
    puts("Enter your name now");
    scanf("%24s",a);
    name = malloc(strlen(a)+1);
    strcpy(name,a);
    puts("Enter your address now ");
    scanf("%24s",a);
    address = malloc(strlen(a)+1);
```

```
        strcpy(address,a);
        puts("Enter your home town now");
        scanf("%24s",a);
        hometown = malloc(strlen(a)+1);
        strcpy(hometown,a);
        puts("Enter your state now");
        scanf("%24s",a);
        state = malloc(strlen(a)+1);
        strcpy(state,a);
        printf("%s\n %s\n %s\n %s\n",name,address,hometown,state);
}


/*********/
/* INPUT */
/*********/
Enter your name now
 John
Enter your address now
 Mainstreet
Enter your home town now
 Miami
Enter your state now
 Florida


/***********/
/* OUTPUT */
/***********/
 John
 Mainstreet
 Miami
 Florida
```

Notice that the same storage locations were used again and again to hold the data read, a pointer was set to point to exactly enough storage to hold the appropriate data, and then the data was copied to those locations. Even though pointers do occupy some storage themselves, it is clear that efficiency is gained by allocating just enough storage for each data field. The real problem is that separate pointers were used for each data field. A more efficient way might be to incorporate a pointer into a data structure that links the instances of the data structure. ■

The next example will show how to use realloc(3C) to allocate additional storage without destroying the old data.

■ **Example 12.1.2**    Each instance of the data structure will be of exactly the same length and will contain two fields, a student's name and a grade for the last test. The records will be stored in contiguous memory accomplished by the use of realloc(3C).

```
#include <stdio.h>

struct student {
  char name[40];
  int  grade;
};

main()
{
  char holdit[40],temp[3];
  int  number, grd;
  char *malloc();
  char *realloc();
  char *gets();
  struct student *beginningptr, *loopptr;
  loopptr = NULL;
  puts("Enter a name followed by a grade on the next line.");
  puts("When finished simply depress the return key instead of an actual name");
  number = 0;
  printf("Enter a name now: ");
  gets(holdit);
  beginningptr = (struct student *)malloc(sizeof(struct student));
  strcpy((beginningptr+number)->name,holdit);
  printf("Enter a grade now: ");
  gets(temp);
  grd = atoi(temp);
  (beginningptr+number)->grade = grd;
  ++number;
  while (holdit[0] != '\0')
  {
    printf("Enter a name now: ");
    gets(holdit);
    if (holdit[0] == '\0')
      break;
    beginningptr = (struct student *)realloc(beginningptr, (number+1)*sizeof (struct
    strcpy((beginningptr+number)->name,holdit);
    printf("Enter a grade now: ");
    gets(temp);
    grd = atoi(temp);
    (beginningptr+number)->grade = grd;
    ++number;
  }
  for (loopptr = beginningptr;(loopptr - beginningptr)<number;loopptr++)
    printf("%s %d \n",loopptr->name,loopptr->grade);
}



/**********/
/* OUTPUT */
/**********/
Enter a name followed by a grade on the next line.
When finished simply depress the return key instead of an actual name
Enter a name now: Jones
Enter a grade now: 98
Enter a name now: Smith
Enter a grade now: 87
Enter a name now: Brown
Enter a grade now: 78
Enter a name now:
Jones 98
Smith 87
Brown 78
```

■ **Example 12.1.3**   In this example, which solves the same problem as Example 12.1.2, each data structure will again be of exactly the same length but will now contain three fields: name of student, grade on last test, and pointer to next record. The records will not necessarily be stored in contiguous memory because of the use of malloc(3C). Because they are not likely to be stored in contiguous memory, the use of pointer arithmetic is inappropriate. A record will be accessed only through a sequence of pointers, one in each record, beginning at the initial record. It will also be necessary to keep track of the last record, and that will be done by defining its pointer field with the value NULL.

```c
#include <stdio.h>

struct student {
  char name[40];
  int  grade;
  struct student *nextptr;
};

main()
{
  int grd;
  char holdit[40], temp[3];
  char *malloc();
  char *gets();
  struct student *beginningptr, *loopptr, *nexttolastptr;
  puts("Enter a name followed by a grade on the next line.");
  puts("When finished simply depress the return key instead of an actual name");
  printf("Enter a name now: ");
  gets(holdit);
  beginningptr = (struct student *)malloc(sizeof(struct student));
  strcpy(beginningptr->name,holdit);
  printf("Enter a grade now: ");
  gets(temp);
  grd = atoi(temp);
  beginningptr->grade = grd;
  beginningptr->nextptr = NULL;
  nexttolastptr = beginningptr;
  loopptr = beginningptr;
  while (holdit[0] != '\0')
    {
      printf("Enter a name now: ");
      gets(holdit);
      if (holdit[0] == '\0')
        break;
      loopptr = (struct student *)malloc(sizeof (struct student));
      strcpy(loopptr->name,holdit);
      printf("Enter a grade now: ");
      gets(temp);
      grd = atoi(temp);
      loopptr->grade = grd;
      loopptr->nextptr = NULL;
      nexttolastptr->nextptr = loopptr;
      nexttolastptr = loopptr;
    }
  for (loopptr=beginningptr;loopptr->nextptr!= NULL;loopptr=loopptr->nextptr)
    printf("%s %d \n",loopptr->name,loopptr->grade);
  printf("%s %d \n",loopptr->name,loopptr->grade);
}
```

```
/**********/
/* OUTPUT */
/**********/
Enter a name followed by a grade on the next line.
When finished simply depress the return key instead of an actual name
Enter a name now: Jones
Enter a grade now: 98
Enter a name now: Smith
Enter a grade now: 87
Enter a name now: Brown
Enter a grade now: 86
Enter a name now:
Jones 98
Smith 87
Brown 86
```
■

### EXERCISES 12.1

1. Revise Example 12.1 so that the necessary information is read from a file and that mailing labels are printed for 10 different people.

2. Revise Example 12.3 so that each record has an additional pointer field that links the records in the reverse order. Check your work by printing the records in the reverse order by following these new pointers.

## 12.2 FILE ACCESS AND FILE LOCKING: CHMOD AND UNLINK()

### Binary and Text Files

It is extremely important to be able to distinguish between binary files and text files, both of which are stored on disk. Both types of files store ordinary ASCII characters in exactly the same way, a single byte being used to represent a single character. The difference lies in how they treat integer and float data (numeric values).

In binary files, the numeric data on the disk is stored exactly as it was stored in internal memory (binary format), while in text files, numeric data on the disk is stored as ordinary (ASCII) characters, with the programmer responsible for converting it to binary format when it is read back into internal memory. (This is if it is to be used in arithmetic calculations.)

■ **Example 12.2.1** Suppose we have the following in a program:

```
int x;
x =26;
```

On a machine that uses 32 bits to store an integer, 26 (16 + 8 + 2) might be stored in internal memory as

```
0000 0000 0000 0000 0000 0000 0001 1010
```

To copy this value to a text file with associated pointer fptr simply write:

```
FILE *fptr;
fprintf(fptr, "%d", x);      /* the conversion to text is
                                done automatically by fprintf()
                                */
```

On the disk, the former integer 26 will now be treated as two separate characters and occupy two bytes, one for the character 2 and one for the character 6:

```
0101 0000 0101 0100
```

To read characters 2 and 6 back into internal memory as integer x, fptr would have to be positioned at the first of those two bytes and then write:

```
fscanf(fptr,"%d",x);      /*the conversion to an integer is
                             done automatically by the function
                             fscanf() */
```

In this instance, nothing is lost; the integer stored in x is the same as the original integer (26). If the programmer had been dealing with float data (with an appropriate declaration of course), it is indeed possible that the number eventually retrieved from the disk would not be the same as the original number written to disk due to round-off errors. ∎

■ **Example 12.2.2**   Suppose we have the following in a program:

```
int x[1];
x[0] =26;
```

On a machine that uses 32 bits to store an integer, 26 (16 + 8 + 2) might be stored in internal memory as

```
0000 0000 0000 0000 0000 0000 0001 1010
```

To copy this value to a binary file with associated pointer file descriptor filedes simply write:

```
write(filedes, x, 4);      /*transfer 4 bytes from the
                             address x of the buffer into the
                             file associated with filedes (a
                             small integer from 0 to 19) */
```

On the disk, the integer 26 will now take four bytes, exactly as in internal memory.

To read 26 back into internal memory at x[0], filedes would have to be associated with the right file, and then:

```
read(filedes,x,4);
```

In this instance, nothing is lost; the integer stored in x[0] is the same as the original number (26). If the programmer had been dealing with float data, the number eventually retrieved from the disk would again always be the same as the original number sent to disk (with *no* round-off errors). ■

■ **Example 12.2.3**  Suppose we have the following in a program:

```
int x[1];
x[0] =26;
```

On a machine that uses 32 bits to store an integer, 26 (16 + 8 + 2) might be stored in internal memory as

```
0000 0000 0000 0000 0000 0000 0001 1010
```

An alternative and perhaps more convenient and efficient way to copy this value to a binary file with associated file pointer fptr is to use the standard I/O package by writing:

```
FILE *fptr;
fwrite(x,4,1,fptr);        /*transfer from address x, one item of
                           4 bytes (each), into the file
                           associated with fptr */
```

On the disk, the integer 26 will now take four bytes, exactly as in internal memory.

To read the integer 26 back into internal memory at x, fptr would have to be associated with the right file, and then:

```
fread(x,4,1,fptr);        /* transfer beginning at address x, one
                          item of 4 bytes (each) from the file
                          pointed to by fptr */                    ■
```

Here is a comparison of binary and text files:

1. Text files can be easily inspected by editing them with vi or by simply using cat to show them.

2. Binary files would typically be created and accessed directly through an application program.

3. Binary files are often more compact (a 10-digit integer still only occupies four bytes).

4. Binary files can often be accessed more quickly because numerical data do not need to be converted back and forth between binary and character form.

5. Binary files are more reliable, particularly when dealing with floating point numbers, since there is no round-off error.

6. Binary files cannot usually be viewed with cat because the data may be stored with ASCII codes that are not printable (remember that the storage on the disk is identical to that in main memory).

It is now time to discuss the concept of permissions using chmod. Suppose a faculty member has designed a program called scheduled whose purpose is to read a file called data pdate it appropriately based on input information available to the students. Assume that data was supplied by the instructor, and that the instructor and all of the students are members the same group. The instructor would like the students to run the program and turn in the revised data file to determine that scheduling has indeed been run and that data has been appropriately modified. (It is considered bad form to simply edit the file data!)

Suppose the instructor has used chmod to set various permissions, as in the following:

```
$ chmod 600 data
```

```
$ chmod 710 scheduling
```

The student now has no permission to do anything directly with data but does have execute permission for scheduling. If the instructor provided the student with r read and w permission to data, the student might decide to simply edit the file to make the appropriate changes without using the program scheduling at all. The purpose here is to show how the student can run scheduling and, during that run, modify data without having read and write permission to data. The secret is in the "set user ID" bit.

Recall the following from Chapter 11: one of the members of the struct stat structure defined in /usr/include/sys/stat.h is named st_mode of data type unsigned short (two-byte integer). It contains a wealth of information in its 16 bits labeled bit 15 down through bit 0.

If the set user ID (uid) bit 11 is on, then the program user temporarily has the identity of the program owner during the execution of the program. Hence, the program owner, the instructor, can temporarily give the student the instructor's permissions during the execution of scheduling by

```
$ chmod u+s scheduling
```

which adds the set uid bit for the user, or

```
$ chmod 4710 scheduling
```

which does the same. Note that the 4 in this case does not refer to read r; it is 4 because the set uid bit is bit 11. (The last digit picks up bits 0–2, the next last digit refers to bits 3–5, the next one, bits 6–8, and the first one, bits 9–11.)

Now suppose that the same situation exists with respect to permissions, except that the students as part of others are in a different group from the instructor. Then the same goals can be accomplished by the following:

```
$ chmod 600 data
$ chmod 2701 scheduling
```

or

```
$ chmod 600 data
$ chmod 701 scheduling
$ chmod u+g scheduling
```

Note also that in this case, the group user ID bit 10 is on, and, hence, the program user temporarily has the identity of the group of the program owner during the execution of the program. Note again that the 2 in this case does not refer to read w; it is 2 because the group uid bit is bit 10. (The last digit picks up bits 0–2, the next last digit refers to bits 3–5, the next one, bits 6–8, and the first one, bits 9–11.)

### File Locking

The next idea to be tackled is that of providing a programming mechanism that permits a file to be accessed by only one user at a time. The concept is called file locking. Most UNIX systems have no direct way of saying "open the file" and "lock it," although System V provides for this idea without, unfortunately, the actual implementation. Berkeley 4.2 does provide a form of file locking.

Suppose the student in the previous example was running scheduling, which, in turn, was manipulating data, and wished to lock out other users from data during that execution. The algorithm for doing this will be embedded in scheduling as follows:

1. Check to determine if the file called lock exists in the same directory as data.
2. If yes, report to scheduling that data is in use and exit scheduling.

**3.** If no, create a file called lock.

**4.** If the user created lock then remove lock at the end of the execution of scheduling.

Most of this is easy to implement. The real problem involves finding the end of the execution of scheduling. There are many ways a program might end. Some of these are (1) data cannot be opened for reading, (2) data is a file with no real data, (3) data cannot be opened for writing, and (4) the program terminates by receiving a signal such as:

```
SIGHUP==1,SIGINT==2, or SIGQUIT==3.
```

Each of the possible ways to terminate scheduling must include the provision for removing lock because otherwise this may be the *last* use of scheduling (unless of course the systems administrator intervenes).

### unlink()

A way to remove a file from within a C program is via the system called unlink(2), which has the following synopsis. One could also use system rm lock.

```
int unlink(path)
char *path;
```

This may fail for various reasons, including a component of the path does not exist, the file does not exist, search permission does not exist on some component of the path, and such. If successful, 0 is returned; otherwise it returns -1 and sets errno to indicate the error.

■ **Example 12.2.4**   Here is an outline of a program to call scheduling to manipulate the file named data and to provide file locking.

```
main()
{
    if(signal(SIGINT,SIG_IGN) ==SIG_DFL)
    signal(SIGINT,unlock);                  /* unlock will be the
                                             function that removes the
                                             file named "lock" */
                                             / * semicolon can be
                                             written for other possible
                                             signals. The initial
                                             reception of SIGINT will
                                             cause the "if" condition to
                                             be checked. The condition
```

will be true because signal() will return the original value associated with SIGINT, namely SIG_DFL. So SIGINT gets the condition SIG_IGN, but then the condition to "unlock." When unlock() is invoked SIGINT gets the condition SIG_IGN again so that additional receptions of SIGINT will be ignored—you do not want termination of the program here because "lock" has not yet been removed; "lock" is removed; and normal exit status (condition code 0) is returned. */

```
if access(lock,0) == 0) {
```

/* if the check to determine if "lock" exists (access mode 0) is successful (a return value of 0) */

```
puts("lock exists=please leave ");
      exit (2);
      }
else if ((fptr =fopen(lock,"w")) == NULL)       {
```

/* if "lock" cannot be opened for writing */

```
      perror(lock);
      exit(1);
}
if (access(data,0) == 0 {
```

/* if the check to determine if "data" exists (access mode 0) is successful (a return value of 0) */

```
if ((fptr =fopen(data,"r")) == NULL)        {
```
/* and if "data" cannot be
opened for reading, remove
"lock" and exit */

```
            perror(data);
            unlink(lock);
            exit(1);
            }
    }
void unlock()
    signal(SIGINT, SIG_IGN);        /*etc for other
                                    possible signals*/

    unlink(lock);
    exit(0);
    }
    }
```

■

## EXERCISES 12.2

1. Complete Example 12.2.4 and test it.
2. Create a file of data and have a friend do the same. Now provide each other the appropriate permissions so that each of you can modify the other's file, but only during the running of a program that you have written.

## 12.3 CHAPTER SUMMARY

1. malloc(), realloc(), calloc(), and free() are used for dynamic memory management.
2. An efficient way to manage space is to allocate a pointer within each instance of the data structure in question.
3. Binary files store data on disk in exactly the same way as it is stored in main memory, while text files treat numeric data on disk as ordinary characters.
4. The set uid bit (11) is useful for ensuring that data sets can only be changed by running specified programs.

# CHAPTER 13

# Program Development:
# cc, make, lint, cb

## 13.1 | *THE cc COMPILER AND ITS OPTIONS*

The cc(1) compiler can actually call a sophisticated command package. It is found in Section 1 of the UNIX manual and consists of:

1. a preprocessor: the input is a .c file and the output is a .i file
2. a compiler: the input is a .c or .o file
3. an optimizer: must provide the -O option to cc
4. an assembler: as(1)—the input is a .s file and the output is a .o file; however, the output may be placed in myfile by using the -o option as in

   ```
   $ as -o myfile myfile.s
   ```

5. a link editor: the output file is a.out; however, the output may be placed in myfile by using the -o option (actually the -o option is an option for the link editor ld(1), not for cc(1) ) as in

   ```
   $ cc -o myfile program.c
   ```

### Compilation Process and Options

The cc(1) command has the following synopsis:

```
cc [options] files
```

Cc itself processes various options and is able to pass certain other options to the various parts of the command package with the proper arguments. Any *C program* must have a name that ends with .c. Such files are the starting files for the components of the command package: namely, preprocessing, compilation, optimization, assembly, and link editing. A .c program's processing may be terminated at the end of any one of the five passes, *provided the appropriate options are specified.*

*Preprocessing* simply refers to processing any preprocessor directives, such as

```
#include myfile
#define x inches
```

■ **Example 13.1.1**

```
$ cc -P program.c
```

will run only the C preprocessor cpp(1) part of cc on program.c and pass the -P option to cpp(1). Note that the P option is totally different from the lowercase p option; the latter counts the number of times each function is called. The output of this will be the file program.i, which will be different from program.c in that the necessary files have been included and all the substitutions for the symbolic definitions have been made. It is also possible to make the output of the preprocessor go to the standard output by giving cc the -E option as in

```
$ cc -E program.c
```
■

*Compiling* simply refers to processing source code (either program.i or program.c) and producing *object code* in a file named program.o. However, this file is still *not* executable. The file program.o will normally be deleted if a program is compiled and link edited all at once, such as in

```
$ cc program.c
```

which simply produces an executable file named a.out. However, the .o file will not be deleted if the -c option is provided to cc. In this case the link phase is not done. The .o file will also not be deleted if several files are compiled (see Example 13.1.3).

■ **Example 13.1.2**  Object code is produced by

```
$ cc -c program.c
```

in program.o, which is still not executable. ■

*Optimizing* of compiled code can be achieved by providing the -O option to cc as in

```
$ cc -O program.c
```

The cc compiler can be forced to compile the source code and produce assembly language code (a .s file) by providing the -S option to cc as in

```
$ cc -S program.c
```

The output is then placed in program.s. This output could then be assembled by invoking the assembler as(1) directly as in

$ <u>as program.s</u>

which places the assembled code in a .o file (program.o).

Two other useful options for cc are:

-g     generates useful information for the symbolic debugger (to be covered later)

-p     adds code that counts the number of times each function is called. This information profile can then be retrieved by the use of prof(1). The mechanics of using the -p option will be discussed in a moment.

We have now discussed all of the phases of the compilation process with the exception of the last one, the *link editing*. To review a bit, files that end in .c are considered to be C source code, files that end in .i are preprocessed C programs, and files that end in .s are assembly language programs. Any files that appear on the command line for cc and that do not end in one of these suffixes will be passed directly to the link editor. The link editor ld(1) has the following synopsis:

`ld [options] filename`

The function of the link editor is to combine object files (.o files) into a single executable file whose default name is a.out. It accomplishes this task by performing relocation of code and resolution of external symbols, such as printf(), sqrt(), and others that must be brought in from the system libraries to be combined with the other code. It also assists by providing additional information valuable for symbolic debugging. There are several options available to ld(1), but the most important of these are the following:

-o myfile     This option places the executable file in myfile rather than the default of a.out. Recall that any file that does not end in .c, .i, or .s is passed to the link editor. Thus,

$ <u>cc -o myfile myfile.c</u>     puts the executable code in myfile, but the -o option is an option for ld(1), not for cc(1). (Myfile.o is not saved in this case.)

-lx

This option causes the library libx.a to be searched. (X can be up to 9 characters.) This searching occurs when the name is encountered; thus, this option should not be placed too early on the command line. It is necessary to place the option after any file that uses the particular library, so that it can be searched after the file has been read. For example, to use the math library libm to get sqrt() for example, one must write the following line in the source code

```
#include <math.h>
```

and invoke the cc compiler in a fashion such as this:

```
$ cc program.c -lm -o program
```

The standard C library need not be specified. It is automatically searched and thus the standard I/O package will always be found.

Recall that the link editor is passed any file that does not end in c, i, or s. In particular, it is passed .o files.

It can be passed .s files also. Study the following example.

■ **Example 13.1.3**   Suppose a user has a program scattered across several files, file1a.c, file1b.c, and file1c.c. He or she does the following compilation:

```
$ cc -o runit file1a.c file1b.c file1c.c
```

The object code files are not deleted because several files are compiled and combined into a single object code file called runit. If an error is now found in file1b.c, then the recompilation will be more efficient if the following is done:

```
$ cc -o runit file1a.o file1b.c file1c.o
```

It is even possible to have any mixture of .o, .c, and .s files to pass to the cc compiler. ∎

Finally, here's a word and an example about the -p option for the cc compiler. Again suppose the source code for a program is distributed in file1a.c, file1b.c, and file1c.c. We would like to get some information concerning each of the functions that are used, including system functions. We need %time (percentage of time in each function), cumsecs (cumulative seconds used in each function), #call(the number of times each function is called), ms/call (milliseconds used per call), and name (the name of the function itself).

The technique to get that information is as follows:

```
$ cc -p -o runit file1.c file2.c file3.c
$ prof runit
```

## EXERCISES  13.1

1. Experiment with the various options discussed in this section.
2. Generate the assembly code for one of your programs and then run it through the assembler.

## 13.2 | PROGRAM MAINTENANCE WITH MAKE

The desirability of modularity in programming is now unquestioned. Most programs of any consequence consist of a set of files, each of which may have been produced by a team of programmers. When a change must be made in one of the files, it's important that recompilation of each of the files take place *only if necessary*. The command make(1) that uses the file with the default name makefile is expressly suited for maintaining, updating, and regenerating modular programs. There are many options available, but the most valuable one is the −f option to rename the file named makefile to, say, makeprog1. This can be accomplished by

```
$ make -f makeprog1
```

The use of the -f option thus permits the user to have a makefile associated with each program or group of programs in question. On the other hand, if program maintenance only requires a single file called makefile then the above command is simply

```
$ make
```

A makefile consists of a set of file dependencies and associated commands. If makefile is not found, then Makefile, s.makefile, and s.Makefile are sought, in that order. The file makefile consists of a sequence of entries that specify dependencies and commands. An example makefile might be as follows.

■ **Example 13.2.1**

```
$ cat makefile
runit : file1.o file2.o file3.o
cc -o runit file1.o file2.o file3.o
$
```

In this instance, there is only one dependency: namely, the file runit depends on (runit is therefore called a *target* file and is separated from its prerequisites by a ":") file1.o, file2.o, and file3.o. There is only a single command that must be run to implement that dependency, namely,

```
cc -o runit file1.o file2.o file3.o
```
■

There are some restrictions that apply to the format of the makefile: (1) a semicolon (;) or a newline can be used to separate the dependency from the command; and (2) lines that begin with a tab and follow a dependency are treated as shell commands that must be executed to update the *target of the dependency*.

Suppose the makefile listed above exists and the user issues the command make. Then the file runit is produced, but how it is produced depends upon the particular circumstances as follows:

1. Suppose this is the first invocation of make, the .o files exist, and the .c files and runit file do not exist (i.e., the prerequisite files exist, but the target and source do not). In this case, the specified shell command is automatically executed and runit is produced, just as if the following had been done:

```
$ cc -o runit file1.o file2.o file3.o
```

2. Suppose the .c files exist, but not the .o files and not runit (i.e., the prerequisite files do not exist, the target does not exist, and the source does exist). In this case, make is smart enough to produce the .o files and then produce runit.

3. Suppose the .c files as well as the .o files exist (i.e., the prerequisite files do exist and the source does exist). In this case, make becomes a bit more sophisticated in its approach. It first compares the dates and times of the various files, and if a .c file has been modified more recently than a .o file that depends on it, whether

that dependence is explicitly stated or not, then the .c file is recompiled. Eventually, after all the necessary recompilations—and only the *necessary* ones—have taken place, the target file is updated.

4. Finally, if the target file, runit, exists, then its date and time of last modification is compared with those dates and times of the files upon which it depends. If any of these prerequisite files have been modified more recently than the target file, then once again all the necessary recompilations are done, and the target file is updated to reflect these recompilations.

Hence, in all cases, make ensures that all *necessary* compilations are done to update the target file to reflect any changes that have been made in prerequisite files that might affect the target. It is obvious that make is an excellent tool to use in large-scale programming projects that require coordinating the work of several teams of programmers.

Aha! But there is even more—common preprocessor directives that occur in several source files can instead be captured in a header file, say, header.h, and have this file #included in each source file that needs it, and then *modify the appropriate dependency*.

■ **Example 13.2.2**   Suppose that in Example 13.2.1, file1.c and file3.c both need header.h. Then makefile should be as follows:

```
$ cat makefile
runit : file1.o file2.o file3.o
cc -o runit file1.o file2.o file3.o
file1.o file3.o : header.h
$
```

This means that runit depends on three object files, and file1.o and file3.o, in turn, depend on header.h. Again, make automatically knows that .o files depend on .c files. So, if header.h has been modified most recently, then file1.o and file3.o will be modified by make, by recompiling *file1.c and file3.c,* of course. Then runit will be modified because it depends on the recently modified file1.o and file3.o. ■

A bit more of streamlining can be done by using the equivalent of UNIX shell variables, called a *macro definition,* in a makefile. Remember that shell variables always have string values—so do macro definitions. In macro definitions, blanks are permitted in these string values without the necessity of enclosing them in single quotes. To get the value of the macro definition, it is necessary to enclose the name of the macro definition in braces and precede it with a dollar sign.

■ **Example 13.2.3**    Recall Example 13.2.2:

```
$ cat makefile
runit : file1.o file2.o file3.o
cc -o runit file1.o file2.o file3.o
file1.o file3.o : header.h
$
```

This could be modified as follows:

```
$ cat makefile
TARGET = runit
OBJECTFILES = file1.o file2.o file3.o
HEADER = header.h
HEADEROBJECTS = file1.o file3.o
${TARGET} : ${OBJECTFILES}
cc -o ${TARGET} ${OBJECTFILES}
${HEADEROBJECTS} : ${HEADER}
$
```

This technique of making macro definitions in makefile is particularly valuable if makefile needs to be modified as .o files are added or deleted. Rather than make several changes throughout makefile, it is only necessary to change the appropriate macro definitions. ■

## EXERCISES  13.2

1. Experiment with all of the features of make that were discussed in the text.

## 13.3 | *PORTABILITY CONSIDERATIONS: LINT(1)*

The UNIX utility lint(1) has the following synopsis:

```
lint [-abhlnpuvx] file1.c ...
```

Its purpose is to find code in file1.c, and so on, that might indicate a bug, nonportability, or simply inefficiency and waste. For example, it will flag the following kinds of problems:

1. source statements that cannot be reached
2. control statements that are not entered at their tops
3. automatic variables that have been declared but never used in the program

4. logical expressions whose values remain constant

5. functions that do not always return values, have a variable number of arguments, or have return values that are unused

The following options are the most useful ones in that they force lint to suppress warnings, which may be of no particular interest to the programmer:

1. -a The use of this option will force lint to suppress any warnings about a long integer value assigned to an int variable, as in

```
int x;
x = 43L;
```

2. -b The use of this option will force lint to suppress any warnings about any break statements that are impossible to reach, as in

```
while (x == 1)
     if (x != 1) break;
```

3. -h The use of this option will force lint to suppress heuristic tests that attempt to improve style and find bugs.

4. -u The use of this option will force lint to suppress any warnings about any functions or external variables that are not both defined and used.

5. -v The use of this option will force lint to suppress any warnings about any arguments in functions that are unused.

6. -x The use of this option will force lint to suppress any warnings about variables that have been defined externally, but never used.

## EXERCISES  13.3

1. Experiment with the various options associated with lint.

## 13.4 | *THE C BEAUTIFIER: CB(1)*

The purpose of the C beautifier is to read (by default) from standard input a C program and write (by default) to standard output a version of the program properly formatted for spacing and indentation. Both input and output may be redirected using < and > symbols on the command line. Moreover, there are various options available to alter the output. The synopsis of cb(1) is as follows:

```
cb [ -s] [-j] [-1 leng] file.c
```

If no options are specified, then all new lines (\n) in the source code are preserved. The −s option puts the code in the format that is used in *The C Programming Language* by *Kernighan* and *Ritchie*. The -j option takes split lines and rejoins them, while the -l option permits the programmer to have lines that are longer than leng to be split.

## EXERCISES 13.4

1. Experiment with the various options available to the C beautifier, cb(1).

## 13.5 | *SYMBOLIC DEBUGGER: SDB(1)*

The symbolic debugger sdb(1) is used with C programs (as well as F77 programs) to inspect files and afford a controlled environment for execution. It can be of help when a program has bugs that are difficult to find and remedy. Its synopsis is as follows:

```
sdb [-w] [-W] [objectfile [corefile [directory]]]
```

where objectfile is an executable program defaulting to a.out that has been compiled with the -g option (debug); corefile is a core image file that is produced after executing objectfile, which may or may not be present, and defaults to core; and source filenames in objectfile are specified relative to directory. The -W option is used to suppress any warnings that might be generated if the .c files corresponding to the objectfiles cannot be located, or if they have been modified more recently.

The file called core, stored in the working directory and explained in core(4), is created when a process terminates because of an error. These possible errors can be found under signal(2). The core file, also known as the core image, is a copy of the program as it was stored in memory (hence the name corefile). Within core there are two parts: (1) one has a copy of the data for the process, including the registers being used at the time of termination; and (2) one has the actual code for the executable file itself.

Further information about the core file that is dumped can be found in three files: /usr/include/sys/param.h, /usr/include/sys/user.h, and /usr/include/sys/reg.h .

■ **Example 13.5.1**      $ <u>sdb a.out /usr/kem</u>

will provide debugging for the file /usr/kem/a.out. ■

When using sdb with the core file, the *current line* refers to the line containing the source statement at which the program stopped. Similarly, the *current file* refers to the file being examined. If the program

ran successfully, then the current line is simply the first line in main().
There are various commands that can be used for examining data in the
program that is being debugged. Some of the more important ones are:

1. **t** prints a stack trace of the terminated program
2. **T** prints the top line of the stack trace
3. **variable/lm** prints the value of the variable with length l and
   format m. For example, x/bd will print the value of x as a *byte* and
   in format *decimal*. Other possible lengths include h (two
   bytes=half word) and l (four bytes=long word). There are many
   possible choices for m
4. **linenumber?lm** prints the value at the address from a.out given
   by linenumber with length l and format m
5. **variable:?lm** prints the value at the address from a.out given
   by variable with length l and format m
6. **variable=lm** prints the address of variable with length l and
   format m
7. **variable!value** sets the variable to the specified value
8. **x** prints the contents of the machine registers

There are also various commands for examining source files that will not
be explored here, but can be found in the UNIX manual under sdb(1).

## EXERCISES 13.5

1. Experiment with the symbolic debugger, sdb(1).

## 13.6 CHAPTER SUMMARY

1. The cc(1) compiler actually consists of a command package including a preprocessor, a compiler, an optimizer, an assembler, and
   a link editor.
2. Programs can be easily and efficiently maintained using the
   make(1) command.
3. Nonportability, bugs, inefficiencies, and waste in programs can
   often be found by running lint(1).
4. C programs can be properly formatted by running the C beautifier,
   cb(1).
5. Bugs in a C program that are difficult to find can often be located
   by running the symbolic debugger, sdb(1).

# Index